People's Tribunals, Human Rights and the Law

People's Tribunals are independent, peaceful, grassroots movements, created by members of civil society, to address impunity that is associated with ongoing or past atrocities. As such, they offer society an alternative history and create a space for healing and reconciliation to take place that may otherwise be stifled by political agendas and legal technicalities. Since the 1960's, People's Tribunals have grown and developed to address many kinds of situations, from genocide to environmental degradation.

This book presents a balance of academic and practitioner perspectives on People's Tribunals. It explores key questions relating to their formation and roles and discusses what they can offer to victims and survivors. The volume provides an introduction to the subject, theoretically informed discussion reflecting different perspectives, and a range of contributions focusing on different types of People's Tribunals and various aspects of their operation. The authors analyse advantages and disadvantages of these movements in a variety of contexts. The impact and contribution they have in the international criminal law and international human rights context is also discussed.

The book will be welcomed by those interested in international criminal law, human rights, environmental justice, transitional justice and international relations.

Regina Menachery Paulose is a US based international criminal law attorney. She obtained her JD from Seattle University School of Law and her LLM in International Crime and Justice from the University of Turin/UNICRI. She was the Chair of the Steering Committee on the UK Child Sex Abuse People's Tribunal and was a panel member on the China Tribunal.

People's Tribunals, Human Rights and the Law

Searching for Justice

Edited by Regina Menachery Paulose

Routledge
Taylor & Francis Group
LONDON AND NEW YORK

First published 2020
by Routledge
2 Park Square, Milton Park, Abingdon, Oxon OX14 4RN

and by Routledge
52 Vanderbilt Avenue, New York, NY 10017

Routledge is an imprint of the Taylor & Francis Group, an informa business

First issued in paperback 2021

British Library Cataloguing-in-Publication Data
A catalogue record for this book is available from the British Library

Library of Congress Cataloging-in-Publication Data
Names: Paulose, Regina Menachery. editor.
Title: People's Tribunals, human rights and the law : searching for justice / edited by Regina Menachery Paulose.
Description: Abingdon, Oxon ; New York, NY : Routledge, 2020. | Includes bibliographical references and index.
Identifiers: LCCN 2019039644 (print) | LCCN 2019039645 (ebook) | ISBN 9780367200060 (hardback) | ISBN 9780429244674 (ebook)
Subjects: LCSH: International law and human rights—Citizen participation. | International criminal law—Citizen participation. | People's Tribunals
Classification: LCC KZ1266 .P44 2020 (print) | LCC KZ1266 (ebook) | DDC 347/.04—dc23
LC record available at https://lccn.loc.gov/2019039644
LC ebook record available at https://lccn.loc.gov/2019039645

ISBN: 978-0-367-20006-0 (hbk)
ISBN: 978-1-03-208388-9 (pbk)
ISBN: 978-0-429-24467-4 (ebk)

Typeset in Galliard
by Apex CoVantage, LLC

Contents

Author biographies

Alan Collins joined Hugh James as a partner in December 2014 and leads a team of specialist abuse solicitors. He qualified as a solicitor in 1990 and later became a solicitor-advocate, allowing him to act for his clients in the higher courts in England, Wales, Scotland and Northern Ireland. He has considerable experience of both criminal and civil litigation. Alan has represented interested parties before public inquiries including the Independent Jersey Care Inquiry, and IICSA (Independent Inquiry into Child Sexual Abuse). He was the advocate to the People's Tribunal which presented its report on sexual abuse to the UK Parliament (in 2016). Internationally, Alan works in Australia, South East Asia, Uganda, Kenya and California representing clients in high profile sexual abuse cases. Alan also spoke at the Third Regional Workshop on Justice for Children in East Asia and the Pacific in Bangkok hosted by Unicef and HCCH (Hague Conference on Private International Law). Alan is also a qualified mediator. Alan is a regular media contributor on serious personal injury and child abuse issues. He has regularly appeared on BBC and ITN news, ABC, CNN, NBC, and Sky News programmes, as well as BBC Radio 4's "Today," and "PM"; Radio 5; BBC and ITV regional television and radio, Australian radio, and US, Chinese, French, Spanish and Danish television. Alan is a regular speaker at conferences on legal issues including APIL; La Trobe University; National Crime Agency; University of Wales; Law Society of Scotland; Strathclyde University; and Dyfed-Powys Police. Alan is a fellow of the Association of Personal Injury Lawyers (APIL) and a director for the Association of Child Abuse Lawyers (ACAL). ACAL is a support group set up by solicitors and other professionals involved in the field of obtaining compensation for victims of abuse.

Azril Mohd Amin was admitted to the Malaysian Bar as an advocate and solicitor of the High Court of Malaya in 2000 and has been in practice since that time. He is a panel member of the Islamic Consultative Council (2016–2018) chaired by HE the Deputy Prime Minister and chairman of Initiatives for Human in Asia (IHRA) which he co-founded in 2016. He has over a decade of experience in law and human rights for the Asia-Pacific region. His involvement with civil societies accelerated in 2013 when he founded and led the MuslimUPRo delegation, a coalition of 16 major

Islamic Civil Society Organisations (ICSOs), to Malaysia's 2nd Universal Periodic Review at the 25th session of the United Nations Human Rights Council in Geneva, Switzerland. In 2014, he founded and became the chief executive of CENTHRA (Centre for Human Rights Research and Advocacy) a full-fledged research and advocacy outfit focusing on issues of Islam and Human Rights. He had since spent much of his time managing projects and establishing triadic relationships for CENTHRA, domestically and internationally. He had spoken at several international conferences, notably at the Reykjavik Roundtable on Human Rights 2016 on the theme "Democratic Accountability, State Sovereignty, and International Governance" (27–29 April 2016); presented his views at the One Day Conference: Myanmar's Democratic Transition and the Rohingya Persecution hosted by The South Asia Research Cluster (SARC) (11 May 2016) at Oxford University, UK; as a Malaysian government representative at the High-Level Roundtable on Freedom of Religion or Belief, held in conjunction with the Commonwealth Heads of Government Meeting (CHOGM) at Lambeth Palace, London, UK from 17–18 April 2018 and presented a paper at "The Islamic Tradition, Human Rights Discourse & Muslim Communities" Conference organised by the Atlantic Council and Oxford Centre for Islamic Studies, Oxford United Kingdom on 5 May 2018.

In March 2017, he led a six-member delegation of investigative lawyers to present expert views at the Permanent People's Tribunal on Genocide Against Rohingya, Kachin, and other minorities. In November 2017, he co-founded and now co-chairs the Malaysian Alliance of Civil Society Organisations in the United Nations Human Rights Council's Universal Periodic Review Process or MACSA, a coalition of 52 civil society organisations with the specific aim and object to investigate, as well as advocate, human rights issues in Malaysia for the UPR Process.

Benjamin Duerr is an international lawyer, diplomat and writer. He publishes about the politics, functioning and innovation of international law. He has worked as legal and policy adviser in government and for non-governmental organisations. He was the legal and advocacy officer at the Dr. Denis Mukwege Foundation of the Congolese Nobel Peace laureate Denis Mukwege on strengthening international law and building a norm against the use of sexual violence as a tactic of warfare. Benjamin Duerr studied political science and diplomacy at the London School of Economics and Political Science (LSE). He also holds an LLM in international law from the United Nations Interregional Crime and Justice Research Institute (UNICRI) in Turin, Italy, with a focus on international criminal and humanitarian law. He developed a specific expertise on the politics of international law and published the first journalistic book in German on the International Criminal Court (ICC). He has been monitoring war crimes trials in The Hague and has written extensively about international law and the international courts and tribunals. As a journalist, he reported on conflicts and human rights from ten African countries for leading international media outlets, including

Al Jazeera English and *Der Spiegel*. He was a fellow of Johns Hopkins University's international reporting project and was named one of Germany's Top 30 Journalists under 30 Years.

Binoy Kampmark is Senior Lecturer in the School of Global, Urban and Social Studies, RMIT University where he lectures in law and politics. He is also contributing editor to CounterPunch and was a Commonwealth Scholar at Selwyn College, Cambridge University. He has written and published extensively on the intersection between international law, politics and human rights. He is also an associate member of the Royal Roads University human security programme and the Nautilus Institute for Security and Sustainability.

David Matas is an international human rights lawyer, author, and researcher based in Winnipeg and currently acts as Senior Honorary Counsel for B'nai Brith Canada and is a co-founder of the International Coalition to End Transplant Abuse in China (ETAC). He has served the government of Canada in numerous positions including as member of the Canadian delegation to the United Nations Conference on an International Criminal Court; the Task Force for International Cooperation on Holocaust Education, Remembrance and Research; and the Organisation on Security and Cooperation in Europe Conferences on Antisemitism and Intolerance. He has also been involved in several different organisations, including the Canadian Helsinki Watch Group, Beyond Borders, Amnesty International and the Canadian Council for Refugees. Dr. Matas has received numerous awards and honours, including the Manitoba Bar Association Distinguished Service Award in 2008, the Order of Canada in 2009, the Canadian Bar Association National Citizenship and Immigration Section Achievement Award in 2009, and the International Society for Human Rights Swiss Section Human Rights Prize in 2010. In 2018, Dr. Matas was awarded an honorary Doctor of Laws degree from the University of Alberta for his outstanding contributions to human rights. In 2006, Dr. Matas co-authored *Bloody Harvest: Organ Harvesting of Falun Gong Practitioners* in China alongside Hon. David Kilgour. Both Dr. Matas and Mr. Kilgour were nominated for the 2010 Nobel Peace Prize for this work. Dr. David Matas is a co-author of the 2016 investigative report *An Update to Bloody Harvest and The Slaughter*. The report meticulously examines the transplant programmes of hundreds of hospitals in China, drawing on media reports, official propaganda, medical journals, hospital websites and a vast amount of deleted websites found in archives. His other works include *Why Did You Do That? The Autobiography of a Human Rights Advocate*; *Justice Delayed: Nazi War Criminals in Canada* with Susan Charendoff; *Closing the Doors: The Failure of Refugee Protection* with Ilana Simon; *No More: The Battle Against Human Rights Violations*; *Bloody Words: Hate and Free Speech*; and *Aftershock: Antisemitism and Anti-Zionism*.

Geoffrey Nice has practised as a barrister since 1971. He worked at the International Criminal Tribunal for the Former Yugoslavia – the ICTY – between 1998 and 2006 and led the prosecution of Slobodan Milošević, former

President of Serbia. Much of his work since has been connected to cases before the permanent International Criminal Court – Sudan, Kenya, Libya – or *pro bono* for victims' groups – Iran, Burma, North Korea – whose cases cannot get to any international court. He works for several related NGOs and lectures and commentates in the media in various countries on international war crimes issues. He has been a part-time judge since 1984 sitting at the Old Bailey and has sat as judge in other jurisdictions, tribunals and inquiries. Between 2009 and 2012 he was vice-chair of the Bar Standards Board, the body that regulates barristers. He is presently the chairman of the International Tribunal into Forced Organ Harvesting from the Prisoners of Conscience in China.

Hamid Sabi is an Iranian lawyer and human rights advocate practising in London, England. He has studied economics at Tehran University (1966–70) and law in Dundee University (1972–74). He was the Secretary General of the Iranian Students Association for the UN (1968–70). He has acted as counsel and expert witness in major international commercial disputes. He was a member of the Executive Committee of the Iran Tribunal, acted as counsel to the Iran Tribunal's Truth Commission (June 2012) and the Rapporteur of the Iran Tribunal Judgment (February 2013). He is presently the counsel to the International Tribunal into Forced Organ Harvesting from the Prisoners of Conscience in China.

Nevenka Tromp expertise is in the study of political violence committed through mass atrocities and in transitional justice in post-conflict societies. Since 1992 she has been a lecturer in East European studies at the University of Amsterdam (UvA). Between 2000 and 2012 she was a member of the Leadership Research Team (LRT) at the International Criminal Tribunal for the Former Yugoslavia (ICTY) and from 2000 to 2006 was the principle researcher in the team prosecuting Slobodan Milošević, the former President of Serbia. Between 2012 and 2013 she was attached at the Dutch Institute for War Documentation. She is the author of *Prosecuting Slobodan Milosevic: The Unfinished Trial.*

Regina Menachery Paulose is an international criminal law attorney (US). She obtained her JD from Seattle University School of Law and her LLM in International Crime and Justice from the University of Torino/UNICRI. She presents and publishes on topics related to international criminal law and transnational crimes. She has participated on two People's Tribunals. She is the co-founder of A Contrario ICL, a blog devoted to international justice issues. She is a board member of the World Peace through Law Section of the Washington State Bar Association and a Co-Chair of the International Refugee Law Section of the American Bar Association.

Ronald Rogo holds a postgraduate degree in international crime and justice from the United Nations Criminal Research Institute (UNICRI) in Turin,

Italy. He currently lectures at the School of Law, University of Nairobi. He has experience representing victims of sexual violence, illegal detention and police abuse. He also currently consults with various non-governmental organisations in Kenya and has conducted legal aid clinics in communities within Kenya. Ronald is also a co-founder of A CONTRARIO ICL, a blog devoted to international justice issues. His research interests include topics in criminal law, international criminal law, sexual violence and disability law among others.

Roya Ghiasi is a human rights activist. She has a degree in education (1976). She was arrested in Iran in 1980s in a number of occasions because of her activities against the Islamic regime. She was banned from any employment or engagement in the field of education for life. Her sister (Kobra Ghiasi) was executed in 1982. Roya Ghiasi emigrated to Switzerland in 1986, where she lives now. She is active in art and theatre in Switzerland. She joined the Executive Committee of Iran Tribunal in 2009 and gave evidence to the Truth Commission (June 2012) on human rights abuses of the political prisoners in Iran and systematic destruction and murder of the opponents of the regime. She has organised a number of conferences and seminars during Human Rights Conferences in Geneva to increase the awareness of abuses of human rights in Iran.

Shadi Sadr is an Iranian human rights lawyer who studied Master of International Law at the University of Tehran. Shadi Sadr is the founder and director of Raahi, a legal centre for vulnerable women. In a wave of repression against civil society, Raahi was closed down by the Iranian authorities in 2007 when Sadr was detained in notorious Evin prison. Sadr has touched the lives of hundreds of individuals through her work and her support for campaigns such as the Stop Stoning Forever Campaign. In July 2009, she was arrested once again and then released, which allowed her to escape to Europe. On May 17, 2010, she was convicted in absentia in a Tehran Revolutionary court of "acting against national security and harming public order" and was sentenced to six years in prison with 74 lashes. Shadi Sadr has received several awards such as Human Rights Tulip and Alexander Prize of Law School of Santa Clara University. In 2010 Shadi Sadr co-founded a new organisation, Justice for Iran (JFI), which aims to address and eradicate the practice of impunity that empowers officials of the Islamic Republic of Iran to perpetrate widespread human rights violations against their citizens and to hold them accountable for their actions. As the Executive Director of JFI, she has overseen the creation and implementation of several research projects on gross violations of the rights of ethnic and religious minorities, LGBTs, women, and those who are persecuted because of their political beliefs. She is also the co-author of *Crime and Impunity: Sexual Torture of Women in Islamic Republic Prisons.* Shadi Sadr served as a jury member for the 2015 International People's Tribunal (IPT) 1965, the 2017 People's Tribunal on Myanmar, and the 2018–19 Independent Tribunal into Forced Organ Harvesting from Prisoners of Conscience in China.

Shokoufeh Sakhi is currently a member of *Pathologies of Solitude* research network, a project hosted at Queen Mary University, London. She has a doctorate in political science from York University, Toronto, with a specialisation in political theory and philosophy. She acted as Executive Committee Director (2013–2014) of the Iran Tribunal Foundation investigating the Iranian state's crime against humanity in the 1980s. She also testified as an ex-political prisoner at the Iranian People's Tribunal hearings (2012). Among many documentaries, she participated in *The Tree That Remembers*, a production of National Film Board of Canada. Her most recent publication is "Ethical-Political Praxis: Social Justice and the Resistant Subject in Iran" in *Iran's Struggles for Social Justice*: Palgrave 2017.

Susie Hughes is Executive Director and leading Co-founder of the International Coalition to End Transplant Abuse in China (ETAC) and is based in Australia. She has extensive experience in the not-for-profit human rights sector focusing on the issue of forced organ harvesting of prisoners of conscience in China. Susie was a member of the ETAC Steering Committee responsible for initiating the China Tribunal and contributed pro bono as director of logistics for the China Tribunal. She has testified before the Australian Parliament on organ trafficking and transplant tourism, and freedom of religion and belief, and has hosted numerous roundtable discussions, Q&A forums and online seminars on forced organ harvesting in China. Susie has also worked in the private education sector as a teacher, teacher trainer, school administrator and board member.

Thamil Venthan Ananthavinayagan LLM (Maastricht University), PhD (NUI Galway) is a lecturer for international law at Griffith College, Dublin. His research interests lie in the field of the United Nations, public international law, international humanitarian law, international human rights law, post-colonialism, transitional justice and third world approaches to international law. He has worked for the German Labour Party, the Friedrich-Ebert-Stiftung and numerous non-governmental organisations in various European countries. He served as assistant to the speaker of the German Health Ministry and worked as junior lawyer for the German Tenants' Association. Finally, he has presented papers in numerous countries and cities, *inter alia* Nottingham, Liverpool, Geneva, Padova, Dublin, Galway, Seattle, Singapore, Belfast, Maastricht. He is the author of *Sri Lanka, Human Rights and the United Nations: A Scrutiny into the International Human Rights Engagement with a Third World State.*

Zachary D. Kaufman JD, PhD, is Associate Professor of Law and Political Science at the University of Houston Law Centre. He also holds appointments at the University's Department of Political Science and Hobby School of Public Affairs. Immediately before joining the University of Houston, Professor Kaufman taught at Stanford Law School and was a senior fellow at Harvard University's Kennedy School of Government. Previously, Professor Kaufman held academic appointments at Yale Law School, Harvard Law

School, Stanford University, and New York University and taught at Yale University's Department of Political Science and George Washington University's Elliott School of International Affairs. Professor Kaufman is the author or editor of three books: *United States Law and Policy on Transitional Justice: Principles, Politics, and Pragmatics* (Oxford University Press, 2016); *Social Entrepreneurship in the Age of Atrocities: Changing Our World* (Edward Elgar Publishing, 2012); and *After Genocide: Transitional Justice, Post-Conflict Reconstruction, and Reconciliation in Rwanda and Beyond* (Oxford University Press, 2009). He is also the author of over 40 articles and book chapters. His work is published by or forthcoming in the *Harvard International Law Journal*, *Harvard Journal on Legislation*, *Yale Journal of International Law*, *Yale Law & Policy Review*, *Yale Human Rights & Development Law Journal*, *Stanford Law & Policy Review*, *Emory International Law Review*, *Southern California Law Review*, *Journal of International Criminal Justice*, *Criminal Law Forum*, and other journals. He has also written for popular outlets, including the *New York Times*, the *Washington Post*, the *Boston Globe*, the *San Francisco Chronicle*, *Foreign Policy*, *Forbes*, *Just Security*, and *Central African Magazine*. He has delivered over 250 lectures around the world and has been interviewed by numerous media outlets, such as National Public Radio, the BBC, CNBC, Voice of America, the *Boston Globe*, and the *Huffington Post*. His research has been supported by competitive grants from Yale Law School, Harvard University, and the International Criminal Justice Resource Centre. Professor Kaufman has served in all three branches of the US government. In the judicial branch, he was a US Supreme Court Fellow and clerk to a judge on the US Court of Appeals for the First Circuit. In the legislative branch, he was a Council on Foreign Relations International Affairs Fellow on the US Senate Foreign Relations Committee. In the executive branch, he served at the US Departments of State and Justice. He also has served at three international war crimes tribunals: the International Criminal Court (where he was the first American to serve) as well as the UN International Criminal Tribunals for Rwanda and for the former Yugoslavia. In the private sector, Professor Kaufman has practised law at O'Melveny & Myers LLP and worked at Google. Professor Kaufman received his JD from Yale Law School (where he was Editor-in-Chief of the *Yale Law & Policy Review*); his D.Phil. (PhD) and M.Phil., both in International Relations, from Oxford University (where he was a Marshall Scholar); and his BA in Political Science from Yale University (where he was the student body president).

Introduction

Dear Reader,

This volume is geared towards introducing you to movements called *People's Tribunals*. This volume critically examines the following questions on People's Tribunals (PT):

- Can PT be considered legitimate responses to injustices?
- What benefits can PT provide over the pursuit of traditional legal avenues?
- Are they *effective* in countering silence on violations of rights and/or addressing crimes?
- At the conclusion of a PT – what is next?

In order to answer these questions we turn to experts who have participated in PT and those who have closely followed the development of PT. Included in the voices of this volume are survivors and victims of mass atrocities who are central to the concept of PT. No volume can be complete without their viewpoint. It is exciting to have many diverse perspectives in one volume relating to these bourgeoning global movements which have mainly utilised international human rights and international criminal law to conduct their work.

This volume approaches the conversation about PT from two different angles. The first angle is general application of legal theory and international law to the concept of a PT. The second angle looks at PT in practice.

It is my hope that this volume brings about more meaningful discussions about how PT can hold perpetrators responsible for human rights violations when there are no other means to do so. It is not a black and white issue and there are plenty more debates to be had regarding their utility and function. This volume brings some of these critical issues to light but I also hope this volume leads to recognition of the importance of victim and survivor movements in an emerging world of cookie cutter responses to injustices. Issues related to justice are not one size fits all. Ultimately, People's Tribunals open up another space for how we reflect, define, and administer justice.

Sincerely,
Regina M. Paulose
International Criminal Law Attorney

1 Can you hear the people sing? Victim/survivor rights in People's Tribunals

Regina Menachery Paulose

Contours and history

People's Tribunals defined

In a previous volume I defined PT as "movements created by citizens, which integrate both local and international participants to take human rights from the abstract level of treaty provisions to a reality of victim's needs." Upon further reflection my initial definition appears problematic. It is evident that in some cases there is no integration of international and domestic participants. These movements go beyond violations of human rights and, as discussed by Dr. Binoy Kampmark in Chapter 8, they also delve into environmental issues. Therefore, for the purposes of this volume I provide a new definition in order to encompass a broader range of possible topics.

People's Tribunals are *movements that are created for the purpose of examining rights violations whereby civil society believes the violation has not been formally recognised or addressed by the state, community, or a legal system.* It is important to recognise that PT is a movement. A PT is a "movement" because each is uniquely set up to address a specific question. Their focus and objectives are limited in scope, even when they may be set up for a longer duration. Further, it is one event on a continuum of activities on a particular issue. Jean-Paul Sarte, a member of the first Russell Tribunal, thought of PT as "critical spaces for reflection, gathering of testimony, and documentation that then require additional political processes to determine what actions out to follow from their findings."[1] Aside from emphasising why they are movements, Sarte also emphasised that the PT may create more activity once completed. A PT can begin to or continue to raise awareness on an issue and/or act as an interruption to a dominant narrative.

1 Zachary Manfredini, 'Sharpening the Vigilance of the World: Reconsidering the Russell Tribunal as a Ritual' [20 March 2018] Humanity Journal <http://humanityjournal.org/issue9-1/sharpening-the-vigilance-of-the-world-reconsidering-the-russell-tribunal-as-ritual/>

History and types of People's Tribunals

There is no specified format for a PT and it is clear that they can be divided into three main categories. Technically, all of them have been inspired by the first category, the International War Crimes Tribunal, sponsored by Bertrand Russell, a British philosopher of maths and anti-war campaigner starting in World War I. The International War Crimes Tribunal, which started in 1966, focused on US foreign policy in Vietnam and became known as the "Russell Tribunal on Vietnam." The Tribunal was composed of academics and philosophers such as Sartre and Simone de Beauvoir. Russell was inspired by the Nazi trials at Nuremberg and created this format to raise "awareness about the impact" of the Vietnam War and to encourage people "to take action to stop these crimes."[2] The Russell Tribunal held two sessions and then unanimously concluded that the US was "guilty" of the crimes charged which included, "genocide, the use of forbidden weapons, maltreatment and killing of prisoners, violence and forceful movement of prisoners" in Vietnam, Laos and Cambodia."[3]

Bertrand Russell died in 1970 but the legacy of peaceful responses through informal tribunals to the injustices committed by state actors, carried on from 1972–1975 with the creation of Russell Tribunal II. This Tribunal was held to address human rights violations in Latin America. Present among this group of intellectuals was Senator Lelio Basso, who eventually created the Permanent People's Tribunals (PPT). The Russell Tribunal II found Brazil, Chile, Uruguay, and Bolivia "guilty of serious, repeated and systematic violations of human rights" as crimes against humanity.[4]

Subsequent to Russell Tribunal II, there have been three more documented Russell Tribunals. In 2001 the Russell Tribunal on Human Rights in Psychiatry was held in Berlin and focused on human rights violations in the psychiatry profession. Specifically, the Russell Tribunal sought to address how "the concept of psychiatric treatment thus becomes a ready weapon" as a tool in fascism and social control.[5] In 2004 a Russell Tribunal was held in Brussels on the issue of coalition-led invasion into Iraq. Finally, the most recent 2009–2014 Russell Tribunal was on Palestine, which sought "to inform and mobilise public opinion and

2 Cody J. Foster, 'Did America Commit War Crimes in Vietnam?' (*New York Times*, 1 December 2017) <>www.nytimes.com/2017/12/01/opinion/did-america-commit-war-crimes-in-vietnam.html>

3 Ibid.

4 Tamiment Library and Robert F. Wagner Labor Archive, 'Historical/Biographical Note' (International War Crimes Tribunal Records) <http://dlib.nyu.edu/findingaids/html/tamwag/tam_098/bioghist.html>, citing *International War Crimes Tribunal, Against the Crime of Silence: Proceedings of the Russell International War Crimes Tribunal, Stockholm, Copenhagen* (New York, Bertrand Russell Peace Foundation, 1968).

5 Thomas Szasz and George Alexander, 'A Summary of the Accusation of the Russell Tribunal on Human Rights in Psychiatry' (June–July 2001) <>www.freedom-of-thought.de/rt/accusation.htm>

relevant institutions and decision-makers in light of continuing failures to uphold international law in the context of the Israeli-Palestinian conflict."[6]

The Russell Tribunal model continues to build upon Bertrand Russell's hope that the "tribunals would build momentum toward a people-driven, international peace movement that did more than protest."[7] It is clear that Bertrand Russell's first PT made a significant impact on the kinds of possibilities for civil society to increase peaceful protest and discourse around human rights issues, applying international human rights norms. Russell's actions inspired Diana Russell and Nicole Van Den Ven to create an International Tribunal on Crimes against Women (ITCW) in 1976. The ITCW focused on crimes committed against women all over the world. The response of the ITCW was tremendous considering 2000 women from 40 countries came together to denounce abuse against women.

After the original Russell Tribunal, two other categories of People's Tribunal have emerged. The second category was created in 1979 by Italian Senator Lelio Basso. Senator Basso was inspired by the first two Russell Tribunals and went on to create the Permanent People's Tribunal (PPT), which is part of the international section of the Lelio Basso Foundation. The "Algiers Charter" forms the basis for activity of the PPT and is a list of people's rights that "that codify the right to a national and cultural identity, the right to self-determination, economic rights, the right to culture, the right to the environment and to common resources, minority rights and the guarantees to these rights."[8] The format of the PPT is similar in each case as it is governed by a "statute" adopted in 1979.[9] The PPT statute allows for groups that have suffered a rights violation to apply for examination by the PPT mechanism or the PPT can issue an advisory opinion.[10] The PPT takes on a wide range of issues. For instance, the PPT explored the working conditions of migrants and refugees, stemming from a series of PPT held from 2017–2018. Additionally the PPT took on the issue of fracking and climate change. At the time of writing, the PPT has issued a total 46 "judgements."

At this juncture, a quick side note is warranted. The Russell Tribunals and the PPT use legal descriptors to make it presumably appear as though it is a legal institution. The reason for the use of certain legal descriptors is unclear. It is my view that these descriptors cause confusion and detract from the critical conversations that are taking place. A PT does not have the power to indict people, issue

6 Russell Tribunal on Palestine, Submission to CERD, Israel's Combined 14th, 15th and 16th Periodic Review (January 2012), p. 1 <https://www2.ohchr.org/english/bodies/cerd/docs/ngos/RussellTribunalOnPalestine_Israel80.pdf>

7 Foster, (note 2).

8 Permanent People's Tribunal, 'Algiers Charter' <http://permanentpeoplestribunal.org/algiers-charter/?lang=en>

9 The Statute that still governs the work of the PPT is from 1979, although it appears a new one is being formulated. That statute can be found on the PPT website. <http://permanentpeoplestribunal.org/statute/?lang=en>

10 Permanent Peoples Tribunal, Statute, Article 3 and 4 (1979) <http://permanentpeoplestribunal.org/wp-content/uploads/2016/06/statute.pdf>

arrest warrants, compel witnesses, and sentence people. Ronald Rogo will discuss in this volume that this is one of the main differences between a PT and a Truth Commission.

Take for example some of the descriptors used in the 2015 International People's Tribunal (IPT) which convened in Washington, DC to examine crimes against the Filipino people by President B. Aquino and President Obama. Building upon the work of the other Philippines PPT, the IPT "indicted" defendants by certified mail and even had its own "Clerk of Court." Without the highly charged legal language which can be found throughout its report, this movement is impressive because of the sheer volume of participants, specifically victims and survivors that came together to discuss these issues, and the amount of documentation it was able to produce.

Besides the legal language that can give the perception that these are "kangaroo courts"[11], PT are criticised for being one-sided and therefore lead to a predetermined outcome. Other criticisms of PT are outlined in chapters by Benjamin Duerr, Dr. Thamil Venthan Ananthavinayagan, Ronald Rogo and Shadi Sadr. A PT can only benefit from having a multitude of voices and perspectives, in support of or contrary to, so that the issues are well balanced and presented in a manner that can truly mobilise public opinion and governments to act. Perhaps some of these criticisms are the underlying reasons for a third category of PT to emerge.

The third categories of PT are those that are completely independent. Their formats are created based on the inquiry, goals, and resources of the civil society group which initiates the process. The ICTW mentioned earlier is one example. Another example is the International Peoples Tribunal on Kashmir (IPTK) which was created in order to document human rights violations in Kashmir. The IPTK was only able to focus on the Indian-controlled side of Kashmir due to difficulties in accessing the Pakistan-controlled side.[12] The IPTK convened from 2008–2009 to 1) examine the failures of governance; 2) to examine the breakdowns in human rights; 3) expand awareness on human rights abuses; 4) develop recommendations for justice; and 5) increase participation of the local and international community toward justice, peace, and security in the region.[13] The IPTK concluded its session with a report, "Buried Alive" which documented the graves

11 Both the Russell Tribunal on Vietnam and the Russell Tribunal on Palestine faced criticism for being biased. *See* Richard Falk, 'People's Tribunals, and the Roots of Civil Society of Justice' (12 May 2015) <>www.opendemocracy.net/en/opensecurity/peoples-tribunals-and-roots-of-civil-society-justice/>

12 The author went on to elaborate that the lack of an investigation into the Pakistani side did not mean that there was a lack of rights violations; however, the Indian administered side is the site of a live conflict. Mallika K. Sarkaria, 'On Trial: Human Rights in Kashmir' (Kennedy School Review, Spring 2009) <>www.questia.com/read/1G1-237943395/on-trial-human-rights-in-kashmir>

13 The Independent People's Tribunal on Kashmir, 'Premise and Objectives' (5 April 2008) <>www.kashmirprocess.org/premise.html>

of those killed in mass atrocities. The IPTK submitted its findings to the United Nations and the European Union. The European Union passed a resolution calling upon India and Pakistan to take action to resolve the issues documented in the report.[14] This eventually led India to create a state-run human rights commission[15] to investigate the 3,000 plus unmarked graves in Kashmir, which is of significant importance given the grassroots efforts undertaken by the IPTK. This is a tremendous "win" for this movement as it proved the fruits of working with civil society and the strength of its documentation efforts to create change. India responded in kind to address the injustices thereby validating the work of the movement in raising awareness on the issue.[16]

Another independent format is the Indian People's Tribunal on Environment and Human Rights created in 1993. This PT focuses on conducting investigations concerning both human rights and environmental justice. This particular format took local movements and gave them a national platform and then issued reports on particular issues.

This volume discusses different examples of independent tribunals, including two different PT in Australia and the China Tribunal. While these movements are diverse and can offer a lot of information regarding certain issues, they also, in some respects, do not escape some of the aforementioned criticisms and found throughout this volume.

Our thoughts, our voices

At this juncture it is important to read why victims, survivors, and activists found PT to be important for their movements. These are their personal experiences. This volume would be incomplete without their perspectives.[17]

> *The following is a statement from C.S. in August of 2018:*
>
> I'd been a victim for 30 years when I was first approached to join the steering committee of the UK child sex abuse People's Tribunal. It took us a year and a half from start to finish. I won't lie – it was the hardest thing I'd ever done.

14 *See* European Parliament resolution of 10 July 2008 on allegations of mass graves in Indian administered Kashmir <>www.europarl.europa.eu/sides/getDoc.do?type=TA&reference=P6-TA-2008-0366&language=EN>

15 *See* Rifat Fareed, 'India Ordered to Probe 2,080 Mass Graves in Kashmir' *Al Jazeera* (3 November 2017) <>www.aljazeera.com/news/2017/11/india-ordered-probe-3800-mass-graves-kashmir-171103114819966.html>

16 I do not mean to suggest that the Human Rights Commission that followed was perfect nor do I suggest that this should have been the only response to the report.

17 These statements were voluntarily submitted for inclusion in this volume by the victims, survivors, and activists. These statements were solely edited for glaring spelling errors and formatting. These statements were specifically sent in for this volume on People's Tribunals. The sole question asked was what did the People's Tribunal mean to them? They were encouraged to be as open and as critical as they would like to be if that was the case.

At the same time I decided to stand up and face what I'd suffered as a child, so along with the need to help others with our work, I had to help myself too.

Working with the judges was life changing for me. Our chair, legal advisor, and judges all inspired me massively. I'd spent my life being ignored by professionals so for these top shelf successful professionals to engage with me and listen to me was truly amazing.

We finished on a high at UK parliament. Our government chose to ignore us but in the UK I felt that was predictable. Personally I finished as a thriver I'd gone from victim to survivor during it and see life differently in many ways now. It was the hardest most emotional rewarding thing I've ever done in life and I will be eternally proud of what we achieved and grateful for the people I met and worked along the way

If you ever get the chance to speak your truth this way my advice . . . do it

The following is a statement from C.S. in July 2018:

I am a survivor of Child Sex Abuse by my father. Child abuse in the family is the most common form by a very high percentage. Helping the UKCSAPT (UK Child Sex Abuse People's Tribunal) produce a Report in 2016 was important for me in a number of ways:

It helped me feel less alone and it was good for me to work with other survivors and campaigners on the Committee. The teamwork (with it's up and downs) helped me mentally on the surface and also sub-consciously.

By helping others, this has helped myself and continues to do so.

The Report mentioned above, written by a panel of experts, produced conclusions that were sent to the Home Secretary (Theresa May at the time), the Independent Inquiry into Child Sex Abuse and other organisations. It may well have pre-empted many of the conclusions of the IICSA Report when it is produced. Playing a part behind the scenes in helping the UKCSAPT Report to be published means I have done something in the National Interest. There are probably 2 million+ survivors in the UK, and many millions more worldwide. To realise the potential impact helps me, and helps others who will benefit from the effects of the UKCSAPT Report.

Although much campaigning was done before the Jimmy Savile revelations, 2012 seems to have been the point after which survivors were more likely to be heard and children more likely to be better protected. The UKCSAPT Report contributes to slowly changing the societal attitude to Child Sex Abuse. The Report's continuing relevance continues to help me.

My fading father continues to be unpleasant (although I am continually improving my reactions to his hate and concentrating more on enjoying and getting the most out of life with my supportive family). I have to continue to look to help other survivors where they feel they need help and I can possibly make a difference.

The UKCSAPT was successful in producing a Report with which survivors were involved behind the scenes and also on the Panel. Survivors are in various stages of recovery so to have a number of survivors working together with campaigners up to the Report stage is a huge achievement. We often have trust issues and can easily find getting on with others very difficult. The UKCSAPT evolved over a couple of years and many of the Committee members were picked from activists on Twitter or experts in the CSA and Human Rights field. A lawyer who was involved with the IICSA said we would not be able to produce a Report. We proved him wrong, even on a shoe-string budget.

From scratch to the Report stage was a convoluted and complex process mainly of relationships between people. I don't think I can offer advice as to how we could have done things differently. I'll just repeat that we produced a Report, and may take things further at some point.

The following is a statement from G.F. in October 2018

The People's Tribunal is such an important part of my life. In short, it gives a voice to survivors who have been made to be silent to hide the abuse. I feel that having fellow survivors on the committee was a massive help and gave confidence to the survivor coming forward, we weren't just strangers in suits. We were just like them!

We defiantly couldn't have done the work we did without the help of the amazing professionals that worked alongside us for free, even paying for themselves to travel to the UK regularly to hold meetings. On a personal level, this restored some faith in me of professionals as a whole and helped me focus less on the ones that had already let so many of us down. It was a blessing for to meet so many professionals that didn't just dismiss us tell us that our past didn't matter as we had heard too many times before!

From my perspective the People's Tribunal was set up though a lack of confidences in the government inquiry. As their inquiry was solely set up of professionals, some of which could potentially be indirectly or directly involved with the abuse in the first place. As survivors we didn't trust that the government inquiry would give a true representation of what had gone on and was afraid it would lead to further cover-ups. I was horrified at how I personally felt that we were blocked from the media!

I was most amazed at how the incredible professionals we had working with us genuinely wanted to help. On a personal level I have realised everyone has the right to say no this isn't right. We can do so much more to prevent abuse to our children I just hope the government can start to adhere to our recommendations so that our children and their children can be save from re-abuse. No, we can't stop it all but there are definitely ways in which we can minimise and stop future abuse.

I would personally like to thank EVERY survivor that had the courage to come forward and give us their statement as I do understand how difficult this would have been but without all those amazing people we wouldn't have been able to accomplish what we did.

So, if I was to sum up I would say for me personally the People's Tribunal brought hope, hope that we can make things better.

The following is a statement from B.E. in December 2018

February 3, 2012 I went to London to meet John and Hamid. I was supposed to meet Hamid and John on the same day at 5 pm. The weather was stormy that day and severe snow storm and extreme weather brought blizzards across Europe. Swedish airports are well equipped because of the country's hard winters and snow has no major impact on the flights. We boarded the plane at Stockholm´s Skavsta airport but were not allowed to fly. Storm caused disruption at London´s Stansted airport and many flights were cancelled after storms hit UK. After five hours of waiting on the plane, we were allowed to fly to London. Stansted airport was still closed and no flights were taking off or landing because of the storm when we approached the airport. The plane had no other choice but to land at Heathrow airport after flying over the sky of London for twenty five minutes. We landed at the Heathrow airport at 6 pm. I called Hamid as soon as I arrived at the airport and told him the story. Because of the delay I had, the meeting was not held that night. We met at John´s home next day. I told John and Hamid about my trip and regretted that the meeting was not held last night because of my delay. When I stopped talking, John asked me: "Where do you get all these motivations that with this physical condition you are doing this."

Two weeks before my trip to London, my disc caused me extreme pain and greatly limited my movement. This would usually take me 3 to 4 week and sometimes more to be able to walk properly again. Until one day before the flight, I could not think I would be able to go to London. On the morning of the flight I felt I was able to walk. I set aside my crutches and while I was walking with difficulty, I went to the airport. Hours of sitting on the plane for people like me, who have problem with their back and walk hardly, it feels like you have been tortured for hours.

In response to John's question, I told him a memory of bitter memories I had from Evin Prison: "It was one of the days of April 1982, if I remember correctly, on Wednesday, May 15th. One of the prison guards opened the door of our room. He was called "Hamza." He was a villager from Azerbaijan and hardly understood Farsi. He hated very much political prisoners, Communists in particular. In a ridiculous tone, he said: Who wants to go to paradise, Raise his hand? There was a deadly silence in the room. Everyone knew he had come to take a number of prisoners for execution. Earlier, in several occasions, he had taken prisoners from the room for executions. From the list he had with him, he read four names. All four were under the age of eighteen and were members of the Mojahedin Khalq. All four had a strong emotional connection with me. Soon I came to the room, we became friends and a mutual trust was established between us. We became like father and sons.

For the first time, after months of interrogation and torture, I came to a room, where eighty political prisoners were kept like a herd of sheep. There was no enough space to walk through the room. The room was 36 square meters. It was lunchtime. I picked up my blindfold and said hello to everyone. I found a tiny place near the door and sat there.

A few moments later, a teenage boy came to me and showed me the corner to the left side of the room near the window and said: "Come and sit there with us." I would prefer do not get close to anyone before to get to know the room and the people who were kept there. But I felt I could trust him. He was a handsome and lovely kind teenager. I was brutally tortured and I did not have a good physical condition and could hardly go. I followed him haltingly and sat with him and his friends in the corner of the room.

When Hamza read the names of these four teenagers, Kiomars, who was relatively short and had body-shaped and blue eyes and was younger than his comrades; Hamid Reza, Mohammad, and Mehran, hugged me tight, cried out loudly and with a loud voice repeatedly said:" I do not want to die, I do not want to die, do not let him take me away." He made everyone cry. Kiomars was the same young man who asked me to join him and his friends when I came to the room.

I said to John: "What could I say to this sixteen-year-old teenage boy at that moment that would relieve him?! Nothing could relieve him. They were taking him to take his life. What could possibly console him at that moment?!"

The only thing that came to my mind in that difficult and deadly moment was to tell him that any displacement does always mean taking prisoners to death. I wish that was the case, but the reality was something else. I promised myself, if I would stay alive and get out of the prison, I would be their voice. He and his three comrades were taken out of the room few moments later and executed on the same day. I could not eat or speak to anyone for one week. It was there I decided if I would go out of prison, I would plead justice for them and thousands of others who were executed by the Islamic Republic of Iran in 1980s. Since I came out of prison, I was trying to carry out my promise. Iran Tribunal is a result of the efforts that I and some of my former co-prisoners carried out for years. Islamic Republic of Iran has introduced a deep and unforgivable wound to the Iranian people. Iran Tribunal has been able to disclose the barbarism and brutality of the Islamic Republic of Iran in 1980s and made them known internationally.

The following is a statement from a Rohingya activist and genocide survivor in January 2019

Under intolerant state policies, the Rohingya are being destroyed in Myanmar facing systematic ethnic, religious and political persecution. Particularly from 1962 military takeover, the Rohingya have faced continuous process of de-legitimisation, institutionalised persecution and worsening abuses culminating in genocide. For nearly six decades they have been systematically deprived of their basic rights and freedoms – freedom of movement, worship, marriage, education, and access, healthcare, employment, trade and business – and even the ability to survive. The UN has described them as "the world's most persecuted minority."

The influx of refugees and boat people into Bangladesh and other countries are regular pheromenon. In 2012 state sponsored deadly violence was carried out killing many hundreds of Rohingya and other Muslims and displacing 120,000 in Rakhine State. Some 145,000 people confined to apartheid-like concentration camps and scores of others have remained in ghettos in Rakhine capital Sittwe and southern towns.

The government continued to restrict movement and block access for food, water, healthcare, education and vital humanitarian assistance forcing the people to flee to neighbouring countries with the peak of forced migration occurring in 2015. Military campaigns had been intensified killing the innocent civilians, raping the women and girls, torching their homes, and destroying their age-old settlements in 2016, causing unprecedented influx across the border into Bangladesh, creating great humanitarian disaster

In response to the well documented unfolding and escalating genocide in Rakhine State, Myanmar, a letter was submitted on 24th November 2016 by Nurul Islam, on behalf of the a group of researchers, academics, activists in coalition with global Rohingya refugees, requesting the Permanent People's Tribunal (PPT) in Rome to take up the urgent case of Myanmar's Muslim Rohingya ethnic minority.

Accordingly, an International Permanent People's Tribunal (IPPT) on Myanmar, was established in 2017 to examine cases regarding violations of human rights of Rohingya and other people. It was a free opinion tribunal, independent from any state authority.

A one-day session was held on 25th July 2017 in Queen Mary University, London, and It heard the testimonies and collected evidences. Then a 5-day session was held in University Malaya in 1917. A seven-man panel tribunal announced its verdict after considering documentary and expert evidence as well as the testimony of some 200 victims of the atrocity committed against the Rohingya, Kachin and other minority groups in Myanmar.

Following five days of hearing, from September 18–22, held at the university Malaya Legal faculty moot court, head judge Daniel Feierstein, who founded the Centre for genocide Studies in Argentina, read out the findings/judgement. He said that Myanmar regime was indicted and found guilty of genocide, war crimes and crimes against humanity. Thus "the tribunal ruled that Myanmar is guilty of genocide against the people of Kachin and Muslim groups there."

Following the judgement, the tribunal also made 17 recommendations, some of them are:

- Myanmar government must cease the acts of violence against the Muslim minorities there.

- Visas and free access must be granted to the United Nation's Fact Finding Mission to probe the atrocities committed against the Rohingya, Kachin and Other Groups in Myanmar.
- Myanmar government must also amend the constitution and abolish discriminatory laws to give citizenship to the oppressed minorities.

The international community must provide financial help to countries such as Bangladesh and Malaysia that are hosting the influx of refugees escaping the violence. The tribunal's findings, judgement and recommendations would be forwarded to international bodies and civil groups to pressure the Myanmar government to act accordingly.

Welcoming the verdict as significant step towards recognising the crimes committed in Myanmar, the organising committee chairman Dr. Chandra Muzaffar said that the tribunal has called the evil by its name by using terms such as crimes against humanity and genocide, and that the tribunal findings and judgement should be used as the basis for international bodies such as the ASEAN, International Criminal Court and super powers to act.

The whole Rohingya people, whether in the homeland or in their places of refuge, have felt encouraged by the judgement of the People's Tribunal. For the first time the voices of the voiceless or oppressed and persecuted Rohingya, Kachin and other Muslims were heard by a group of international legal experts in a strong people's court, thereby their cases have received international legal attention.

The following is a statement written by A.M. in April 2019

I remember organising a small table petition in 2006 in the city close to where I lived at the time. It was the year that evidence and news of forced organ harvesting from prisoners of conscience in China first began to emerge. Only a small number of courageous witnesses had stepped forward, and investigative evidence was very much in its infancy. Those who were aware of the severity of the human rights situation in China were quick to take a stand, knowing the plausibility of the evidence, given the Chinese regimes brutality. But for many, there were just too many hurdles in their minds to be able to believe.

It might have seemed a futile act, standing there in a shopping centre on a Saturday morning, collecting signatures. But this is where the advocacy began, working to give a voice to those who didn't have one. Thirteen years later, I believe the China Tribunal has once again given a voice to those who don't have one, to allow witnesses and families to tell their stories. This time, I truly believe they have been heard.

In the beginning, there were many in the international community who didn't want to listen. The Chinese Communist Party had perfected years of severe domestic and international propaganda against Falun Gong, one of the main victim groups effected by organ harvesting. Their voices were drowned out by the noise of a behemoth machine. Evidence was therefore treated with disbelief, and disdain. Many doors remained firmly closed. I believe that the China Tribunal can help to open those doors. It is truly independent in its nature, rigorous in its process and eminent in its choice of panel. The decisions and judgements it makes cannot be ignored, or dismissed.

Not long after evidence began to emerge, independent investigators began to take on the issue of organ harvesting, with a deeply inspiring fervour and resilience. As their evidence continued to grow, so did the realisation of the scale and severity of the situation. Their reports were published, and the stance of the international community began to shift. Speeches and resolutions started to appear in government houses, media reports began to emerge – people were starting to talk about it. Yet, as the months rolled into years, many governments, institutions and organisations retracted away from it.

Forced organ harvesting from prisoners of conscience in China is an incredibly complex issue. There is no one single piece of evidence that tells the whole story. It takes time to absorb and process the information, to carefully put the pieces of the puzzle together, and to understand the wider context. It is not an easy task to take this on, and frankly, an incredibly emotionally distressing subject to engage with. For these reasons, many simply didn't. But the China Tribunal has. They have painstakingly worked through all the investigations and research. They have cross-examined and corroborated evidence, and sought consultation and critique. They have sat face to face with witnesses, looking each in the eye as they described the horrors they have seen. They have done the hard work, for those who could not.

From could not to will not. Wilful ignorance is an uncomfortable topic, but it is one that exists here. China has huge foreign investment globally. Money buys silence. Governments are muted. Institutions and organisations alliances and allegiances are massaged. Media outlets are manipulated. There are many who could act, and should act, but wilfully choose not to. Their reasons will be many and varied, yet all have the same consequence.

Advocacy to try to end forced organ harvesting comes with a great sadness. It is not a historical act, something that has a defined beginning, middle and end. It is still unfolding as I write this, and with every day that goes by, more people suffer and die in the most horrible of ways. It is my deep hope that the China Tribunal can make most change here. By applying a clear, independent judgement based on rule of law, laws which no one can act outside of, more governments, institutions and organisations will find themselves in a position where they can do nothing but act, and China may finally be held to account.

The following statement is a statement written by J.Z. in April 2019

April 7, 2019 is a day that I shall never forget. On that day, I was invited, as a labor camp survivor, to testify regarding my personal experiences related to forced organ harvesting, before "The Independent Tribunal into Forced Organ Harvesting from Prisoners of Conscience In China."

For me, the procedure seemed simple. I had already submitted my testimony in writing, and the tribunal members only needed to question me further on anything they felt needed clarification.

However, nobody knew how long I had waited, what a journey I had traveled, and how grateful I was to be given such an opportunity!

I was first arrested on July 20, 1999, two days before the nationwide crackdown on Falun Gong officially started in China. I was arrested three more times after that, before being thrown into a forced labor camp without trial.

The physical and mental torture I suffered in the camp was beyond description. Nothing compared, however, to the humiliation I endured in order to be let out of the camp; so that I could expose the astonishingly inhumane crimes being committed inside those jails and labor camps.

I was forced to firstly give up, and then betray my beliefs. Under the pressure of daily brainwashing sessions, I felt my thoughts being defiled and taken away. I felt that I was becoming an empty shell of a human – a non-human, without thoughts, free will, dignity, or even a soul. No regime has ever tried to deprive people of their own thoughts, their very soul, on top of murdering their bodies on such a large scale.

Only after I paid such a price was I released. I had never expected, however, that it would take so long for the world to listen to, or try to find out what was happening to their fellow human beings in China. Thirteen years have passed since live organ harvesting of Falun Gong practitioners was first exposed to the world. How many people have been murdered during those years?

Today this unprecedented evil has expanded to target other minority groups in Chinese society, most notably, millions of Uyghurs have been detained, blood and DNA tested (a necessary step before killing people on demand for their organs). A video recently circulated on Chinese social media showed a teenage boy admitting that his brother had abducted and killed five children, before selling their organs.

This indicates that Chinese society is "imitating" its government's behavior; treating human beings as mere live organ banks, without a soul, without dignity.

How far do things have to go? What will it take for us to do something to stop this kind of evil?

I was so grateful that the People's Tribunal was willing to start a serious investigation into this issue. When I saw the tribunal members sitting there, carefully examining all the evidence and documents, and vigorously asking questions, I knew we were one step closer to the "end of the tunnel."

The role of the victim and survivor in PT

By now, it should be clear that the success attributed to these movements is a result of victim and survivor engagement. Prior to elaborating on this point, it is important for us to discuss the landscape of victim and survivor rights in international criminal law. Then a discussion will follow on how the PT process can improve its relationships with survivors and victims' by making two recommendations. The first is a need for mental health resources for victim and survivors and the second is the need for a Victim/Survivor Framework.

Victims' rights in international law

National victims' rights movements have had a positive impact on how victim and survivor rights were created within the international community and inevitably within international criminal proceedings.[18] In 1985 the United Nations issued its "Declaration of Basic Principles of Justice for Victims of Crime and Abuse of Power" (Basic Principles). The Basic Principles sets forth international standards on victims' rights. In summary these standards ask states to provide victims 1) treatment with compassion and dignity; 2) expeditious, fair, and inexpensive redress; 3) information regarding the roles of victims; 4) representation of victims views and concerns; 5) proper assistance (mental health and/or social assistance); 6) unnecessary delay; and 7) protection of privacy. The Basic Principals suggests that informal mechanisms be utilised where appropriate and that restitution made where possible.

Late professor Cherif Bassouini has pointed out that the Basic Principles are primarily concerned with "victims of domestic criminal law and are only applicable in the event that the domestic criminal law of a given State has incorporated the applicable international human rights or humanitarian norm."[19] Bassouini asserted that one of the reasons a Convention on Victims' Rights does not exist is illustrated in the adoption of the Basic Principles. Governments shortened the Basic Principles to avoid responsibility they may owe victims and wanted to focus instead on crimes committed by non-state actors.[20]

Subsequently in 2006 the UN adopted the "Basic Principles and Guidelines on the Right to a Remedy and Reparation for Victims of Gross Violations of International Human Rights Law and Serious Violations of International Humanitarian Law" (Guidelines). These Guidelines focus on the right of victims to benefit from remedies and reparation. The Guidelines provide for certain obligations outside of reparations, which include:

a Take appropriate legislative and administrative and other appropriate measures to prevent violations;
b Investigate violations effectively, promptly, thoroughly and impartially and, where appropriate, take action against those allegedly responsible in accordance with domestic and international law;

18 For more of a discussion on the impact of crimes on victims and a short history of victim rights movements. *See* UNODC, *Handbook on Justice for Victims* (New York, 1999) <>www.unodc.org/pdf/criminal_justice/UNODC_Handbook_on_Justice_for_victims.pdf>

19 M. Cherif Bassiouni, 'International Recognition of Victims' Rights' [2006] 6(2) Human Rights Law Review 203–279, 217.

20 Ibid., 247–248.

c Provide those who claim to be victims of a human rights or humanitarian law violation with equal and effective access to justice, irrespective of who may ultimately be the bearer of responsibility for the violation; and
d Provide effective remedies to victims

The Guidelines "seek to rationalize through a consistent approach the means and methods by which victim's rights can be addressed."[21] The Guidelines contain a "right to truth" provision in principle 24. "Truth can help provide an historical record, educate people, promote forgiveness and prevent future victimization. Truth is an imperative, not an option to be displaced by political convenience."[22] While international criminal proceedings seek the truth through their own means, the "right to truth" is the philosophical bedrock of why People's Tribunals are formed.

The victim in international criminal law proceedings

Within the international tribunals the rights of victims have gradually increased and now involve more victim participation in proceedings. "The Nuremberg and Tokyo tribunals were the first international courts to prosecute war criminals. Unfortunately, neither court addressed the protection and rights of victims."[23] Minor changes were made with the advent of the ad hoc tribunals such as the International Criminal Tribunal for the Former Yugoslavia (ICTY) and the International Criminal Tribunal for Rwanda (ICTR). The ICTY did not allow for victims to participate in proceedings and the ICTR allows for participatory rights in specific and limited circumstances. Essentially, the main role for the victims and survivors in both ad hoc tribunals was as a witness. The fact that victims and survivors had this main role in the ICTY and ICTR inspired the victims' rights scheme at the International Criminal Court (ICC). The ICC moved away from the role of the victim and survivor solely as a witness and created functions whereby victims could actively participate at different stages of the proceedings and broadly participate as well.[24]

The criticisms of the ICTY and ICTR[25] in how they approached the victims' rights issues also likely inspired the Extraordinary Chambers of the Courts of Cambodia to be the first hybrid court in 2003 to allow victims to act as civil parties at trial. The sheer amount of victims which were able to participate as a result of a strong framework in these trials should be commended.[26] The Special

21 Ibid., 251.
22 Ibid., 276.
23 Michael Bachrach, 'The Protection and Rights of Victims Under International Criminal Law' [2000] 34(1) The International Lawyer 12.
24 Miriam Cohen, 'Victims' Participation Rights Within the International Criminal Court: A Critical Overview' [2009] 37(3) Denver Journal International Law and Policy 357.
25 *See* Charles P. Trumbull IV, 'The Victims of Victim Participation in International Criminal Proceedings' [2008] 29 Michigan Journal of International Law 777.
26 Zdunczyk Varney and Gaudard, The Role of Victims in Criminal Proceedings [December 2017] ICTJ Briefing <>www.ictj.org/publication/role-victims-criminal-proceedings>

Tribunal for Lebanon and the Kosovo Special Chambers also give an opportunity for victims and survivors to participate thus making the ICTY and ICTR victim model a framework of the past. Although victims' rights framework under international criminal law suffers from a lack of "commonly shared understanding"[27] between different disciplines, the international criminal law system has finally recognised that victims and survivors play a greater role than merely facilitating a conviction.

People's Tribunals and victim/survivor role

Knowing within the international criminal law penal system that victim and survivor rights are continuing to go through an evolution, how is the victim and survivor role defined within a PT?

In PT movements the participation of the victim and survivor is critical yet their roles vary because of the unique mandates that each PT may choose. In *most* cases the people who have pushed for an informal tribunal are generally victims and activists who are interested in the particular issue. One could argue that because the victims and survivors are the creators of most PT, mental health resources and a Victim/Survivor Framework (V/S F) is unnecessary. After all, they can outline what it is needed and can ensure that those needs are met. However, not all PT movements are formed by victims and survivors. In some cases, there are no victims and survivors on the steering committees themselves. Further, even if there are victims and survivors on the steering committees the need still exists for information to be provided as to the scope and nature of their participation and likely impact.

The Russell Tribunals are all silent on this particular issue. The PPT has a statute but the PPT statute is completely void of any references to a framework or charter for victims. The closest language the statute uses is "respect for the fundamental rights of peoples, minorities and individual." Interestingly, under Article 15, the PPT offers the accused government a chance to participate at all stages of the proceedings when a case is brought against the government. The Statute further states that if the government chooses not to cooperate, the PPT will still communicate "all relevant acts" to the government. The Algiers Declaration states under Article 27 that perpetrators will "carry personal penal liability" for violations of the Declaration and Article 28 states that people have the right to "enforce" fundamental rights which have been disregarded. Perhaps, it could be argued that Article 28 translates into a victim's right to access justice; however that is not clear from the wording. Therefore, the foundational documents regarding the PPT are silent as to the participatory rights of victims within the PPT mechanism.

However, the independent tribunals also face the same issue, in most cases. There is a lack of a specific V/S F. The United Kingdom Child Sex Abuse

27 Bassiouni, (note 19), 204.

People's Tribunal (UKCSAPT) can be set apart from most PT.[28] The UKCSAPT was set up by victims and survivors of child sex abuse. The mandate of the UKCSAPT states that it was created to "provide a safe space free from interference and scrutiny to allow survivors, supporters, and witnesses to speak freely regarding institutional child sex abuse."[29] Aside from the role of survivors in the Steering Committee, and specific language in the mandate, the UKCSAPT also provided victim and survivor counselling support during the entire time the tribunal was in effect. The UKCSAPT partnered with three other civil society organisations that provided free counselling and referral services for those who wanted to participate. This was constantly advertised throughout social media and on the website the UKCSAPT had at the time. The UKCSAPT went to great length to ensure anonymity and confidentiality of all who participated in the process. This service was critical to the success of all those who participated in the tribunal process. For those PT that have not been set up, such as the one Zachary D. Kaufman will suggest in Chapter 11, there are two recommendations that can assist in creating a greater empowering experience for victims and survivors.

Recommendations

Given the volume of PT movements that have taken place, it is time for two large considerations to be folded into these movements so that they can continue to grow with support of victims and survivors. The PT movements need to consider providing victims and survivors' access to mental health resources and need to consider creating a V/S F at the start of each PT.

Survivor resources

It should be noted that access to mental health resources is a problem within the international legal system. In a general sense, there is still considerable debate as to whether the processing of human rights violations with victims has any therapeutic value whatsoever.[30] In a narrower sense, the impact of mental health for a victim participating in the criminal justice system is not necessarily beneficial. As one scholar noted, "experiencing the criminal justice system can be a further source of suffering for victims rather than an opportunity for them to overcome their trauma."[31] Basia Spalek, one of the expert panellists of the UKCSAPT, states

28 The other PT that had some services available to the victims and survivors was the Women's Court, discussed in Chapter 5 by Dr. Nena Tromp.

29 UKCSAPT, 'Healing and Justice: In Defence of the Survivors of Child Sex Abuse' para. 5, p. 5, March 1, 2016, <>www.ukcsapt.wordpress.com>

30 *See* S. M. Meffert, S. Shome, T. C. Neylan, K. Musalo, H. V. Fineberg, M. M. Cooke, E. P. Goosby, et al. 'Health Impact of Human Rights Testimony: Harming the Most Vulnerable?' [2016] 1(1) BMJ Global Health e000001. doi:10.1136/bmjgh-2015-000001.

31 Mina Rauschenbach and Damien Scalia, 'Victims and International Justice, a Vexed Question?' [June 2008] 90(870) International Review of the Red Cross 446.

that even if a victim may participate more in a case that does not necessarily mean that there are emotional and psychological benefits.[32]

Regardless, PT movements need to provide victims and survivors certain mental health resources for participating. Mental health and trauma often are overlooked components, even in final PT reports. PT movements need to ensure that there are resources which can help victim and survivors throughout the entire duration of PT. These movements, as the reader will learn, can at times be lengthy processes. The UKCSAPT illustrates survivors on the steering committee detailed the necessity for resources to be provided so that no survivor was left to handle re-traumatization on their own. This was a critical request made by the survivors for other victims and survivors and assisted greatly in the amount of people who participated through the evidentiary process.

Another example where the need for these services was clear was during the China Tribunal. During the proceedings of the China Tribunal, several victims and survivors came forward over the course of two different sessions to detail their accounts of horrific torture and abuse in Chinese prisons. It became evident that for many of these survivors the recollection of the torture was painful and traumatic. Further, it became clear that many people in the room (hearings were public), including the interpreters were impacted by these narratives. In this particular situation, the need for some kind of mechanism to assist people was evident.

Incorporating a mental health component to the PT movement can make these movements stronger and provide victims and survivors the continued strength should they choose to continue after a PT is concluded.

VS framework

Even though the international community's Basic Principles and Guidelines were created by national and international victim groups for a more participatory framework, it is logical that PT adopt similar kinds of instruments.

The V/S F for each PT should incorporate some or all of the Basic Principles and Guidelines since these are already accepted rights within the international community. What is incorporated of course will depend on the aims of the PT and its resources. In the cases of the Russell Tribunals and the PPT, while for the most part their framework stays the same for each PT, they should reconsider at the start of each PT the needs of the groups that they are seeking to assist. Given the PT completed as of this volume, each V/S F should consider the following:

- What is the purpose of this PT and what does it aim to accomplish?
- What is expected of the victim and survivor during this process?
- What security measures are in place to survivors and loved ones if they participate?

32 *See* Basia Spalek, *Crime Victims: Theory, Policy and Practice* (London, Palgrave Macmillan, 2006).

- What will be done with the victim statement after the conclusion of the PT and the issuance of the final report?
- How can a victim and survivor participate at the beginning, during, and after the conclusion of the PT?

Aside from these questions that should be answered by the steering committee at the start of every PT, there should also be an emphasis on the "right to truth" principle outlined in the Guidelines. While some of this may seem logical, the reality is that these steps ensure a transparent and open process and continues to build trusting relationships with victims and survivors. In particular, a V/S F will assist in effectuating the long-term changes these movements seek to garner.

Conclusion

This chapter began with a new working definition of a PT. We have reviewed the history of PT starting with the Russell Tribunal until the advent of the independent PT. These movements offer a chance for peaceful protest and a counter narrative to emerge as a result of the hard work of those who participate. Finally this chapter discussed the necessity of examining victim's rights in the context of the PT. The two recommendations which have been made, 1) for an increase of mental health resources to be provided to victims and survivors and 2) a Victim/Survivor Framework to be created for each PT, offers a chance for the PT process to become more robust and allows for significant engagement by the citizens themselves in the process. As with all types of movements, PT shows promise as a more accessible tool for civil society to utilise.

References

Basic Principles and Guidelines on the Right to a Remedy and Reparation for Victims of Gross Violations of International Human Rights Law and Serious Violations of International Humanitarian Law 2005.

Bassiouni, M. C., 'International Recognition of Victims' Rights' [2006] 6(2) Human Rights Law Review.

Cohen, M., 'Victims' Participation Rights Within the International Criminal Court: A Critical Overview' [2009] 37(3) Denver Journal International Law and Policy.

Declaration of Basic Principles of Justice for Victims of Crime and Abuse of Power 1985.

Falk, R., 'People's Tribunals, and the Roots of Civil Society of Justice' (*Open Democracy*, 12 May 2015) <www.opendemocracy.net/en/opensecurity/peoples-tribunals-and-roots-of-civil-society-justice/> accessed 21 February 2019.

Foster, J., 'Did America Commit War Crimes in Vietnam?' (*New York Times*, 1 December 2017) <www.nytimes.com/2017/12/01/opinion/did-america-commit-war-crimes-in-vietnam.html> accessed 25 January 2019.

Indian People's Tribunal <www.iptindia.org/> accessed 3 March 2019.

International People's Tribunal, Documents of the International People's Tribunal (IBON International, Philippines, 2015).

Manfredini, Z., 'Sharpening the Vigilance of the World: Reconsidering the Russell Tribunal as Ritual' (*Humanity Journal*, 20 March 2018) <http://humanityjournal.org/issue9-1/sharpening-the-vigilance-of-the-world-reconsidering-the-russell-tribunal-as-ritual/> accessed 17 January 2019.

Odink, J., 'Appendix I: The Permanent Peoples' Tribunal' [1998] 11(2) Netherlands Quarterly of Human Rights.

Parker, I., 'Russell Tribunal on Human Rights in Psychiatry & "Geist Gegen Genes"' (*Psychology in Society*, 30 June–2 July 2001) <www.pins.org.za/pins/pins27/pins27_article12_Parker.pdf> accessed 15 March 2019.

Paulose, R., 'Imagining People's Tribunals as the Promoter of Human Rights' in *Human Rights and Power in Times of Globalisation* (Leiden, Brill Nijhoff Publishers, 2018).

Permanent People's Tribunal <http://permanentpeoplestribunal.org/?lang=en> accessed February 2019.

Rauschenbach, M. and Scalia, D., 'Victims and International Justice, a Vexed Question?' (*International Review of the Red Cross*, June 2008).

Sarkaria, M., 'On Trial: Human Rights in Kashmir' (*Kennedy School Review* 2009) <www.questia.com/read/1G1-237943395/on-trial-human-rights-in-kashmir> accessed 3 March 2019.

Spalek, B., *Crime Victims: Theory, Policy and Practice* (London, Palgrave Macmillan, 2006).

The Independent People's Tribunal on Kashmir <www.kashmirprocess.org/premise.html> accessed 3 January 2019.

Tognoni, G., 'The History of the Permanent People's Tribunal' in Andrew Byrnes and Gabrielle Simm, eds., *People's Tribunals in International Law* (Cambridge University Press, 2018)

Trumbull, C., 'The Victims of Victim Participation in International Criminal Proceedings' [2008] 29 Michigan Journal of International Law.

2 Political will and the people's will

The role of People's Tribunals in international justice

Benjamin Duerr

People's Tribunals and formal courts in international law

Accountability for grave crimes is a relatively new concept in international relations and law. Although there were attempts to establish International Criminal Courts before, an international criminal law regime started to emerge only in the 1990s.[1] The decisions of the United Nations Security Council to create two international criminal tribunals to hold to account perpetrators of the conflict in Yugoslavia and the Rwandan genocide set in motion a development that led to the creation of several other special courts and tribunals. Such institutions were established, for example, to prosecute crimes committed in the conflicts in Sierra Leone and Kosovo, following the fall of the Khmer Rouge regime in Cambodia and after the end of the dictatorship of Hissène Habré in Chad. With the adoption of the Rome Statute in 1998, which entered into force in 2002, the ICC came into being – the first permanent international court mandated to investigate and prosecute the core international crimes: genocide, crimes against humanity, war crimes and the crime of aggression.

As a subset of international law, international criminal law has its sources in treaties, customary law, general principles of law, and judicial decisions and writings of the most qualified publicists.[2] War crimes have their origin in the laws and customs of war. One of the first attempts to regulate warfare and forbid certain acts was made in 1863 by Francis Lieber who wrote the "Instructions for the Government of the Armies of the United States in the Field."[3] It prohibited rape, killing, wounding or maiming the population of the invaded country. Later, the 1899 and 1907 Hague Conventions on the Laws and Customs of War on Land, together with the Geneva Conventions, became the cornerstones of international humanitarian law, which regulates the conduct of warfare and criminalises certain acts.

1 Robert Cryer, *An Introduction to International Criminal Law and Procedure* (Cambridge University Press, 2010), 3.
2 Statute of the International Court of Justice, 38(1)(a)-(d).
3 David M. Crowe, 'War Crimes and Genocide in History, and the Evolution of Responsive International Law' [2009] 37 Nationalities Papers 6, 769.

The crime of genocide emerged after World War II and is codified in the Genocide Convention of 1948.[4] Crimes against humanity began to emerge at the same time and include various offences "committed as part of a widespread or systematic attack directed against any civilian population."[5] They form the core international crimes and are offences over which International Criminal Courts and tribunals have been given jurisdiction.

PT claim to apply the sources of international criminal law and engage with it in similar ways. PTs emerged about two decades prior to the birth of modern international criminal tribunals. As Regina Menachery Paulose points out in Chapter 1, a group of intellectuals alongside British philosopher Bertrand Russell are seen as the founders of today's PT. In November 1966, Russell, then 94 years old, and other distinguished European intellectuals, including Jean-Paul Sartre, Vladimir Dedijer, a jurist from Yugoslavia, British historian Isaac Deutscher, and the Italian jurist Lelio Basso constituted the Russell Tribunal on War Crimes in Vietnam.[6] The tribunal was inspired by the set-up and procedures of the Nuremberg Military Tribunal and organised under the umbrella of the Russell Peace Foundation. It was thus independent of political power and state authorities and did not have a formal legal basis. Crucially, it also lacked political support from governments. A few days before the opening of the tribunal in April 1967, the American-friendly director of the hotel in Paris, where the hearings were to take place, cancelled the booking of Russell's group.[7] Before the incident, French president Charles De Gaulle had already refused Sartre's request to host the tribunal.[8] Public sessions were therefore held in the capitals of Sweden and Denmark, Stockholm and Copenhagen. At the end, the panel issued a verdict, finding that the US was committing war crimes, and that the conflict amounted to genocide against the people of Vietnam.[9] Australia, New Zealand and South Korea were found guilty as accomplices to the crimes, and Thailand, the Philippines and Japan complicit in initiating and conducting the Vietnam War.

Russell died shortly after, in 1970, but his idea of PT lives on. Since the first Russell Tribunal on Vietnam more than 80 PT have been established, including tribunals for Iraq in 2004 and Palestine in 2009.[10] They feature multiple commonalities which put them in a particular position in relation to international law,

4 Convention on the Prevention and Punishment of the Crime of Genocide, adopted by the General Assembly on 9 December 1948.

5 Rome Statute of the International Criminal Court, 7(1).

6 Ken Coates, 'Russell Tribunals' (Bertrand Russel Peace Foundation) <www.russfound.org/The_Spokesman/KCTrib104.html> accessed 16 February 2019.

7 'Russell "Tribunal" Loses Paris Hotel "Courtroom"', *New York Times* (New York, 12 April 1967).

8 Coates, (note 9).

9 Gabrielle Simm and Andrew Byrnes, 'International Peoples' Tribunals in Asia: Political Theatre, Juridical Farce, or Meaningful Intervention?' [2014] 4 Asian Journal of International Law 105.

10 Ibid.

distinguishing them from other forms of activism on the one hand, and from formal courts on the other hand.

First, PT are not legal entities. Most citizens' tribunals operating in the field of transitional justice are established by the PPT discussed in Chapter 1.[11] The PPT is based on a statute which defines its purpose and establishes its legal basis.[12] This does not, however, give PT the same legal authority of international courts and tribunals.

While the latter are established through a treaty or United Nations resolution, PT are implemented via their own structures. They are, therefore, not an entity under international law. The Rome Statute of the ICC, on the other hand, states in Article 4, para. 1 that "[t]he Court shall have international legal personality." Even without such an explicit provision, it is clear that international tribunals enjoy a form of legal personality that PT do not. In an Advisory Opinion, the International Court of Justice (ICJ) held that the fact that states have deferred certain powers to an institution and equipped it with rights and responsibilities gives it personality under international law.[13] Since PT are not created by states, and consequently do not have powers deferred to them, they cannot claim legal personality in the way international organisations can. The lack of legal personality is a central feature that not only distinguishes PT from formal courts, but also critically impacts their functioning, as will be discussed ahead.

Second, PT focus on state responsibility, rather than on individuals. The statute of the PPT holds in Article 1 that the tribunal's competence "extends to serious and systematic violations of the rights of peoples, whether committed by States, by authorities other than States, or by private groups or organizations." Only exceptionally it would focus on the responsibility of individuals, or on "single violations of rights of an individual." By trying to establish state responsibility for grave crimes, instead of individual criminal culpability, PT build their cases around a different legal concept. In this respect, it is important to note the peculiar application of formal legal norms by People's Tribunals: under international law states can be held accountable for wrongful acts only, not for crimes.[14] PT thus use international criminal law and apply it to states and entities instead of individuals.

Third, PT look at broader patterns of violence. Based on the PPT statute, it claims competence "to give judgements on any international crime, specifically

11 Tribunale Permanente dei Popoli, <http://permanentpeoplestribunal.org/?lang=en> accessed 17 February 2019.

12 Statute, 'Permanent Peoples' Tribunal' <http://permanentpeoplestribunal.org/wp-content/uploads/2016/06/statute.pdf> accessed 17 February 2019.

13 Reparation for injuries suffered in the service of the United Nations, Advisory, Opinion: ICJ Reports 1949 <www.icj-cij.org/files/case-related/4/004-19490411-ADV-01-00-EN.pdf> accessed 24 February 2019.

14 Draft Articles on Responsibility of States for Internationally Wrongful Acts, 2001, International Law Commission, (UN Doc A/56/10, 43, UN Doc A/RES/56/83, Annex, UN Doc A/CN.4/L.602/Rev.1, GAOR 56th Session).

on crimes against peace and humanity, any infringement of the fundamental rights of peoples and minorities, grave and systematic violations of the rights and freedoms." Unlike international criminal tribunals, which focus on the responsibility of individuals and establish their role in the commission of very specific acts, People's Tribunals look at patterns of violence, large-scale crimes and long-term abuses. As Alan Collins points out in Chapter 9, the focus of a body like the UKCSAPT is to establish patterns of abuse and institutional failure, rather than judging individuals for specific crimes. Although the UKCSAPT does not apply international law and does not operate in the field of transitional justice, it shows, more generally, how citizen and survivor-driven initiatives can expose systemic gaps, scrutinise government action, and put a spotlight on a societal problem.

Fourth, PT claim to act on the principle of universal jurisdiction and, therefore, assume a much broader temporal and geographical jurisdictional basis than formal courts. PPT, for example, claim in Article 2 of their statute jurisdiction over jus cogens crimes – acts that can be prosecuted irrespective of the location where they have been committed.[15] While there is no full agreement as to which crimes have reached jus cogens status, it is widely agreed that aggression, genocide, crimes against humanity, war crimes, piracy, torture, slavery, and slave-related practices are among them.[16] The international community considers these crimes to be so grave that they are prohibited under any circumstances, and that their commission creates certain "obligations of a state towards the international community as a whole"[17] – a phrase widely understood to include the obligation to prosecute these crimes.[18] The principle of universal jurisdiction allows their prosecution by any state and at any time, even when crimes have been committed abroad or by foreign nationals. Many of the PT that address large-scale crimes and abuses committed during a conflict are set up abroad, mainly because of the political situation where the crimes have been committed, or because of a large activist diaspora or refugee community abroad. Such tribunals in exile use the principle of universal jurisdiction to give legitimacy to their jurisdiction.

With their relatively broad jurisdictional scope, PT differ significantly from international courts and tribunals which operate in a narrowly defined space. Tribunals like the ICTY and its sister, the ICTR, were established through resolutions of the Security Council.[19] The ICC is based on a multilateral treaty – the

15 'Final Report on the Exercise of Universal Jurisdiction in Respect of Gross Human Rights Offences' (*International Law Association Committee on International Human Rights Law and Practice* 2000) <www.scribd.com/document/131960356/ILA-Report-on-Universal-jurisdiction-2000> accessed 21 February 2019.

16 Cherif Bassiouini, 'International Crimes: Jus Cogens and Obligatio Erga Omnes' [1996] 59(4) Law and Contemporary Problems 68.

17 *Belgium v Spain* (1970) 3 ICJ 32.

18 Bassiouini, (note 19), 74.

19 ICTY Statute Adopted on 25 May 1993 by Resolution 827 <>www.icty.org/x/file/Legal%20Library/Statute/statute_sept09_en.pdf>, and Statute of the ICTR <http://legal.un.org/avl/pdf/ha/ictr_EF.pdf> accessed 21 February 2019.

Rome Statute – which has to be ratified, accepted or approved by signatory states.[20] These documents limit the jurisdiction of the institutions to a specific period of time, a clearly defined geographical area, and certain crimes. The ICTR, for example, was only allowed to prosecute persons for violations of international humanitarian law committed in the territory of Rwanda, and Rwandan citizens responsible for such crimes in the territory of neighbouring states, between 1 January and 31 December 1994.[21] The ICC, the only permanent international court and the centrepiece of international justice, has a mandate to prosecute crimes committed after the Rome Statute entered into force on 1 July 2002[22] and, without a referral by the Security Council, only on the territory of States Parties or by their nationals.[23]

The non-existence of jurisdictional limits is a big advantage of PT, because it allows them to operate in contexts in which formal courts are blocked for political reasons, or which are neglected by the international community. As discussed by Azril Mohammed in Chapter 7, the People's Tribunal on Myanmar is a clear example: plans for the PT emerged in 2013 when the systematic crimes committed by the Myanmar state against the Rohingyas and other minorities received little attention.[24] As the situation worsened and accountability through international institutions became elusive because of contrasting political interests,[25] the International Tribunal on Myanmar's Crimes against Rohingya and Kachin Peoples became one of the few fora to hear the testimony of victims and experts.[26] Only later the UN was seized with the matter and established the Independent Investigative Mechanism for Myanmar. Importantly, the Mechanism only collects, analyses, and preserves evidence, but does not hold hearings, establish individual criminal liability or issue verdicts. As a consequence, informal justice process through the PT remains one of the most inclusive avenues for accountability in the region so far. The next section will look in depth at the role of People's Tribunals in situations where formal courts and institutions are blocked.

20 Rome Statute, (note 8), 125.

21 Statute of the ICTR, (note 22), Art. 1.

22 Rome Statute, (note 8), 11.

23 Ibid., 13–14. The only exception is a referral by the Security Council under Chapter VII of the Charter of the United Nations.

24 Permanent People's Tribunal, State Crimes Allegedly Committed in Myanmar against the Rohingyas, Kachins and Other Groups, Judgment, September 2017 (online) <http://permanentpeoplestribunal.org/wp-content/uploads/2017/11/PPT-on-Myanmar-Judgment-FINAL.pdf> accessed 23 March 2019.

25 Human Rights Council, Report of the independent international fact-finding mission on Myanmar (A/HRC/39/64), 12 September 2018 (online) <https://documents-dds-ny.un.org/doc/UNDOC/GEN/G18/274/54/PDF/G1827454.pdf?OpenElement> accessed 23 March 2019.

26 Human Rights Council, Resolution adopted by the Human Rights Council on 27 September 2018 (A/HRC/RES/39/2), para. 22.

People's Tribunals and the crisis of international justice

International law depends on the willingness of states to enforce and develop it. In the absence of own police forces, international courts are particularly dependent on the cooperation of governments to arrest suspects, enforce decisions, and accept the jurisdiction of the courts in the first place.

Since its emergence after World War II, international criminal law has experienced a rapid growth, particularly following the end of the Cold War in the 1990s – an evolution that is often described as a process of different phases or layers.[27]

The first layer consists of international criminal tribunals, established by the UN Security Council in the 1990s. Acting under Article VII of the Charter of the United Nations, the Council decided in 1993 to create a court to prosecute "persons responsible for serious violations of international humanitarian law committed in the territory of the former Yugoslavia since 1991" – the ICTY.[28] A year later, following the genocide in Rwanda, the Council created the ICTR and gave it the competence to hold persons responsible for grave crimes "committed in the territory of neighbouring States, between 1 January 1994 and 31 December 1994."[29] Binding Security Resolutions as a basis for the tribunals provided a high level of legitimacy and a strong enforcement mechanism. At the same time, however, the establishment became a political decision, as the adoption of a Security Council resolution is a political process and depends on the willingness of governments. The voting pattern of Council members shows that this political will is shifting and reveals an opportunistic approach of the five permanent members (P5).[30] Instead of a long-term strategy or coherent vision and policy on international accountability, their voting behaviour shows a focus on short-term benefits. They support an international court when it is not against their national interests. In addition, the P5 tend to shield their nationals from international accountability.[31] These dynamics limit the efficiency and fairness of the courts.

A second layer of international justice is the emergence of hybrid courts, including the Extraordinary Chambers in the Courts of Cambodia, the Special Court for Sierra Leone, and the Special Tribunal for Lebanon. They are usually established on the request of the government and often located in the countries where the crimes were committed and combine international and domestic law. They are usually set up through an agreement between the respective governments and the United Nations. They have been hailed for their flexibility and

27 See for example Jean-Marc Sorel, 'International Criminal Tribunals: The Light and the Dark Sides of a Recent Grand Ambition' [2011] 1 Revue Tiers Monde 205.

28 ICTY Statute, (note 22), 1.

29 Ibid.

30 David P. Forsythe, 'The UN Security Council and Response to Atrocities: International Criminal Law and the P-5' [2012] 34(3) Human Rights Quarterly 842.

31 Ibid., 843.

proximity to the victims and communities they are supposed to serve. However, hybrid or mixed courts have been criticised for their strict focus on prosecutions and purely legal processes and the failure to take long-term interests of the conflict-affected countries into account, such as reconciliation or capacity-building of local institutions.[32]

The third development was the establishment of a permanent International Criminal Court. The plans originated in a report of the International Law Commission which concluded that the creation of such a court is desirable and feasible.[33] Upon the request of the UN General Assembly, a committee developed a draft statute in the early 1950s, but a vote in the General Assembly was postponed. Only in 1989, following a request from Trinidad and Tobago, the project was revived and the draft statute completed. The General Assembly established the Ad Hoc Committee on the Establishment of an International Criminal Court and the Preparatory Committee on the Establishment of an International Criminal Court which prepared a text for a diplomatic conference, which was to take place in 1998 in Rome. After a month of negotiations in Rome, 120 states voted in favour of the statute, seven against, and 21 abstained.[34] Within four years after the resumption of the International Law Commission's work, the international community agreed on a treaty to establish the ICC – the Rome Statute – which entered into force on 1 July 2002 after the required 60 states had ratified it.[35]

None of the institutions of the three layers can act fully independently. They were established through political processes and depend on the support of governments. While the number of tribunals proliferated and the number of states that acceded to the Rome Statute increased significantly since the mid-1990s, this process has slowed down in recent years.[36] The international community has only shown greater hesitation to create new tribunals, for example in Syria.[37] It has also reduced its commitment and support to existing institutions, most notably the ICC. Governments have become reluctant to increase financial contributions; the retreat from multilateral institutions and agreements is seen as a

32 Parinaz Kermani Mendez, 'The New Wave of Hybrid Tribunals: A Sophisticated Approach to Enforcing International Humanitarian Law or an Idealistic Solution with Empty Promises?' [2009] 20 Criminal Law Forum 60.

33 United Nations, 'Establishment of an International Criminal Court – Overview' (United Nations) <http://legal.un.org/icc/general/overview.htm> accessed 13 March 2019.

34 Fanny Benedetti and John L. Washburn, 'Drafting the International Criminal Court Treaty: Two Years to Rome and an Afterword on the Rome Diplomatic Conference' [1999] 5(1) Global Governance 27.

35 John Washburn, 'The Negotiation of the Rome Statute for the International Criminal Court and International Lawmaking in the 21st Century' [1999] 11 Pace International Law Review 362.

36 For an overview of the State Parties and their accession, see UNTC, United Nations Treaty Collection <https://treaties.un.org/pages/ViewDetails.aspx?src=IND&mtdsg_no=XVIII-10&chapter=18&lang=en> accessed 13 March 2019.

37 Alex Whiting, 'An Investigation Mechanism for Syria: The General Assembly Steps into the Breach' [2017] 15 Journal of International Criminal Justice 232.

threat to the international rule of law in general; and rising nationalism means that countries are less willing to defer power to supranational courts.[38] More specifically, the ICC faces the withdrawal of States Parties, budget constraints, and a lack of support from governments in carrying out its work. In 2014, for example, the prosecutor had to freeze her investigations in Darfur, Sudan due to a lack of cooperation from Security Council members.[39] A few months later, in March 2015, the ICC terminated the proceedings against the Kenyan president Uhuru Kenyatta,[40] after the prosecutor had to withdraw the charges, saying the Government of Kenya failed to cooperate and contributed to the collapse of the investigation.[41] In 2017, the withdrawal of Burundi from the Rome Statute took effect,[42] and in 2019 the Philippines left.[43] These developments not only weakened the institutions, but also, according to observers, have caused a crisis of the international criminal justice project as a whole.[44] They argue that the diminishing political support for the international rule of law and the seemingly declining interest of states in international criminal law – and the ICC in particular – create an accountability or "impunity gap"[45] that needs innovative solutions.[46]

Are PT a possible solution? Since they are established without the involvement of governments, they can operate freely from interference and political will. While Bertrand Russell acknowledged at the constitutional meeting of the first Russell Tribunal that the lack of political support meant the PT would be unable to compel policy makers to appear before the tribunal or enforce decisions, he said that the independence from political interests of governments was an advantage. "I believe that these apparent limitations are, in fact, virtues. We are free to

38 See for example Joseph Powderly, 'International Criminal Justice in an Age of Perpetual Crisis' [2019] 32(1) Leiden Journal of International Law 1.

39 ICC, 'Statement to the United Nations Security Council on the Situation in Darfur, Pursuant to UNSCR 1593 (2005)' (*International Criminal Court*, 12 December 2014).

40 ICC, 'The Prosecutor v. Uhuru Muigai Kenyatta, Decision on the Withdrawal of Charges Against Mr. Kenyatta' (ICC-01/09-02/11-1005, 13 March 2015).

41 ICC, 'Statement of the Prosecutor of the International Criminal Court, Fatou Bensouda, on the Withdrawal of Charges Against Mr. Uhuru Muigai Kenyatta' (5 December 2014) (online) <www.icc-cpi.int/Pages/item.aspx?name=otp-statement-05-12-2014-2> accessed 23 March 2019.

42 United Nations, 'Burundi: Withdrawal' <https://treaties.un.org/doc/publication/cn/2016/cn.805.2016-eng.pdf> accessed 13 March 2019.

43 Ibid.

44 David Luban, 'After the Honeymoon: Reflections on the Current State of International Criminal Justice' [2013] 11 Journal of International Criminal Justice 509.

45 See for example Makau W. Mutua, 'Closing the "Impunity Gap" and the Role of State Support for ICC: Contemporary Issues Facing the International Criminal Court' (2016) <https://ssrn.com/abstract=3026289> accessed 24 February 2019.

46 Sam Muller, Nathalie Dijkman, Peter Polakovic, Maurits Barendrecht and Laura Kistemaker, 'Legal Futures of the International Criminal Court' (*HiiL Innovating Justice*, September 2017) <www.amnesty.nl/content/uploads/2018/10/170928HiiL-ICC-Report-FIN.pdf?x90110> accessed 24 February 2019.

conduct a solemn and historic investigation, uncompelled by reasons of State or other such obligations."[47]

Given their independence, PT can be created in situations where international courts lack jurisdiction, or where there is no political will to set up and finance an international or hybrid tribunal. Cassese identified various conditions that need to be fulfilled for the international community to set up a formal court.[48] These aspects include, first, geopolitical interests which need to be in favour of establishing a tribunal in a specific country; and second, the support of an affected state to establish a tribunal. In light of these preconditions for a formal court to intervene, it is no surprise that PT tend to emerge in situations where either geopolitical or national interests prevent the establishment of an international court, the referral of the situation to the Security Council, or the initiation of a *proprio motu* investigation of the ICC. Most recently, PT have been held over crimes committed against the Rohingyas, Kachins and other minority groups in Myanmar; the conflict between Turkish armed forces and Kurds; the crimes committed against migrants trying to enter Europe; the conflict between Israel and Palestine; and the war in Iraq.[49] As of this writing, none of these situations has been formally investigated by a tribunal; therefore, PT shed a light on these crimes. Thus, in situations in which the formal accountability mechanisms are either absent or non-functioning, PT can make an important contribution by documenting and acknowledging criminal acts and abusive behaviour.[50] Richard Falk, who participated in different tribunals, went so far to suggest that citizens possess "a residual right and duty to implement the norms of international law bearing on war and peace when official institutions fail to discharge their responsibilities," and that People's Tribunals enable them to claim this right.[51]

PT thus can play an important role in addressing crimes that would otherwise go unnoticed. They provide victims, who would otherwise be left without redress, a forum to tell their story. PT do, however, more than merely fill a gap left by formal institutions of international justice. Their set-up offers different advantages to courts.

On a societal level, the forum of People's Tribunals can contribute to a broader process of reconciliation and dealing with the past. Payam Akhavan explained how a PT in Iran offered a "therapeutic process" for a nation that had suffered

47 Coates, (note 9).

48 Antonio Cassese, 'The Fight of Internationalized Courts and Tribunals in the Fight Against International Criminality' in Andre Nollkaemper and Jann K. Kleffner (eds), *Internationalized Courts Criminal Courts: Sierra Leone, East Timor, Kosovo, and Cambodia* (Cesare P. R. Romano, 2004).

49 For an overview of the jurisprudence of the Permanent Peoples' Tribunal (PPT). See <http://permanentpeoplestribunal.org/category/jurisprudence/?lang=en> accessed 24 February 2019.

50 Simm and Byrnes, (note 12), 121.

51 Richard Falk, *The Costs of War: International Law, the Un, and World Order After Iraq* (Taylor & Francis Ltd, 2007), 173.

decades of violence under a totalitarian regime and imposed silence.[52] Due to the geopolitical complexities, chances were slim for a formal international court to be established in Iran. The PT also offered advantages a criminal court could not have provided. Akhavan argues that doing justice in a society that has experienced a high level of violence for a long time requires more than the punishment of individuals in order "to effect a broader political and cultural transformation."[53] By exposing the population and the regime to the stories of victims, the normalisation of violence and the silence that dominated for a long time was broken. The PT offered the possibility to uncover decades of violence more effectively than a formal court could have. International courts and tribunals have a mandate to prosecute individuals and establish their criminal liability, but do not necessarily prioritise the advancement of transitional justice, reconciliation, or societal healing. Criminal justice requires the investigation of specific crimes and therefore leads to the prosecution of a relatively small number of individuals and acts only. PT, on the other hand, shed light on patterns of violence and its underlying causes in ways criminal courts usually do not.

By focusing on the principle of state responsibility, rather than individual criminal accountability, PT uncover patterns of violence and scrutinise government action.[54] The international community has set up various formal bodies, mechanisms, and procedures to control and examine state behaviour and enforce state responsibilities. These bodies include the European Court of Human Rights of the Council of Europe, the Inter-American and African Union human rights systems with the Inter-American Court and the African Commission on Human and Peoples' Rights, and the bodies and procedures of the United Nations system, including the Human Rights Council. Similar to the courts and tribunals, the politicisation of their establishment and processes can limit their effectiveness and impair their legitimacy.[55] They are inter-governmental bodies comprised of government delegates, rather than independent experts. Such a setup provides a forum for member states to pursue their national interests, particularly when great powers are involved.[56] The Human Rights Council, for example has been criticised for enabling China to undermine the participation of NGOs, for addressing the Syria conflict only selectively, for failing to mention human rights abuses around the Olympic games in Beijing, and for being silent on Russia's aggression towards Georgia and South Ossetia.[57]

52 Payam Akhavan, 'Is Grassroots Justice a Viable Alternative to Impunity? The Case of the Iran People's Tribunal' [2017] 39(1) Human Rights Quarterly 96. For more detailed discussion about the Iran Tribunal see Chapter 6.

53 Ibid., 97.

54 Simm and Byrnes, (note 12), 105.

55 Rosa Freedman and Ruth Houghton, 'Two Steps Forward, One Step Back: Politicisation of the Human Rights Council' [2017] Human Rights Law Review 1.

56 Gerd Oberleitner, *Global Human Rights Institutions* (Polity, 2007), 47.

57 Freedman and Houghton, (note 58), 2.

The fact that PT are established without the involvement of governments does not mean, however, that they are not politicised. A fundamental critique that weighed particularly heavily on the Russell Tribunal for Vietnam is that PT are set up with and serve a particular political agenda.[58] The Russell Tribunal on Vietnam was perceived as hostile to US policy, with a predetermined verdict.[59] Not even its founders denied that it served a particular political objective: In his opening remarks, Russell said "[w]e arouse consciousness in order to create mass resistance."[60] Sartre explained that the tribunal "worked for" the American people but that it also sought to "work on them."[61] It "worked for" the people because it gave them a framework and instrument to scrutinise policies of their government. But, in Sartre's understanding, it was also meant to "work on" the people because the revelations and charges placed a responsibility on them to act and resist. The tribunal was, therefore, meant first and foremost as a mechanism and catalyst for public and political action.

Thus, unlike truth and reconciliation commissions, which have emerged as another form to shed light on large-scale past abuses and the role of governments, the primary objective of PT is not necessarily to establish a balanced, objective historic record, but rather to use law and legal principles to achieve a political objective.

This emphasis on legal processes – including for example the application of international law, the hearing and weighting of evidence, and the pronouncement of a verdict – distinguishes PT from other forms of activism, such as speeches or demonstrations.[62] Unlike other forms of transitional justice and activism, they enter a sphere that is considered an exclusive domain of states. President de Gaulle, who refused to host Russell's Tribunal on Vietnam in France, argued that "[j]ustice of any sort, in principle as in execution, emanates from the State."[63] The Russell Tribunal, "through its very form, . . . would be acting against the very thing which it is seeking to uphold." De Gaulle was of the opinion that the lack of a formal legal basis made the tribunal illegitimate.

It is important to notice, however, that institutions can derive their legitimacy from different sources. Legitimacy has been defined as the "quality that leads people (or states) to accept authority – independent of coercion, self-interest, or rational persuasion – because of a general sense that the authority is justified."[64] In this sense, legitimacy has normative and sociological aspects:[65] an institution

58 Tor Krever, 'Remembering the Russell Tribunal' [2017] 5(3) London Review of International Law 483.

59 Ibid.

60 Karen Engle, Zinaida Miller and D. M. Davis, *Anti-Impunity and the Human Rights Agenda* (Cambridge University Press, 2016), 295.

61 Ibid., 485.

62 Simm and Byrnes, (note 12), 105.

63 'Text of de Gaulle's Letter Banning War Crimes Tribunal' [1967] 5 World Outlook 19, 483.

64 Daniel Bodansky, 'The Legitimacy of International Governance: A Coming Challenge for International Environmental Law?' [1999] 93 American Journal of International Law 600.

65 Harry Hobbs, 'Hybrid Tribunals and the Composition of the Court: In Search of Sociological Legitimacy' [2016] 16(2) Chicago Journal of International Law 494.

can be perceived as legitimate because of its foundation in law, or because the population considers it legitimate. In addition to the moral or psychological acceptance, an international institution can also derive its legitimacy from the belief in certain values and goals by the majority of a population – a concept Cassese called "purposive legitimacy."[66] Similarly, his notion of "universal value legitimacy" of an institution is based on the values common to the whole community in which the institution operates. In such a view, a court or PT enjoys universal value legitimacy because it is based on generally accepted norms of international law, such as jus cogens.

PT tend to base their legitimacy on what Thomas Franck called "symbolic validation,"[67] aspects such as the reading of a judgement, the detailed reasoning based on accepted laws and norms, and the participation of distinguished individuals or organisations associated with the tribunal generate legitimacy in society. From such a point of view, legitimacy, as opposed to legality, is derived from a perception of acceptability of certain values, rather than from the idea that an institution or its decision need to be conform with formal legal standards.[68] This form of public legitimacy has been described as the beliefs of the population that an institution has "the right to exercise authority in a certain domain."[69] It is thus not the foundation that legitimises PT, but people who trust them.

PT should, therefore, not be seen as a better or worse option to international courts, but as a complementary tool to, first, hold perpetrators of grave crimes accountable; second, fill a gap when formal institutions are not existing or not functioning;[70] and, third, push for the development and advancement of international law.

The Russell Tribunal, for example, stimulated the debate about the concept of genocide which is defined under international law as acts committed with the intent to destroy, in whole or in part, "a national, ethnical, racial or religious group."[71] The wording of the article has been widely criticised for being too narrow and for excluding other groups.[72] In relation to the crimes in Vietnam, the Russell Tribunal broadened the definition and introduced the notion of cultural genocide: the intent to wipe out a language, religion, national feeling, culture or tradition.[73]

66 Antonio Cassese, 'The Legitimacy of International Criminal Tribunals and the Current Prospects of International Criminal Justice' [2012] 25 Leiden Journal of International Law 492.
67 Thomas M. Franck, *Fairness in International Law and Institutions* (Clarendon Press, 1995), 34.
68 Tullio Treves, 'Aspects of Legitimacy of Decisions of International Courts and Tribunal' [2017] 38 Estudos Jurídicos e Políticos 75, 20.
69 Erik Voeten, 'Public Opinion and the Legitimacy of International Courts' [2013] 14(2) Theoretical Inquiries in Law 414.
70 Simm and Byrnes, (note 12), 120.
71 Convention on the Prevention and Punishment of the Crime of Genocide (1948), 2.
72 See for example Benjamin Whitaker, 'Revised and Updated Report on the Question of the Prevention and Punishment of the Crime of Genocide Prepared by Mr. B. Whitaker' (*UN Economic and Social Council* 1985) <www.legal-tools.org/doc/99c00c/pdf/> accessed 13 March 2019.
73 Simm and Byrnes, (note 12), 119.

Another example for the contribution of PT to and the influence of People's Tribunals on international law – and vice versa – is the Tokyo Women's Tribunal which was held in 2000. The negotiations of the Rome Statute led to the development of NGOs networks and stimulated the establishment of a People's Tribunal to shed light on the rapes and sexual slavery committed during World War II by the Imperial Japanese Army against women in East Asia.[74] The Women's International War Crimes Tribunal for the Trial of Japan's Military Sexual Slavery focused on the responsibility of nine individuals and the Japanese state for the crimes against humanity of rape and sexual slavery.[75] Importantly, the indictment was framed as a continuation of the International Military Tribunal for the Far East (IMTFE) which was held between 1946 and 1948 to try crimes committed during World War II.[76] As the IMTFE indictment did not cover the sexual slavery system, the Tokyo Women's Tribunal filled a gap and drove accountability for sexual violence crimes. The Tribunal was held at a time when the use of large-scale sexual violence in wars started to receive increasing awareness among prosecutors. In their verdict, the judges focused on the experience of the women who were enslaved as "comfort women," and gave a definition of sexual slavery that better reflected, in their view, the nature of the crimes.[77] The Tribunal's conclusion was seen as a criticism of the narrow definition of sexual slavery which the Preparatory Commission for the Elements of Crime presented for the then-new ICC.[78]

The Tokyo Women's Tribunal thus was an example of the role PT can play in international justice: it filled a gap and offered a forum to victims of grave crimes, who did not have access to the formal international court; it was based on and applied international law and legal principles and processes; and it highlighted shortcomings in the formal system and drew attention to a neglected aspect of international criminal law.

Conclusion

People's Tribunals hold hearings, hear witnesses and issue verdicts. They apply international law and claim jurisdiction on the basis of established legal concepts, such as the principle of universal jurisdiction. They claim to use law and legal principles like a court, but pursue activist and political objectives. The emphasis on law is what distinguishes them from other forms of activism. This chapter

74 Ibid., 111.

75 For information about the cases and the tribunal see 'The Prosecutors and the Peoples of the Asia-Pacific Region v. Hirohito Emperor Showa et al. – Asser Institute', <www.internationalcrimesdatabase.org/Case/981/The-Prosecutors-and-the-Peoples-of-the-Asia-Pacific-Region/> accessed 13 March 2019.

76 Tina Dologopol, 'The Judgment of the Tokyo Women's Tribunal' [2003] 28(5) Alternative Law Journal 243.

77 Ibid., 245.

78 Ibid.

highlighted four aspects that most PT have in common and clearly distinguishes their design and workings from formal courts. First, PT are not set up by states, and are not formal legal entities. Second, they usually focus on state responsibility, rather than criminal accountability of individuals. Third, they often uncover broader patterns of violence and abuse, rather than specific crimes. Fourth, PT use the principle of universal jurisdiction as a legal basis and, therefore, claim much broader temporal and geographical jurisdiction.

Whereas formal international courts have very specific mandates which depend on political factors, PT can operate more independently. Political factors, such as geopolitical interests and the willingness of the local post-conflict government to cooperate, determine whether an international tribunal will be created or the ICC can step in. Since the end of the Cold War, the expansion of international criminal law and the establishment of various international and hybrid courts have been indicators of a growing commitment of the international community to accountability for grave crimes. In recent years, however, the trend has stalled and the international justice project is perceived to experience a crisis. Governments are reluctant to establish new courts and transfer sovereignty to international institutions. The ICC not only experienced a slowdown in new accessions but even faces several withdrawals, leading to a net decline of the number of States Parties. In an environment where formal courts are blocked, People's Tribunals offer an alternative accountability mechanism. Recent People's Tribunals for crimes committed in Myanmar, the conflict between Turkish armed forces and Kurds, and in the war between Israel and Palestine highlight the potential for alternative mechanisms to document and acknowledge large-scale criminality. The case of Iran showed the PT offered the possibility to uncover decades of violence against the people more effectively than a formal court could have.

An additional benefit of PT is their activist approach to the development of international law. The Russell Tribunal for Vietnam and the Tokyo Women's Tribunal, for example, have stimulated the debate about the concept of genocide and the push for accountability for sexual violence crimes. Both put a specific conflict or aspect of it in the spotlight and attracted global attention. Moreover, the Women's Tribunal helped to unify victims of sexual slavery and formulate their demand for state responsibility, which a few years later led to the establishment of the Asian Women's Fund[79] – a fund by the Japanese government to compensate the victims, which was, however, rejected because it fell short of officially recognising the crimes and the state's responsibility.[80] By seriously engaging with international law, People's Tribunals have agenda-setting power and the possibility to shape the discourse. Rather than being a second-best option when formal

79 Rumi Sakamoto, 'The Women's International War Crimes Tribunal on Japan's Military Sexual Slavery: A Legal and Feminist Approach to the "Comfort Women" Issue' [2001] 3(1) New Zealand Journal of Asian Studies 57.

80 Norimitsu Onishi, 'Japan's "Atonement" to Former Sex Slaves Stirs Anger' *New York Times* (25 April 2017) <www.nytimes.com/2007/04/25/world/asia/25japan.html> accessed 23 March 2019.

institutions do not exist or are not functioning, People's Tribunals can, firstly, fill gaps and give victims a forum to tell their story; and, secondly, highlight shortcomings of the formal international legal system and contribute to its development and advancement.

References

Akhavan, Payam, 'Is Grassroots Justice a Viable Alternative to Impunity? The Case of the Iran People's Tribunal' [2017] 39 Human Rights Quarterly 1.

Bassiouini, Cherif, 'International Crimes: Jus Cogens and Obligatio Erga Omnes' [1996] 59 Law and Contemporary Problems 4.

Belgium v Spain (1970) 3 ICJ 32.

Benedetti, Fanny and Washburn, John L., 'Drafting the International Criminal Court Treaty: Two Years to Rome and an Afterword on the Rome Diplomatic Conference' [1999] 5 Global Governance 1.

Bodansky, Daniel, 'The Legitimacy of International Governance: A Coming Challenge for International Environmental Law?' [1999] 93 American Journal of International Law.

Cassese, Antonio, 'The Fight of Internationalized Courts and Tribunals in the Fight Against International Criminality' in Andre Nollkaemper and Jann K. Kleffner, eds., *Internationalized Courts Criminal Courts: Sierra Leone, East Timor, Kosovo, and Cambodia* (Cesare P. R. Romano, 2004).

Cassese, Antonio, 'The Legitimacy of International Criminal Tribunals and the Current Prospects of International Criminal Justice' [2012] 25 Leiden Journal of International Law.

Coates, Ken, 'Russell Tribunals' (Bertrand Russel Peace Foundation) <www.russfound.org/The_Spokesman/KCTrib104.html> accessed 16 February 2019.

Convention Against Torture and Other Cruel, Inhuman or Degrading Treatment or Punishment 1985.

Convention on the Prevention and Punishment of the Crime of Genocide, Adopted by the General Assembly 9 December 1948.

Convention on the Prohibition of the Development, Production, Stockpiling and Use of Chemical Weapons and on Their Destruction 1999.

Convention on the Prohibition of the Use, Stockpiling, Production and Transfer of Anti-Personnel Mines and on Their Destruction 1997.

Crowe, David M., 'War Crimes and Genocide in History, and the Evolution of Responsive International Law' [2009] 37 Nationalities Papers 6.

Cryer, Robert, *An Introduction to International Criminal Law and Procedure* (Cambridge University Press, 2010).

Dologopol, Tina, 'The Judgment of the Tokyo Women's Tribunal' [2003] 28 Alternative Law Journal 5.

Draft Articles on Responsibility of States for Internationally Wrongful Acts, 2001, International Law Commission (UN Doc A/56/10, 43, UN Doc A/RES/56/83, Annex, UN Doc A/CN.4/L.602/Rev.1, GAOR 56th Session).

Engle, Karen, Miller, Zinaida, and Davis, D. M., *Anti-Impunity and the Human Rights Agenda* (Cambridge University Press, 2016).

Falk, Richard, 'International Law and the United States Role in Viet Nam: A Response to Professor Moore' [1967] 76 The Yale Law Journal 6.

Falk, Richard, *The Costs of War: International Law, The Un, and World Order After Iraq* (Taylor & Francis Ltd, 2007).

Final Report on the Exercise of Universal Jurisdiction in Respect of Gross Human Rights Offences' (*International Law Association Committee on International Human Rights Law and Practice* 2000) <www.scribd.com/document/131960356/ILA-Report-on-Universal-jurisdiction-2000> accessed 21 February 2019.

Forsythe, David P., 'The UN Security Council and Response to Atrocities: International Criminal Law and the P-5' [2012] 34 Human Rights Quarterly 3.

Franck, Thomas M., *Fairness in International Law and Institutions* (Clarendon Press, 1995).

Freedman, Rosa and Ruth Houghton, 'Two Steps Forward, One Step Back: Politicisation of the Human Rights Council' [2017] 0 Human Rights Law Review 1–17 <https://research.reading.ac.uk/ungop/wp-content/uploads/sites/13/publications/HRLR-2017.pdf>.

Hobbs, Harry, 'Hybrid Tribunals and the Composition of the Court: In Search of Sociological Legitimacy' [2016] 16 Chicago Journal of International Law 2.

Human Rights Council, Report of the Independent International Fact-Finding Mission on Myanmar (A/HRC/39/64), 12 September 2018 (online) <https://documents-dds-ny.un.org/doc/UNDOC/GEN/G18/274/54/PDF/G1827454.pdf?OpenElement> accessed 23 March 2019.

ICC, Statement of the Prosecutor of the International Criminal Court, Fatou Bensouda, on the Withdrawal of Charges Against Mr. Uhuru Muigai Kenyatta, 5 December 2014 (online) <www.icc-cpi.int/Pages/item.aspx?name=otp-statement-05-12-2014-2> accessed 23 March 2019.

ICC, 'Statement to the United Nations Security Council on the Situation in Darfur, pursuant to UNSCR 1593 (2005)' (International Criminal Court, 12 December 2014).

ICC, The Prosecutor v. Uhuru Muigai Kenyatta, Decision on the Withdrawal of Charges Against Mr. Kenyatta (ICC-01/09-02/11-1005, 13 March 2015).

Krever, Tor, 'Remembering the Russell Tribunal' [2017] 5 London Review of International Law 3.

Luban, David, 'After the Honeymoon: Reflections on the Current State of International Criminal Justice' [2013] 11 Journal of International Criminal Justice.

Mendez, Parinas Kermani, 'The New Wave of Hybrid Tribunals: A Sophisticated Approach to Enforcing International Humanitarian Law or an Idealistic Solution with Empty Promises?' [2009] 20 Criminal Law Forum.

Muller, Sam, Dijkman, Nathalie, Polakovic, Peter, Barendrecht, Maurits and Kistemaker, Laura, 'Legal Futures of the International Criminal Court' (*HiiL Innovating Justice*, September 2017) <www.amnesty.nl/content/uploads/2018/10/170928HiiL-ICC-Report-FIN.pdf?x90110> accessed 24 February 2019.

Mutua, Makau W. 'Closing the "Impunity Gap" and the Role of State Support for ICC: Contemporary Issues Facing the International Criminal Court' (2016) <https://ssrn.com/abstract=3026289> accessed 24 February 2019.

New York Times, 'Russell "Tribunal" Loses Paris Hotel "Courtroom"', *New York Times* (New York, 12 April 1967).

Oberleitner, Gerd, *Global Human Rights Institutions* (Polity, 2007).

Onishi, Norimitsu, 'Japan's "Atonement" to Former Sex Slaves Stirs Anger' *New York Times* (New York, 25 April 2017) <www.nytimes.com/2007/04/25/world/asia/25japan.html> accessed 23 March 2019.

Permanent Peoples' Tribunal <http://permanentpeoplestribunal.org/wp-content/uploads/2016/06/statute.pdf> accessed 17 February 2019.

Permanent Peoples' Tribunal <http://permanentpeoplestribunal.org/category/jurisprudence/?lang=en> accessed 24 February 2019.

Permanent People's Tribunal, State Crimes Allegedly Committed in Myanmar Against the Rohingyas, Kachins and Other Groups, Judgment, September 2017 (online) <http://permanentpeoplestribunal.org/wp-content/uploads/2017/11/PPT-on-Myanmar-Judgment-FINAL.pdf> accessed 23 March 2019.

Powderly, Joseph, 'International Criminal Justice in an Age of Perpetual Crisis' [2019] 32 Leiden Journal of International Law 1.

Reparation for Injuries Suffered in the Service of the United Nations, Advisory, Opinion: ICJ Reports 1949 <www.icj-cij.org/files/case-related/4/004-19490411-ADV-01-00-EN.pdf> accessed 24 February 2019.

Rome Statute of the International Criminal Court 1998.

Sakamoto, Rumi, 'The Women's International War Crimes Tribunal on Japan's Military Sexual Slavery: A Legal and Feminist Approach to the "Comfort Women" Issue' [2001] 3 New Zealand Journal of Asian Studies 1.

Simm, Gabrielle and Byrnes, Andrew, 'International Peoples' Tribunals in Asia: Political Theatre, Juridical Farce, or Meaningful Intervention?' [2014] 4 Asian Journal of International Law 105.

Sorel, Jean-Marc, 'International Criminal Tribunals: The Light and the Dark Sides of a Recent Grand Ambition' [2011] 1 Revue Tiers Monde 205.

Statute of the International Court of Justice.

Statute of the International Criminal Tribunal for the Former Yugoslavia 1993.

Statute of the International Criminal Tribunal for Rwanda 1994.

'Text of de Gaulle's Letter Banning War Crimes Tribunal' [1967] 5 World Outlook 19.

'The Prosecutors and the Peoples of the Asia-Pacific Region v. Hirohito Emperor Showa et al. – Asser Institute' <www.internationalcrimesdatabase.org/Case/981/The-Prosecutors-and-the-Peoples-of-the-Asia-Pacific-Region/> accessed 13 March 2019.

Treves, Tullio, 'Aspects of Legitimacy of Decisions of International Courts and Tribunal' [2017] 38 Estudos Jurídicos e Políticos 75.

Tribunale Permanente dei Popoli <http://permanentpeoplestribunal.org/?lang=en> accessed 17 February 2019.

United Nations, Burundi: Withdrawal <https://treaties.un.org/doc/publication/cn/2016/cn.805.2016-eng.pdf> accessed 13 March 2019.

United Nations, 'Establishment of an International Criminal Court – Overview' (United Nations) <http://legal.un.org/icc/general/overview.htm> accessed 13 March 2019.

United Nations, Philippines: Withdrawal <https://treaties.un.org/doc/Publication/CN/2018/CN.138.2018-Eng.pdf> accessed 13 March 2019.

UNTC, United Nations Treaty Collection <https://treaties.un.org/pages/ViewDetails.aspx?src=IND&mtdsg_no=XVIII-10&chapter=18&lang=en> accessed 13 March 2019.

Voeten, Erik, 'Public Opinion and the Legitimacy of International Courts' [2013] 14 Theoretical Inquiries in Law 2.

Washburn, John, 'The Negotiation of the Rome Statute for the International Criminal Court and International Lawmaking in the 21st Century' [1999] 11 Pace International Law Review.

Whitaker, Benjamin, 'Revised and Updated Report on the Question of the Prevention and Punishment of the Crime of Genocide Prepared by Mr. B. Whitaker' (*UN Economic and Social Council*, 1985) <www.legal-tools.org/doc/99c00c/pdf/> accessed 13 March 2019

Whiting, Alex, 'An Investigation Mechanism for Syria: The General Assembly Steps into the Breach' [2017] 15 Journal of International Criminal Justice.

3 People's Tribunals and truth commissions

Ronald Rogo

People's Tribunals and power to the people

"Power to the people!" Revolutions have thrived on this call. Some governments have fallen in the heat of the excitement. But how, pray tell, do the people get back the power that legitimately belongs to them? Can this power be returned back to the people? The activists and politicians have been short on these details. PT seems as part of the answer for grassroots development of justice.

Bertrand Russell's name is synonymous with the development of People's Tribunals.[1] A philosopher, Russell became impatient with the invasion of Vietnam by the American government. His plea for an investigation on the atrocities by the American government fell on deaf ears. As discussed in Chapter 1 and 2, as a result, Russell grouped a panel of respected people and started the Russell Tribunal.[2] Although the American government pretended to ignore him, it quietly worked with their allies to ensure that Russell would struggle in his endeavours.

The Russell Tribunal lacked comprehensive legal status in the nations it operated. However, in spite of this, it is promoted as a court that belonged to the people where issues of injustice, long ignored by the international community, are investigated and prosecuted.[3] The Russell Tribunal made history. For the first time an independent body, without any form of state backing, was holding

1 In Chapter 1, Regina Menachery Paulose defines People's Tribunals. People's Tribunals have also been defined as a process initiated by civil society that involves the presentation to a body of eminent persons of evidence and arguments that seek to establish whether a state, international organisation, corporations or, less frequently, specified individuals have committed breaches of international law or of another body of law or norms. It may evaluate the adequacy of existing international law, institutions or structures with broader notions of law or justice including 'peoples' law.

Andrew Byrnes and Gabrielle Simm (eds), *Peoples' Tribunals and International Law* (Cambridge University Press, 2018), 3–4.

2 Ibid., 11.

3 Simona Fruadatario and Giani Tognoni, 'The Participation of Peoples and the Development of International Law the Laboratory of the Permanent Peoples' Tribunal' in Andrew Byrnes and Gabrielle Simm (eds), *Peoples' Tribunals and International Law* (Cambridge University Press, 2018), 140.

the world's most powerful country to account for mass atrocities committed elsewhere in its name. This was distinct from the Nuremburg and Tokyo trials two decades before where justice only swung in the direction of the victorious nations.

The place of PT in the pursuit of justice has always been controversial. For example, Dorothy Thompson describes it as "a mob indoctrinated with its own self-importance and hypnotized by the slogans of its secular-religious credo."[4] In relation to the process of PT, she adds that the witnesses are simply there in pursuit of a premeditated end. She adds that the mob is called upon to bear witness, with no challenge to the credibility of the witness if only his testimony serves the end previously ordained. Further, she concludes that there is need to "take the conduct of justice out of the hands of the multitude; away from the mob and the market place where rumour, hearsay, passion, prejudice, malice and mass emotion so easily hold sway."[5] PT have also been described as "patently political projects, trying to sway public opinion by filling some of the information gaps and silences in public discourse that serve to deflect disagreement and vilify dissent."[6] But is the work of the PT simply "political theatre?"[7] A careful analysis will show that there are benefits that these bodies have introduced.

First, PT have brought to the world's attention the atrocities that have long been ignored.[8] These human rights abuses are often ignored largely because of the effect of politics on the justice system. The realities regarding the "inequality of states"[9] sometimes force the international community to turn a blind eye to obvious instances of abuse. For example, before PT, the American government had never been held liable for illegal invasion of Vietnam and the subsequent deaths that occurred. The government in Syria has openly breached international law and regional politics has diluted calls for accountability. Since PT have limited government influence they are able to lift the veil and investigate cases that the international community generally ignores. Through PT we get to know and understand the nature and impact of these "silent" human rights abuses. As we are reminded of them they remain in the world's conscience, constantly reminding us of the need to respond appropriately.

Second, PT have acted as a source of historical record of events. PT emphasise what happened rather than just the guilt or innocence of the perpetrators.[10] This contrasts with ordinary trials where rules of procedure and evidence limit what the

4 Dorothy Thompson, 'The People's Tribunal: The Antithesis of Justice' [April 1954] 40(4) American Bar Association Journal 289.

5 Ibid., 289–290.

6 Dianne Otto, 'Impunity in a Different Register: People's Tribunals and Questions of Judgment, Law, and Responsibility' in Karen Engle et al (eds), *Anti-Impunity and the Human Rights Agenda* (Cambridge University Press) 291.

7 Zachary Manfredi, 'Sharpening the Vigilance of the World: Reconsidering the Russell Tribunal as Ritual' [2018] 9(1) Humanity Journal 75–76.

8 Fruadatario and Giani Tognoni, (note 3), 133.

9 Ibid., 134.

10 Fruadatario and Giani Tognoni, (note 3), 133.

victim is allowed to say. In PT, however, the victims are able to relay in detail what happened to them, without the legal restrictions of evidentiary rules. They act as "critical spaces for reflection, gathering of testimony, and documentation."[11] This record would be useful when a responsive future government chooses to take action to hold the perpetrators accountable and ensure reparations to the victims. Such historical records are also very important if we are to genuinely avoid repeating the same mistakes.

Third, building on what has been written in Chapters 1 and 2, PT have been a source of relief for the victims of the offences.[12] While much has been said about the lack of enforcement capacity, its contribution to the victims' healing process has been underemphasised. Most of the judgements have recognised the victims and emphasised the emotional trauma that they underwent and continue to suffer.[13] This is important since any trial process does not just serve the ends of justice but it also provides the platform for catharsis to the victim. When the victim is shunned and ignored, healing will never take place. The voice of the victim in the PT set-up is very important.[14]

In addition, PT offer an alternative vision of international criminal law.[15] Looking at the workings of CPT we see what is wrong with our current system. The politicisation of international justice, detailed in several chapters in this volume, is one problem.[16] Double standards in the application of international justice norms genuinely affect the legitimacy of international criminal law. Relevant questions on this issue include: Is justice just for the victors? Which stories will make the front headline during investigations? Who funds the process of getting this justice? Who decides which atrocities should be investigated? What of the other

11 Manfredi, (note 7), 76–78.

12 Fruadatario and Giani Tognoni, (note 3), 139–140. One of the stated aims of the Indonesian tribunal included to contribute to the healing process of the victims and their families of the genocide and crimes against humanity in Indonesia in and after 1965; . . . to prevent the reoccurrence of violence against victims of the genocide and crimes against humanity in and after 1965 and to ensure the fair trial of perpetrators of such violence.

(Final Report of the IPT 196 Findings and Documents of the International People's Tribunal on Crimes Against Humanity Indonesia 1965, 20 July 2016, IPT 1965 Foundation, The Hague, Jakarta <www.tribunal1965.org/en/tribunal-1965/tribunal-report/> accessed 20 March 2019), 11). See also Byrnes, (note 1), 19, Gabrielle Simm, 'Peoples' Tribunals, Women's Courts and International Crimes of Sexual Violence' in Andrew Byrnes and Gabrielle Simm (eds), *Peoples' Tribunals and International Law* (Cambridge University Press, 2018), 61 <>www.cambridge.org/core/terms>. https://doi.org/10.1017/9781108368360.004 accessed 20 March 2019.

13 Fruadatario and Giani Tognoni, (note 3), 139–140.

14 Dianne Otto, 'Beyond Legal Justice: Some Personal Reflections on People's Tribunals, Listening and Responsibility' [2017] 5(2) London Review of International Law 226.

15 Fruadatario and Giani Tognoni, (note 3), 134. See also Marcos Zunino, 'Subversive Justice: The Russell Vietnam War Crimes Tribunal and Transitional Justice' [1 July 2016] 10(2) *International Journal of Transitional Justice* 211; Manfredi, (note 7), 76–78; Ibid., 225.

16 Fruadatario and Giani, (note 3), 134–135.

"smaller atrocities"? Commenting on the inadequacies of international criminal law, Zachary Manfredi stated:

> tribunals serve as "courts of the victors," selectively applying justice while ignoring the violence of major Western state actors and their allies; tribunals remove justice concerns from local jurisdictions and disrupt more "traditional" frameworks for post conflict reconciliation; international indictments stifle domestic peace processes by mitigating the ability of accused groups to participate in negotiations; and the case law of the tribunals codifies a body of precedent that systematically criminalizes the actions of less technologically advanced actors, while providing exceptions for the "targeted killings" of the most sophisticated militaries.[17]

It has also been recognised that international law is limited in its ability to promote universal access to fundamental rights.[18] PT thus "offer fertile ground for re-examination of the aims and purposes of international criminal and human rights law."[19] For example, Sir Geoffrey Nice, a contributor to this volume and former prosecutor of the ICTY, acknowledged that despite its gravity the massacres in Iran would never have been investigated by any formal body.[20] Even if a formal investigation were to begin, the states will interfere with the proceedings towards a given agenda.[21]

PT, on the other hand, offer an alternative perspective on how international law should work. They have emerged out of "the need to fill the gap between violations of human rights and the promises of international law."[22] They have therefore become "an experimental laboratory of possible paths that are increasingly necessary when aiming for a law for and by peoples."[23] In addition, PT also seeks to influence and bend international law. For example, the Bhopal People's Tribunal sought to "make recommendation to influence international law . . . the Secretary General of the United Nations, and appropriate UN bodies."[24] PT therefore hope that by staging an alternative methodology to justice, change will be effected in the international legal order.[25]

17 Manfredi, (note 7), 75.
18 Ibid., 134–135.
19 Manfredi, (note 7), 75–77.
20 Owen Bowcott, 'Tribunal to Investigate 1980s Massacre of Political Prisoners in Iran' *The Guardian* (18 October 2012) <>www.theguardian.com/world/2012/oct/18/iran-tribunal-investigates-massacre>
21 Otto, (note 14), 235.
22 Fruadatario and Giani, (note 3), 137–138. See also Byrnes and Gabriel, (note 1), 3–4 where it was stated that "a foundational premise of international peoples' tribunals is that states do not have an exclusive monopoly on the creation, interpretation and application of international law".
23 Fruadatario and Giani, (note 3), 135.
24 'From the Permanent Peoples' Tribunal, Bhopal: 10 Years Later Why the Permanent Peoples' Tribunal?' [Fall 1994] New Solutions 12.
25 Otto, (note 14), 230.

The process of accountability that is wholly led by the ordinary citizen also empowers the citizen. Through PT the citizen becomes aware about their ability to make a difference: to ask questions, to get facts and to give an opinion that can hold the powerful accountable. The relatively simple procedures and plain language used in PT saves the ordinary person from the "manifold intricacies of the law, its peculiar pedantic language, its references to precedent, its minutiae of interpretation, its seemingly archaic ritual."[26]As stated by Dorothy Thompson, justice within the PT is "naturally rough and ready."[27]

The underlying message from the discourse on People's Tribunals is the centrality of the people in enforcing human rights.[28] As a result, the citizen recognises his "rights to decision, election, action and liberation."[29] Describing the power of the initial Russell tribunal, Russell stated: "We have no armies and no gallows. We lack power, even the power of mass communication. It is overdue that those without power sit in judgment over those who have it."[30] Citizens are empowered and encouraged to be more vigilant about human rights abuses, especially those perpetrated by the state.[31] An empowered civil society, however, is likely to be a government's worst nightmare. It is no surprise that throughout this volume are examples of governments who have chosen to ignore various PT. This begs the question: if PT were as ineffective as they were made out to be, then why were they opposed so much? On the other hand, it is also important to note that PT could increase the expectations of the ordinary individual.[32] This, in turn, could conceivably lead to disappointment when these expectations are not met.

PT have also affirmed that the search for justice need not be expensive. The common argument against the function of the ICC and the *ad hoc* tribunals established after incidences of mass atrocities has been the exceedingly huge costs involved in the process. However, PT, perhaps because they are not funded by the taxpayers, have been relatively cheaper to run. This may be in large part because most of all the people engage the process in an entirely pro bono capacity. This could, however, be seen as an indicator of the absence of a solid process that considers the right of the accused persons. Sceptics of PT consider justice as a necessarily expensive process. The accused person, for example, always needs an advocate, and there ought to be mechanisms to protect vulnerable witnesses among others.

26 Thompson, (note 4), 289–290.

27 Ibid.

28 Fruadatario and Giani, (note 3), 134.

29 Ibid., 138–139.

30 "The force of our Tribunal lies in the impeccability of its procedures and the thoroughness of its investigations": Opening Statement to the First Tribunal Session by Bertrand Russell (Stockholm).

31 Manfredi, (note 7), 75.

32 Gabrielle Simm, 'Peoples' Tribunals, Women's Courts and International Crimes of Sexual Violence' in Andrew Byrnes and Gabrielle Simm (eds), *Peoples' Tribunals and International Law* (Cambridge University Press, 2018), 61–69.

Lastly, PT, for all their faults, are a timely reminder to perpetrators that, in spite of their political networks and connections today, they will eventually be held accountable in the future.[33] However, it is doubtful whether this reality can effectively prevent future conflict.[34]

Truth justice and reconciliation commissions

TRC have emerged as a common international mechanism and are seen to be an essential element of national post-conflict reconciliation. They are truth-seeking bodies set up to investigate past records of human rights violations and are mostly initiated in countries emerging out of conflict or political turmoil. The five characteristics of TRC are that they focus on past forms of abuses, which they later investigate; they are established by the state; they are created for a period when the country is under transition; and they are temporary.[35] TRC have developed out of a mixture of lack of jurisdiction by the courts, weak judicial bodies and need for restorative justice that unites the perpetrators with the victims.[36] Generally, the choice of a TRC in post-conflict countries is sometimes seen as the most strategic way for the country to move forward.[37] Proponents of TRC believe that "restorative justice is more effective and more moral than criminal justice, for it produces both common values and a new collective identity . . . and, as a result, social consensus."[38] TRC are set up with the assumption that their processes will lead to reconciliation between the perpetrators and the victims, enabling the country to move forward together. That is, in the long run, it is better for reconciliation rather than individual justice to prevail.

The initial TRC were established in Latin America and Africa in the 1980s. These were, however, criticised for obfuscating the truth and justice.[39] For example, the Ugandan Commission of Inquiry into the Disappearances of People in Uganda was established 25 January 1971 by President Idi Amin Dada.[40] Its

33 Bowcott, (note 20).

34 Payam Akhavan, 'Beyond Impunity: Can International Criminal Justice Prevent Future Atrocities?' [2001] 95(1) The American Journal of International Law 7.

35 Priscilla Hayner, *Unspeakable Truths: Facing the Challenge of Truth Commissions* (New York, Routledge, 2001).

36 David Androff, 'Truth and Reconciliation Commissions (TRCs): An International Human Rights Intervention and Its Connection to Social Work' [2010] 40 British Journal of Social Work 1960, 1962.

37 Pierre Hazan, *Judging War Judging History: Behind Truth and Reconciliation* (Stanford University Press, 2010), 33.

38 Ibid.

39 Hayner, (note 35).

40 Commission of Inquiry into the Disappearances of People in Uganda since 25 January, 1971: Charter <www.usip.org/sites/default/files/resources/collections/truth_commissions/Uganda74-Report/Uganda74-Charter.pdf> accessed 20 March 2019; Alejandro Chavez-Segura, 'Can Truth Reconcile a Nation? Truth and Reconciliation Commissions in Argentina and Chile-Lessons for Mexico' [2015] 6(2) Latin American Policy 226, 232.

mandate was to investigate the accusations of disappearance of Ugandans in the hands of Ugandan military officers. The Commission's report was never published and the president continued on the path of human rights abuse with impunity. Similarly, Bolivia established a Commission to inquire into the disappearance of Bolivians. However, it was disbanded before a final report had been produced. The Commission on the Truth for El Salvador was established in 1992 pursuant to the Salvadoran Peace Accords to address conflict and identify human rights violations following a civil war that saw 75,000 lives lost, assassinations of various people and other gross violations of human rights such as rape that had become the way of life in El Salvador. However, one week after the publishing of the perpetrators' names, the Salvadoran government passed a blanket amnesty law covering all crimes related to the civil war. Thus the perpetrators were never investigated nor prosecuted.[41] Decades later a feeling of impotence, abandonment and deception prevails among the populace.

The South African Truth and Justice Commission is perhaps the most studied TRC.[42] It was set up after the end of apartheid in South Africa in 1994 to investigate gross human rights violations during the apartheid regime between 1960–1994. This TRC was to help lead the nation away from a divided past to a future founded on recognition of human rights and democracy. Some people have argued that after the South African TRC, the nature of TRC changed.[43] For example, this was the first commission to be given the power to grant amnesty to perpetrators. This enabled it to get detailed accounts from individual perpetrators and institutions. Unlike other countries, the Commissioner was given powers of subpoenas, search and seizure which were essential for thorough investigation. The Commissioners could also summon and question any person- including those who did not apply to the TRC.

Additionally, it was the first TRC to create witness protection. Its hearings included aspects of enquiry where institutional and special hearings were included and non-governmental organisations gave their contributions. It is also important to note that the Moroccan TRC was the first such body established among the Arabic nations in the Middle East and Northern Africa. TRC have also been established in Chile, Argentina, Sierra Leone, Peru, Timor-Leste, Morocco, Liberia, and Solomon Islands, among others. There may be further critiques of this mechanism that could be borrowed from Dr. Thamil Venthan Ananthavinayagan's analysis using Third World Approaches to International Law in Chapter 4.

41 Heather Parker, 'Truth and Reconciliation Commissions: A Needed Force in Alaska?' [2014] 34(1) Alaska Law Review 46.

42 Steven D. Roper and Lilian A. Barria, 'Why Do States Commission the Truth? Political Considerations in the Establishment of African Truth and Reconciliation Commissions' [2009] 10 Human Rights Review 373, 376.

43 Michal Ben-Josef Hirsch, Megan MacKenzie and Mohamed Sesay, 'Measuring the Impacts of Truth and Reconciliation Commissions: Placing the Global "success" of TRCs in Local Perspective' [2012] 47(3) Cooperation and Conflict 386, 395; Hazan, (note 37), 33.

As many legal scholars and writers have argued, truth alone is not enough for TRC to be effective. After all, the horrors of past abuse can, at best, only be articulated by "moments of truth."[44] Justice, equity and reparations must remain front and centre of any discussions about reconciliation.

The truth justice and reconciliation commission in Kenya

The path towards the establishment of a TJRC in Kenya has been iterative. Soon after the removal of the dictatorship in 2002, the new government sought to establish a TJRC. To roll out the process it first established a taskforce to get views on the suitability of a Truth Justice and Reconciliation Commission. The taskforce found that:

> Kenyans want a truth, justice, and reconciliation commission established immediately. The overwhelming majority of Kenyans, over 90 per cent of those who submitted their views to the Task Force, want the government to establish an effective truth commission, a vehicle that will reveal the truth about past atrocities, name perpetrators, provide redress for victims, and promote national healing and reconciliation. Kenyans believe that a truth commission will renew the country's morality in politics, law, in the economy, and throughout the society. They want a state founded on the rule of law and respect for the human rights of every individual who resides in Kenya. In other words, Kenyans want a human rights state.[45]

The taskforce recommended the establishment of "an effective and credible truth commission, one that will address past abuses, recreate the state, banish impunity, and set Kenya on an irreversible trajectory to democracy and respect for basic freedoms."[46] However, such a Commission was not established as recommended. Instead the report of the taskforce was shelved and ignored. It is only after the 2007–2008 post-election violence in Kenya that discussions on the need for a TJRC re-emerged. However, even then, there are those who believe that the TJRC was imposed by international mediators during the conflict, as part of the peace building effort. As a result it was never fully supported by the Kenyan ruling class.[47] Perhaps this explains the challenges the Kenyan TJRC would face later on.

44 Hannah Arendt quoted in Pierre Hazan, (note 37).

45 See Report of the Task Force on the Establishment of a Truth, Justice and Reconciliation Commission, p. 9 <www.knchr.org/Portals/0/Transitional%20Justice/Kenya_Report_of_the_Task_Force_on_the_Establishment_of_a_Truth_Justice_and_Reconciliation_Commission_August_26th_2003.pdf?ver=2018-06-08-100201-947> accessed 20 March 2019.

46 Ibid.

47 Kimberley Lanegran, 'The Kenyan Truth, Justice and Reconciliation Commission: The Importance of Commissioners and Their Appointment Process' [2015] 1(3) Transitional Justice Review 41, 53.

Kenya's TJRC was established to start operating from 9 March 2009[48] to investigate and document the extensive human rights violations committed in Kenya during the British colonial period and under the administrations of the first three presidents. It also was supposed to investigate atrocities committed during the 2007–2008 post-election violence.[49] These periods were characterised by corruption, torture, enforced disappearances, extrajudicial killings, political assassinations and displacement of communities.

The main objective of the TJRC in Kenya was to:

> seek and promote justice, national unity, reconciliation and peace, among the people of Kenya by inquiring into the human rights violations in Kenya and recommending appropriate redress for persons and communities who have suffered injury, hurt, damage, grievance or those who have in any other manner been adversely affected by such acts and omissions.[50]

It was hoped that the end result of the process would be "desire for development, concern for gross human rights violations, abuse of power and misuse of public office."[51]

The TJRC was given powers to "recommend prosecution of perpetrators; determine redress for victims; facilitate the granting of amnesty; provide a platform for non-retributive truth-telling; provide a forum for hearing victims; and provide a forum for confession."[52] One of the unique features of the Kenyan TJRC was that it was the first commission with the mandate to "investigate economic crimes."[53] Since economic crimes were a common occurrence in the country, this mandate was clearly not in line with the UN recommendations that were "comprehensive but narrow enough to be manageable in time and scope . . . realistic and commensurate with resources and time assigned to the Commission."[54]

The operations of the Kenyan TJRC were embroiled in controversies from the beginning. First, there were challenges regarding the membership of some of the commissioners. The commission was caught up in internal wrangling. There were allegations that some of its members had been serving the former dictatorial regime and therefore had a significant role in the abuse of citizens' rights. While the challenge on the suitability of some of the commissioners fizzled out, the challenge on the chairperson's moral authority remained and grew stronger.

48 TJRC Act, Section 1.

49 See ICTJ "Kenya" https://www.ictj.org/our-work/regions-and-countries/kenya.

50 Preamble to the Truth, Justice and Reconciliation Commission Act, 2008.

51 Ibid.

52 TJRC Act section 5.

53 Ibid. See also Lanegran, (note 47), 53–54.

54 Report from OHCHR Fact-Finding Mission to Kenya (6–28 February 2008) <www.ohchr.org/documents/press/ohchrkenyareport.pdf> accessed 20 March 2019.

There were allegations that the chair of the Commission was also a suspect in past human rights abuse during his time as a government official.[55] Since the chair was a high ranking member of the previous governments under investigation it was inevitable that he would both be a suspect and a witness in some cases. It was feared that this, in turn, would create conflict of interest that would inevitably interfere with the Commission's operations. In effect therefore, although the TJRC was created by the government, albeit reluctantly, the selection of and continued participation of the chair would ensure that it continued to have a voice in it.[56]

Demands for the resignation of the chairperson and concern regarding his continued stay in office took up to one year of the TJRC's two-year mandate.[57] The chairperson's initial reluctance to step aside led to the resignation, in protest, of the vice chairperson of the Commission. A court case was also filed,[58] where the applicants sought an order prohibiting the Chairperson from running the affairs of TJRC. The applicants also sought orders quashing the chairperson's oath of office. They argued that the chairperson took his oath before he had been formally appointed and his name published in the official government gazette. The Court however found that the chairperson's appointment involved many bodies – the Selection Panel, the Minister for Justice, Parliament, and the president. His selection, the Court held, could not be challenged without questioning the decision of all these bodies.

After this, there were demands that the Chief Justice should appoint a tribunal to investigate the suitability of the chairperson to continue as such. The Chief Justice yielded to these demands and appointed a tribunal to investigate the chair's suitability to continue in office. The tribunal was supposed to report back to him in six months. However, the chair of the TJRC managed to get stay orders from court preventing the tribunal from continuing to operate.[59] He was then able to run down the clock until the six months were over and the tribunal's mandate was over. Attempts by the other commissioners to get the Chief Justice to appoint another Tribunal to investigate the chair were however unsuccessful. Later, the Commissioners filed an application seeking to have the court order the Chief Justice to create such a tribunal.[60] They argued that the chairperson had already been adversely mentioned by other witnesses and he would bring

55 For more discussion on this see David Anderson, 'Remembering Wagalla: State Violence in Northern Kenya, 1962–1991' [2014] 8(4) Journal of Eastern African Studies 658–659 <https://doi.org/10.1080/17531055.2014.946237> accessed 20 March 2019; Lanegran, (note 47), 41.

56 Lanegran, (note 47), 41–66.

57 Ibid., 41–59.

58 *R v Truth, Justice and Reconciliation Commission & Another Ex-parte Augustine Njeru-Kathangu & 9 Others* [2009] eKLR.

59 *BethuelKiplagat v Chief Justice of the Republic of Kenya &4 Others* [2011] eKLR.

60 *Truth Justice and Reconciliation Commission v Chief Justice of the Republic of Kenya & Another* [2012] eKLR.

the TJRC's report into disrepute. Further, they stated that they still needed the chairperson as a witness in their investigations on political assassinations. The Court however held that the Chief Justice had no powers to set a tribunal to investigate the past conduct of a commissioner. Such information, the Court held, ought to have been provided to the Selection Panel before the appointment of the commissioners. The Court further stated that "it is not for fellow Commissioners or the Commission to question the return of the Chairman and put obstacles and hurdles into the path of his return when none of the allegations have been considered, investigated and determined."[61]

Cleared of all charges, the chairperson returned to the Commission during the writing of the report. When his colleagues protested his presence, he assured them that he would not be involved in the report writing stage.[62] However, strangely enough, the chairman was one of the people who criticised the methodology used to collect information and the conclusion of the report.[63]

Financial challenges were also plenty. The Act established a TJRC Fund that would get direct funding from the Consolidated Fund.[64] This provision was made in order to shield the TJRC from political interference. However, in the end, it played a limited role in actualising the TJRCs actual receipt of budget monies. The government still controlled the budget strings. Most donor countries and non-governmental organisations that had pledged to support the TJRC's operations also withdrew because of the controversies that followed it.

In addition, the TJRC also faced political challenges.[65] The support of the leaders in government was at best "ad hoc and inconsistent."[66] First, the President failed to appoint another person to replace the vice chairperson who had earlier resigned. It was also clear that the government was not comfortable with the proceedings in the TJRC. For example, the government failed to provide documentation related to the Wagalla massacre that occurred in north eastern Kenya in 1984.[67] This was a government-led operation against residents of north Eastern Kenya that involved "torture, brutal beatings, rape, and sexual violence, burning of houses and looting of property"[68] and resulted in the deaths of almost one thousand innocent victims.[69] The government also refused to release reports of previous commissions of inquiry that could assist the TJRC in its investigations.

61 Ibid.

62 Lanegran, (note 47), 41, 64–65.

63 Kiplagat doubts TJRC report will pass test of time, Wambui Ndonga, 23 May 2013 <www.capitalfm.co.ke/news/2013/05/kiplagat-doubts-tjrc-report-will-pass-test-of-time/> accessed 20 March 2019.

64 TJRC Act, Section 44.

65 Lanegran, (note 47), 41–61.

66 Kenya Transitional Justice Network, 'Summary: Truth Justice and Reconciliation Commission Report' 4 <www.acordinternational.org/silo/files/kenya-tjrc-summary-report-aug-2013.pdf> accessed 20 March 2019.

67 Anderson, (note 55).

68 Ibid., 658–670.

69 Ibid.

In spite of all these hurdles the TJRC stumbled on to the end of its term. After recording 42,465 statements, collecting 1,828 memoranda and analysing relevant documentation the report was finally released in May 2013.[70] The TJRC Report indicted the governments of the first three presidents for human rights abuse and for economic crimes. State security agencies, especially Kenya police and Kenya Army, were found to have been perpetrators of bodily integrity violations of human rights in Kenya such as massacres, enforced disappearances, torture and ill-treatment and sexual violence. The Commission also found that historical grievances over land were the most important driver of conflicts and ethnic tension in Kenya. Close to half of the memoranda received by the Commission related to or touched on claims over land. In addition, the British government was also found liable for sexual assault of Samburu women by its soldiers. The TJRC found a link between economic crimes and gross violations of human rights such as killing and torture of those who attempt to combat it. This undermined the quality of public services on which the poor depend on to meet their basic needs and the minority groups and indigenous people were displaced due to corruptly approved infrastructure and developments.

Even after the final report had been submitted to the president it was not released to the public as was required.[71] In addition, the minister responsible was required to table the report in Parliament within 21 days after its publication[72] and thereafter follow up on its implementation with bi-annual reports on the status of its implementation.[73] All these steps were not taken. As if that is not enough there were other court cases subsequently filed by various individuals in order to prevent tabling of the report in the Kenyan Parliament,[74] to quash some of the references in the report[75] challenging the factual finding of the

70 Kenya Transitional Justice Network, (note 66).

71 TJRC Act Section 48(3) Required the Commission to Publish Its Report in the Kenya Gazette and in at Least Three Local Newspapers.

72 TJRC Act, Section 48(4).

73 Ibid., Section 50.

74 *Njenga Mwangi & Another v Truth, Justice and Reconciliation Commission & 4 Others* [2013] eKLR.

75 *Republic v Truth, Justice and Reconciliation Commission & Another Ex-Parte Beth Wambui Mugo* [2016] eKLR <http://kenyalaw.org/caselaw/cases/view/118960/> accessed 20 March 2019. The Petitioner alleged that she did not benefit from irregular allocation of land during the Kenyatta presidency and sought to quash such findings in the Report. The judge stated that the Attorney General displayed a "lackadaisical attitude" and did not participate. In any event, it quashed the references to the Petitioner as she had not been invited to defend herself in the TJRC's proceedings. However, in *Republic v Truth Justice and Reconciliation Commission & 3 Others Ex-parte Ngengi Muigai* [2015] eKLR, a case with similar arguments failed ostensibly because the Petitioner faced "no imminent threat of the implementation of the recommendation against him". Other cases seeking their names to be expunged from the Report included *Heildah Awuor Ogol v Truth, Justice and Reconciliation Commission & Another* [2016] eKLR.

report[76] among other complaints. Demand for release of the report to the public later became a political point of contention. Thus, support or opposition to the demand largely depended on which side of the political divide one belonged to.

While attempting to tackle the past injustices the TJRC lost the present goodwill. Apart from a few opposition leaders and non-governmental organisations that continued to demand the release of the report, the majority of Kenyans either remained blissfully ignorant about the report's existence or simply had chosen to forget and move on. As stated previously, the government was also, at best, completely nonchalant about the TJRC. One of the major reasons for their indifference was because a number of the government officers in the executive office and legislature had been adversely mentioned. For example, the current president is a son of the first president whose regime was found guilty of significant human rights abuses. As a result, very few of the TJRC's recommendations have been implemented to date. For example, the president was required to apologise on behalf of the previous regimes to victims of torture and extrajudicial killings. This has never happened in spite of the negligible financial cost involved. Perhaps sensing the government's reluctance to embrace the TJRC process and the waning public support, eventually very few perpetrators were willing to admit liability. Gabrielle Lynch describes one of the sessions for persons adversely mentioned as a denial session:

> I heard not a single admission of personal responsibility or guilt. Instead, testimonies were characterized by five discursive strands of responsibility denied: denial through a transfer of responsibility, denial through a questioning of sources, denial through amnesia, denial through a reinterpretation of events and an assertion of victimhood, and denial that events constituted a wrongdoing.[77]

There is little doubt that the Kenyan TJRC was ineffective. The air of impunity continues with the ruling class. Reporting on the process of the TJRC, Godfrey Musila states:

> The transitional justice debate has become entangled – perhaps irredeemably – in coalition government politics and power struggles which in turn seem to revolve around pro-reform and pro-status quo elements. The legitimacy of

76 *Kiriro Wa Ngugi& 6 Others v Truth, Justice and Reconciliation Commission & 6 Others* [2013] eKLR where the petitioner argued the report is "not an accurate, complete and historical record of violations and abuses of human rights and economic crimes inflicted on persons by the State, public institutions and holders of public office between 12th December 1963 and 28th February 2008".

77 Gabrielle Lynch, 'Transitional Justice: Impunity, Project Kenya and Burying the TJRC Report' (8 September 2018) <www.theeastafricanreview.info/op-eds/2018/09/08/when-killers-become-victims-impunity-project-kenya-and-burying-the-tjrc-report/> accessed 20 March 2019.

> the process is therefore in doubt, and the greater public and civil society organizations have been largely excluded from the process.[78]

Although the TJRC sought to heal the divisions in the country and unite the country little reconciliation[79] has been achieved. Little wonder that the country continued to suffer post-election violence even after the 2017 general elections. With little reform within the general policy level there is little hope for significant fundamental change. As Payam Akhavan, states:

> Accountability is ultimately effective when it conforms with the broader policy context within which it operates . . . Postmortem justice without a corresponding commitment of military, political, and economic resources significantly dilutes the message of accountability and under-mines its long-term viability in preventing crimes.[80]

The Kenyan TJRC experience is an example of a mock process that was conducted to meet the demands of the international community. It also shows how, ultimately, without buy-in from the political class it is very difficult to have genuine reconciliation.

Differences and similarities of TRC and PT

TRC and PT both operate where there have been gross human rights abuses. Often, these abuses have not been recognised or addressed by the formal justice systems. Sometimes, the time lapse between the abuse and the determination to take action can be very long. This would significantly reduce the probability of successful criminal prosecution. The number of victims or perpetrators are also often too many to process in court. Hence, there is always a need for alternative ways of addressing such atrocities.

TRC are concerned with the status of the victim.[81] The victims are provided with an opportunity to talk about their abuse and fears. Unlike criminal trials the narrative is not given under the shadow of astronomical legal fees or fear of cross examination.[82] Instead, the opportunity for showing respect for the victim's

78 Geoffrey M. Musila, 'Options for Transitional Justice in Kenya: Autonomy and the Challenge of External Prescriptions' [November 2009] 3(3) *International Journal of Transitional Justice* 445–464.

79 Alejandro Chavez-Segura, defines to include the absence of violent conflict and creation to a culture of respect for fundamental rights instead of abuse and coercion, Segura, (note 40), 227.

80 Akhavan, (note 34), 7–30.

81 Robert Amea and Seidu Alidu, 'Truth and Reconciliation Commissions: Restorative Justice, Peacemaking Criminology and Development' [2010] 23(3) Criminal Justice Studies 253.

82 Ibid; Jonathan Allen, 'Balancing Justice and Social Unity: Political Theory and the Idea of a Truth and Reconciliation Commission' [1999] 49(3) The University of Toronto Law Journal 315, 331.

narrative is an end in itself that ought to be respected. PT are also concerned with the victim. These concerns include questions regarding victim compensation and how the fears of reoccurrence of the abuse and impunity can be addressed. Thus the two bodies are more restorative in nature than ordinary criminal trials. The two bodies also make recommendations to the state in order to revert the victim as close to a holistic state.[83]

Like PT, TRC are also interested in establishing the truth.[84] Their hearings are geared towards developing a "macro-historical record that can . . . serve as a reminder of the violence in the social conscience."[85] As a result the proceedings of the TRC act as legitimate records of the events of the past. The reports can also later be used in prosecution of the perpetrators and sharing our liability.[86]

The strict rules of evidence applicable in courts are also not applicable in both institutions.[87] In TRC the main focus is getting to establish the cause of the human rights abuse, the perpetrators and hopefully get some form of reconciliation through recriminations.[88] Dr. Nevenkana Tromp provides greater detail in Chapter 5 when she discusses the Women's Court.

PT and TRC are both often product of pressure from the civil society.[89] This happens through lobbying. As this volume highlights, the international crimes against ethnic minorities of Myanmar and lack of justice prompted a PT on the crimes in Myanmar. The inability of society to appropriately address child sex abuse led survivors to form the UKCSAPT. The Iranian government's complete denial of its involvement of torture and abuse prompted survivors decades later to push for a PT to provide their narrative.

Differences

Although both may be a product of civil society pressures, some authors have argued that TRCs emerge whenever there is a stalemate among the political contestants.[90] They are therefore seen as part of the post-regime transitional process in order to preserve the stability of the country while holding the leaders of the former regime accountable.[91] As stated by Elin Skaar, they "appear most frequently as sole solutions [to human rights abuses] in the cases where there is a heavy element

83 Androff, (note 36).
84 P Von Zyl, 'Justice Without Punishment: Guaranteeing Human Rights in Transitional Societies' in C Villa-Vicencio and W Verwoerd (eds), *Looking Back, Reaching Forward: Reflections on the Truth and Reconciliation Commission in South Africa* (Cape Town, South Africa, University of Cape Town Press, 2000), 42–57.
85 Androff, (note 36).
86 Ibid.
87 Allen, (note 82), 315–329.
88 Hirsch, MacKenzie and Sesay, (note 43), 386.
89 Androff, (note 36), 300.
90 Audrey Chapman and Patrick Ball, 'The Truth of Truth Commissions: Comparative Lessons from Haiti, South Africa and Guatemala' [2001] 23(1) Human Rights Quarterly 1.
91 Hirsch, MacKenzie and Sesay, (note 43), 386–389.

of pre-regime transition bargaining."[92] Since the post-transition democratic nations are too weak, it is assumed that they will not be able to handle the rigours of a full trial of the former regime's perpetrators.[93] The TRC will then be formed so as to mark "a decisive break with the official sponsorship of human rights violations that characterized the past."[94] On this point it has been stated as follows:

> Truth commissions, in general, and the TRC, in particular, purport to be attempts to balance the independent forces of both justice and reconciliation. . . . If, on the other hand, unity, peace, and reconciliation have clear priority, this would in many cases be best served by a general amnesty.[95]

PT, on the other hand, are not necessarily associated with regime change. The main purpose of the PT is mainly to ensure grassroots participation in the process of holding leaders accountable.[96] As we have seen with most PT, it can be established even without change of government accompanying it.

PT usually take the format of an ordinary criminal trial where there is an accused person and his accusers. TRC however are not criminal trials.[97] The purpose of the TRC is to recall and uncover the truth about the past atrocities, and through this exercise hopefully encourage reconciliation. There could be people who are adversely mentioned but the TRC can only recommend future prosecution. There is no determination of guilt or innocence as happens in PT.

Although TRC have in the past been seen to be grassroots oriented and with effect on the grassroots,[98] there is a sense in which this characterisation does not always hold. First, they are established by legislation passed by Parliament. They also get their officials selected by the government and get funding from the central government. As a result, as we have seen with the Kenyan TJRC, they are liable to manipulation by the government. The TRC in Columbia and Timor were also used to whitewash the actions of the people in authority.[99]

The PT, unlike the TRC, are independent bodies. Their legitimacy draws from the demand by the people for investigations and accountability. However, TRC are established by the ruling regime under a law established by the legislative body.[100]

92 Elin Skaar, 'Truth Commissions, Trials – or Nothing? Policy Options in Democratic Transition' [1999] 20(6) Third World Quarterly 1109, 1122.
93 Allen, (note 82), 315–319.
94 Ibid.
95 Ibid., 315–320.
96 Fruadatario and Giani, (note 3), 135–136.
97 Segura, (note 40), 229.
98 Hirsch, MacKenzie and Sesay, (note 43), 386–388.
99 Ibid., (note 43), 154. See also See comments on the Ugandan Truth Commission and the truth process in Yugoslavia-Jelena Subotić, *Hijacked Justice: Dealing with the Past in the Balkans* (Ithaca, Cornell University Press, 2009), 55; Joanna R. Quinn, 'Constraints: The Un-Doing of the Ugandan Truth Commission' [2004] 26 Human Rights Quarterly 423.
100 The Greensboro Truth Commission is however given as an example of a TRC that was wholly set up and proceeded without the state participation. See Androff, (note 36), 297.

Questions regarding their legitimacy are therefore significantly reduced. However, in the same vein, the TRC could be seen as tools that governments use to launder their past.[101]

Similarly, TRC also enjoy international support in their establishment.[102] For example, the Sierra Leonean TRC was a product of the Lome Peace Accord where the United Nations was also a party. PT however operate on their own and the government and international legal order is likely to ignore them.[103]

TRCs have more focus on the restorative aspect of justice than PT. The victims provide their testimonies without any interruption or cross examination common in the other tribunals. The perpetrators are also allowed to participate with the sole purpose of acknowledging the harm caused and suffered.[104] The idea is that after the hearings the relationship between the perpetrator and the victim can be restored. Deterrence is not an objective of the TRC.[105] The TRC also are interested in institutional reform in order to prevent future violence.[106]

Amnesty for the perpetrators has been a tool used by TRC to navigate the transition period. The perpetrators are promised that they would not be prosecuted if they are willing to confess to the truth. As a result, it is hoped that more perpetrators would be willing to participate in the process.[107] On the other hand, PT are set up to fight a *de facto* amnesty granted by the state through its unwillingness to investigate past atrocities. In the view of proponents of PT, leaders should be accountable for their actions.

Conclusion

From the preceding it is clear that PT and TRC are well-developed and distinct bodies used to deal with gross human rights violations. While the two bodies share some similarities, they also have stark differences. TRC are established, funded and can be controlled by the state. As a result, they can also be used to whitewash the political players. This is mainly through the tool of amnesty. However, even where no amnesty has been granted, TRC will depend on political players to implement the recommendations. Ultimately, however, the choice of the body to use and how effective or ineffective this body will be depends to a large extent on the level of recognition, and therefore legitimacy, that it

101 Roper and Barria, (note 42), 373–388.

102 Ibid., 386–387.

103 The China Tribunal, Chapter 10, has received publicity and its summary report was even used by the Republican National Convention in the United States to call attention to the horrific suffering of victims of forced organ harvesting. See Eva Fu, 'RNC Unanimously Passes Resolution Opposing Forced Organ Harvesting in China' *The Epoch Times* (7 August 2019) <>www.theepochtimes.com/rnc-unanimously-passes-resolution-opposing-forced-organ-harvesting-in-china_3033869.html>

104 Androff, (note 36).

105 Hirsch, MacKenzie and Sesay, (note 43), 386–395.

106 Amea and Seidu Alidu, (note 81), 253.

107 Androff, (note 36).

enjoys with the people. From the preceding one can surmise that where the state authorities are willing to acknowledge past atrocities TRC will be an appropriate vehicle. However, where they are not then PT would be effective.

Bibliography

Books

Byrnes, A. and Simm, G. (ed), *Peoples' Tribunals and International Law* (Cambridge University Press, 2018).

Hayner, P., *Unspeakable Truths: Facing the Challenge of Truth Commissions* (New York Routledge, 2001).

Hazan, P., *Judging War Judging History: Behind Truth and Reconciliation* (Stanford University Press, 2010).

Subotić, J., *Hijacked Justice: Dealing with the Past in the Balkans* (Ithaca: Cornell University Press, 2009).

Vicencio, C. V. and Verwoerd, W. (eds), *Looking Back, Reaching Forward: Reflections on the Truth and Reconciliation Commission in South Africa* (Cape Town, South Africa, University of Cape Town Press, 2000).

Articles

Akhavan, P., 'Beyond Impunity: Can International Criminal Justice Prevent Future Atrocities?' [2001] 95(1) The American Journal of International Law.

Allen, J., 'Balancing Justice and Social Unity: Political Theory and the Idea of a Truth and Reconciliation Commission' [1999] 49(3) The University of Toronto Law Journal.

Amea, R. and Alidu, S., 'Truth and Reconciliation Commissions: Restorative Justice, Peacemaking Criminology and Development' [2010] 23(3) Criminal Justice Studies.

Anderson, D., 'Remembering Wagalla: State Violence in Northern Kenya, 1962–1991' [2014] 8(4) Journal of Eastern African Studies 658, 670 <https://doi.org/10.1080/17531055.2014.946237> accessed 20 March 2019.

Androff, Jr. K. D., 'Truth and Reconciliation Commissions (TRCs): An International Human Rights Intervention and Its Connection to Social Work' [2010] 40 British Journal of Social Work 1960, 1971.

Androff, Jr. K. D., 'Can Civil Society Reclaim Truth? Results from a Community-Based Truth and Reconciliation Commission' [2012] 6(6) The International Journal of Transitional Justice 296, 297.

Bowcott, O., 'Tribunal to Investigate 1980s Massacre of Political Prisoners in Iran' *The Guardian* (18 October 2012) <www.theguardian.com/world/2012/oct/18/iran-tribunal-investigates-massacre>

Boyle, M. and Kobayashi, A., 'In the Face of Epistemic Injustices? On the Meaning of People-Led War Crimes Tribunals' [2015] 33 Environment and Planning D: Society and Space 697, 702.

Chapman, A. and Ball, Patrick, 'The Truth of Truth Commissions: Comparative Lessons from Haiti, South Africa and Guatemala' [2000] 23(1) Human Rights Quarterly.

Chavez-Segura, A., 'Can Truth Reconcile a Nation? Truth and Reconciliation Commissions in Argentina and Chile-Lessons for Mexico' [2015] 6(2) Latin American Policy 226, 229.

Hirsch, M. B-J., MacKenzie, M. and Sesay, M., 'Measuring the Impacts of Truth and Reconciliation Commissions: Placing the Global "success" of TRCs in Local Perspective' [2012] 47(3) Cooperation and Conflict 386, 395.

Lanegran, K., 'The Kenyan Truth, Justice and Reconciliation Commission: The Importance of Commissioners and Their Appointment Process' [2015] 1(3) Transitional Justice Review 41, 61.

Lynch, G., 'Transitional Justice: Impunity, Project Kenya and Burying the TJRC Report', 8 September 2018.

Manfredi, Z., 'Sharpening the Vigilance of the World: Reconsidering the Russell Tribunal as Ritual' [2018] 9(1) Humanity Journal 75.

Musila, M. G., 'Options for Transitional Justice in Kenya: Autonomy and the Challenge of External Prescriptions' [November 2009] 3(3) International Journal of Transitional Justice 445–464.

Otto, D., 'Beyond Legal Justice: Some Personal Reflections on People's Tribunals, Listening and Responsibility' [2017] 5(2) London Review of International Law 230.

Parker, H., 'Truth and Reconciliation Commissions: A Needed Force in Alaska?' [2014] 34(1) Alaska Law Review 46.

Quinn, R. J., 'Constraints: The Un-Doing of the Ugandan Truth Commission' [2004] 26 Human Rights Quarterly 423.

Roper, D. S. and Barria, A. L., 'Why Do States Commission the Truth? Political Considerations in the Establishment of African Truth and Reconciliation Commissions' [2009] 10 Human Rights Review 373, 388.

Simm, G., 'Peoples' Tribunals, Women's Courts and International Crimes of Sexual Violence' in Andrew Byrnes (ed), *Peoples' Tribunals and International Law* (Cambridge University Press, 2018), 61, 69.

Skaar, E., 'Truth Commissions, Trials – or Nothing? Policy Options in Democratic Transition' [1999] 20(6) Third World Quarterly 1109, 1122.

Thompson, D., 'The People's Tribunal: The Antithesis of Justice' [April 1954] 40(4) American Bar Association Journal 289, 290.

Zunino, M., 'Subversive Justice: The Russell Vietnam War Crimes Tribunal and Transitional Justice' [1 July 2016] 10(2) International Journal of Transitional Justice 211.

Zyl, P. V., 'Justice Without Punishment: Guaranteeing Human Rights in Transitional Societies' in C. Villa-Vicencio and W. Verwoerd (eds), *Looking Back, Reaching Forward: Reflections on the Truth and Reconciliation Commission in South Africa* (Cape Town, South Africa, University of Cape Town Press, 2000), 42–57.

Websites

International Center for Transitional Justice, "Kenya" www.ictj.org (accessed 20 March 2019).

Bowcott, Owen, 'Tribunal to Investigate 1980s Massacre of Political Prisoners in Iran' *The Guardian* (18 October 2012) <www.theguardian.com/world/2012/oct/18/iran-tribunal-investigates-massacre>

Chief Prosecutor of the Kuala Lumpur War Crimes Commission V. George W Bush & Anthony L. Blair, Transcript of Judgement <www.globalresearch.ca/chief-prosecutor-of-the-kuala-lumpur-war-crimes-commission-v-george-w-bush-anthony-l-blair/27821> Accessed 20 March 2019.

Commission of Inquiry into the Disappearances of People in Uganda Since 25 January, 1971: Charter <www.usip.org/sites/default/files/resources/collections/truth_commissions/Uganda74-Report/Uganda74-Charter.pdf> accessed 20 March 2019.

Final Report of the IPT 196 Findings and Documents of the International People's Tribunal on Crimes Against Humanity Indonesia 1965, 20 July 2016, IPT 1965 Foundation, The Hague, Jakarta <www.tribunal1965.org/en/tribunal-1965/tribunal-report/> accessed 20 March 2019.

Final Verdict International Peoples' Tribunal Washington, DC, USA <https://internationalpeoplestribunaldotorg.files.wordpress.com/2015/09/international-peoples-tribunal-ipt-2015-final-verdict.pdf> accessed 20 March 2019.

Kenya Transitional Justice Network, 'Summary: Truth Justice and Reconciliation Commission Report', 4 <www.acordinternational.org/silo/files/kenya-tjrc-summary-report-aug-2013.pdf> accessed 20 March 2019.

Kiplagat Doubts TJRC Report Will Pass Test of Time, Wambuindonga (23 May 2013) <www.capitalfm.co.ke/news/2013/05/kiplagat-doubts-tjrc-report-will-pass-test-of-time/> accessed 20 March 2019.

Lynch, Gabrielle, Transitional Justice: Impunity, Project Kenya and Burying the TJRC Report (8 September 2018) <www.theeastafricanreview.info/op-eds/2018/09/08/when-killers-become-victims-impunity-project-kenya-and-burying-the-tjrc-report/> accessed 20 March 2019.

Permanent People's Tribunal <http://permanentpeoplestribunal.org/algiers-charter/?lang=en> accessed 20 March 2019.

The Permanent People's Tribunal <www.tppcanada.org/a-propos-du-tpp/session-canada> accessed 20 March 2019.

Report from OHCHR Fact-Finding Mission to Kenya (6–28 February 2008) <www.ohchr.org/documents/press/ohchrkenyareport.pdf> accessed 20 March 2019.

Report of the Task Force on the Establishment of a Truth, Justice and Reconciliation Commission, p. 9 <www.knchr.org/Portals/0/Transitional%20Justice/Kenya_Report_of_the_Task_Force_on_the_Establishment_of_a_Truth_Justice_and_Reconciliation_Commission_August_26th_2003.pdf?ver=2018-06-08-100201-947> accessed 20 March 2019.

Russell Tribunal on Palestine <www.russelltribunalonpalestine.com/en/about-rtop> accessed 20 March 2019.

4 Panem et circences?

People's Tribunals from a TWAIL perspective

Thamil Venthan Ananthavinayagan

Introduction

International justice, quo vadis? Christine Schwoebel-Patel writes that:

> [S]eemingly, a dialectic between human rights critique and its more mainstream projects has evolved. Although the grounds which led to such self-reflection in human rights law (commitments to universality in view of a pluralistic world, the moral tone adopted, the hypocrisy of 'Western' states in their rhetoric for human rights protection, to name but a few) are much the same in international criminal law, ICL is a field of international law which is confident, charging ahead, with much fewer apparent anxieties. The apparent lack of critique means that significant shifts which have taken place through the rising prominence of the discipline are not questioned in a way which goes beyond an effectiveness critique.[1]

There have been many attempts to ask for the recognition of different systems of justice, including the call for a modern-colonial relationship of "traditional customary law." Does this secure a deep transformation of monocultural state-centric notions of justice central to national and international legal systems? The 2007 United Nations Declaration on the Rights of Indigenous Peoples highlights

> [C]onvinced that the recognition of the rights of indigenous peoples in this Declaration will enhance harmonious and cooperative relations between the State and indigenous peoples, based on principles of justice, democracy, respect for human rights, non-discrimination and good faith.[2]

However, the differentiation that this declaration establishes between law and collective systems of life and individual – positivist – rationalist law and its

1 Christine E. J. Schwoebel, 'The Comfort of International Criminal Law' [2013] 24(2) Law and Critique 169–170.

2 United Nations Declaration on the Rights of Indigenous Peoples 2007.

Eurocentric modern/colonial/capitalist roots should be pondered carefully because "[t]he firm intention to respect the customs, does not always imply the will to taken away from them from the action of progress, development and civilization under the control of the Nation-State."[3]

Ineffectuality, Eurocentrism, and elitist distance is considered to be the *Achilles heel* of international criminal law. With ineffectuality the author refers to the increasing disparity between cases concerning crimes committed by the Western hemisphere and the Eastern hemisphere.[4] With elitist distance the author invokes the technocratic and detached nature of the international criminal justice system.[5] Some scholars emphasise the possibility to opt for legal petitions to courts on behalf of small states. With this minor insurrection of the small and weak states, these see their only chances to echo their grievances and demand for accountability.[6] It also criticised that the major international tribunals' lack of enforcement mechanisms (in particular of the ICC), limited jurisdictional scope, inability to extradite suspects from noncompliant states, consistent underfunding, and notorious sluggishness in producing verdicts perpetuate a certain bias towards international institutions.[7] More recently, the Pre-Trial Chamber at the ICC has rejected the prosecutor's request, filed nearly eighteen months ago, to open an investigation of war crimes and crimes against humanity in Afghanistan, including allegations that United States forces and the Central Intelligence Agency committed acts of torture there.[8] This, in consequence, will reinforce the view of many states in the Global South that the ICC and international criminal justice at large are ineffective and contribute towards the exoneration of the Western hemisphere in their strife towards universalisation of their values.[9]

Postcolonial criticism of international criminal law centres around the effects of the tribunals' work: the perception as the "courts of the victors," selective

3 See also: Rosalba Icaza, 'The Permanent People's Tribunals and Indigenous People's Struggles in Mexico: Between Coloniality and Epistemic Justice?' [2015] 1(15020) Palgrave Communications 1.

4 See also: Hiroyuki Tosa, 'Global Constitutional Order and the Deviant Other: Reflections on the Dualistic Nature of the ICC Process' [2018] 18(1) International Relations of the Asia-Pacific 45.

5 Terrence Chapman and Stephen Chaudoin, 'People like the International Criminal Court – as Long as It Targets Other Problems in Other Countries' *Washington Post* (20 January 2011) <www.washingtonpost.com/news/monkey-cage/wp/2017/01/20/people-like-the-international-criminal-court-as-long-as-it-targets-other-problems-in-other-countries/> accessed 11 August 2019.

6 Zachary Manfredi, 'Sharpening the Vigilance of the World: Reconsidering the Russell Tribunal as Ritual, Humanity: An International Journal of Human Rights' [2018] 9(1) Humanitarianism and Development 75.

7 For an interesting view: Ray Murphy, 'Many Criticisms of International Criminal Court Have Validity *Irish Times* (6 June 2013) <www.irishtimes.com/opinion/many-criticisms-of-international-criminal-court-have-validity-1.1418128> accessed 11 August 2019.

8 ICC Pre-Trial Chamber, ICC-02/17, 12 April 2017.

9 Oumar Ba, 'International Justice and the Postcolonial Condition' [2017] 63(4) Africa Today 44, 52.

application of international justice, with sheer ignorance towards the empire of violence perpetrated by Western state actors and their allies; the removal of international justice concerns in domestic criminal jurisdictions; the disruption and hinderance of more “traditional” frameworks for post-conflict justice.[10] Moreover, international indictments stifle domestic peace processes by mitigating the ability of accused groups to participate in negotiations; and the case law of the tribunals codifies a body of precedent that systematically criminalises the actions of less technologically advanced actors, while providing exceptions for the “targeted killings” of the most sophisticated militaries.[11] Meanwhile, in this environment, advocates and human rights activists cannot achieve justice in a political vacuum.[12] Against this background, Ronald Rogo wrote in the previous chapter correctly that PT are products of civil society pressure.

To this end, the next section will give an explanation on what TWAIL is, while analysing the legitimacy rooted in peoples’ justice as opposed to victors’ justice. The third section will inform about the international legal system as compromised by geopolitical fiat and will provide a reinterpretation of global justice form a TWAIL perspective. The fourth section will provide the conclusion.

Third world approaches to international law – an explanation

First of all, it is pertinent to clarify on what TWAIL is. Speaking with Reynolds, Xavier, Bhathia and Natarajan, TWAIL is

> [i]s a movement encompassing scholars and practitioners of international law and policy who are concerned with issues related to the Global South. The scholarly agendas associated with TWAIL are diverse, but the general theme of its interventions is to unpack and deconstruct the colonial legacies of international law and engage in efforts to decolonise the lived realities of the peoples of the Global South.[13]

To further this, Makau Mutua explains that:

> [T]he regime of international law is illegitimate. It is a predatory system that legitimizes, reproduces and sustains the plunder and subordination of the Third World by the West. Neither universality nor its promise of global order and stability make international law a just, equitable, and legitimate code of global governance for the Third World. The construction and

10 Stephen Holmes, ‘Why International Justice Limps’ [2002] 69(4) Social Research 1061, 1065.

11 Manfredi, (note 6).

12 Holmes, (note 10).

13 Usha Natarajan, John Reynolds, Amar Bhatia and Sujith Xavier, ‘Introduction: TWAIL – on Praxis and the Intellectual’ [2016] 37(11) Third World Quarterly 1946.

> universalization of international law were essential to the imperial expansion that subordinated non-European peoples and societies to European conquest and domination. Historically, the Third World has generally viewed international law as a regime and discourse of domination and subordination, not resistance and liberation. This broad dialectic of opposition to international law is defined and referred to here as Third World Approaches to International Law (TWAIL).[14]

The TWAIL perspective, in this vein, helps to reinvent the value of criticism and reimagine contemporary international law.

> [T]WAIL perspective helps scholars to understand and appreciate the current internal contradictions embedded within international law, particularly in the perpetuation of injustice against the Third World, even as it concerns international human rights law. Thus, TWAIL has helped to demonstrate the discrepancy between the contradictory languages that international law adopts in its different subject streams.[15]

Against this background, we need to disentangle the difficult relationship between new, people-led tribunals and the formalised, institutions-led tribunals. At the heart of this argument is the claim that there exists a fundamental incommensurability between international law and subaltern ethics.[16] Christine Chinkin points out that there is an advantage with regards to PT, as there is no predetermined formula and no particular process.[17] Given life under conditions of colonial and neocolonial violence, at the core of subaltern ethics is the belief that the violence, killing, and torture is propounded by its own visions of morality. Subaltern ethics lead over to adjudications in relation to issues such as the rights of citizens, but not to the realm where states assume sovereign authority over the means of violence.[18] What falls within the purview of the sovereign authorities are, and not limited to, the rights of dissidents to possess and use nonconventional weapons; the right of states to recruit spies and to practice shoot-to-kill policies; the right of vigilantes to police their own communities and to dispense justice during times of war (or peace for that matter); the right of prisoners to be given political status

14 Makau Mutua and Antony Anghie, 'Proceedings of the Annual Meeting' [2000] 94 American Society of International Law 31.

15 Opeoluwa Adetoro Badaru, 'Examining the Utility of Third World Approaches to International Law for International Human Rights Law' [2008] 10 International Community Law Review 379, 383.

16 see also: Alex Jeffrey and Michaelina Jakala, 'The Hybrid Legal Geographies of a War Crimes Court' [2014] 104 Annals of the Association of American Geographers 652–667.

17 Christine Chinkin, 'People's Tribunals: Legitimate or Rough Justice' [2006] 24 Windsor Y. B. Access Justice 201–211.

18 Mark Boyle and Audrey Kobayashi, 'In the Face of Epistemic Injustices? On the Meaning of People-Led War Crimes Tribunals' [2015] 33 Environment and Planning D: Society and Space 697–698.

and to be released early as part of peace processes; the right of civilians to appropriate the property of others if it serves the purposes of a political cause; the right of police informers and whistle-blowers; the right of indicted "on the runs" to return to homelands without facing trials; and the right of victims of violence to seek compensation and redress.[19] Both systems, international legal and subaltern systems, have their pitfalls and reveal a severe lack of coherence. This chapter will not endeavour to offer solutions to or advocate for ethical relativism. There are many legal issues in the subaltern juridical systems, as well as abhorrent practices or non-practices in the international legal system.[20] It is not about an argument about whether justice is delivered to others, while it would be necessary (or not) to discuss justice being delivered to the Global South as a "just" justice and to entertain the idea that there exist radically other traditions of ethics, justice, and law. Certainly, this insight has proven central to the success of many reconciliation and peace processes.[21]

International law's criminal justice project is a Western project – it is time to accept and realise this fact in legal history. With the West the author refers to

> [a] civilization independent of locale. Finally, one hears today of a West that includes not only nations populated by European stock, but also non-Western nations that have assimilated Western institutions, techniques, and to some extent values: Japan, for instance.
>
> What the West means in a given context, therefore, depends entirely upon who is invoking the term and for what purpose. But it is fair to say that virtually all definitions of Western civilization drew a line somewhere across Europe placing Germany (at times), Poland and Eastern Europe (at times), and Russia and the Balkans (at all times) beyond the pale of Western civilization.[22]

The Nuremberg trials were the display of US American hegemony.[23] Reynolds and Sujith Xavier correctly hold that

> [T]he irony of Nuremberg, in seeking to claim the moral high ground following military victory over the Nazis by holding Nazism's particular brand of racial supremacy to legal account, was that the adjudicating states either condoned (or practiced as official policy) their own versions of racial mythologies. There was no question of a similar normative conception of criminal accountability attaching to British and French violence in the colonies, or to the subjugation of native Americans and African Americans in the United States. Third World jurists were wise to such selectivity and structural biases from the

19 Ibid.
20 Ibid.
21 Ibid.
22 William H. McNeill, 'What We Mean by the West' [1997] 41(4) Orbis 513–514.
23 Wolfgang Kaleck, *Double Standards: International Criminal Law and the West* (1st edition, Oslo, 2015).

> outset. India's Judge Radhabinod Pal was the most prominent among a range of Asian and Latin American voices of scepticism; his 1,235-page dissent from the judgement of the Tokyo Tribunal denounced the Japanese prosecutions as 'vindictive retaliation' and imperialism by the war's victors. With the atomic bombing of Japan and acts of imperial aggression and annexation by Allied powers exempted from any form of judicial scrutiny, Pal maintained that the Tribunal was structurally incapable of being just. He was sharply critical of the decision by the Allies to mandate the Tribunal to retroactively prosecute previously undefined crimes. This, Pal asserted, brought international law back to its colonial foundations and its facilitation of conquest.[24]

Since the 1960s, over 80 international people's or citizens' tribunals have been established outside formal state and international structures. Many have emulated the forms and procedures of state-sponsored international tribunals, and sought to investigate whether states, international organisations, and transnational corporations have violated established norms of international law, while also seeking to infuse it with more progressive values.[25] The perceptions of PT are met with confused ideas on indigeneity and deprecation. The critics highlight the lack of a formal basis that exists in the state-sponsored international order, the lack of traditional judicial proceedings, the biased and politicised tribunals composed of questionable members and the lack of enforceability within the international legal system or any state system of the "verdicts" or "judgments" of such bodies.[26]

Bertrand Russell, who headed the first PT of its kind, however, stressed that

> [I] can recall many wars. Much injustice has been recorded quietly during these decades. In my own experience I cannot discover a situation quite comparable. I cannot recall a people so tormented, yet so devoid of the failings of their tormentors. I do not know any other conflict in which the disparity in physical power was so vast. I have no memory of any people so enduring, or of any nation with a spirit of resistance so unquenchable. I will not conceal from you the profundity of my admiration and passion for the people of Vietnam. I cannot relinquish the duty to judge what has been done to them because I have such feelings. Our mandate is to uncover and tell all. My conviction is that no greater tribute can be provided than an offer of the truth, born of intense and unyielding inquiry. May this Tribunal prevent the crime of silence.[27]

24 John Reynolds and Sujith Xavier, '"The Dark Corners of the World": TWAIL and International Criminal Justice' [2016] 14 Journal of International Criminal Justice 959, 962.

25 Gabrielle Simm and Andrew Byrnes, 'International Peoples' Tribunals in Asia: Political Theatre, Juridical Farce, or Meaningful Intervention?' [2014] 4 Asian Journal of International Law 103.

26 Ibid.

27 Bertrand Russell, 'Autobiography, Bertrand Russell – Speech to the First Meeting of Members of the War Crimes Tribunal, London, 13 November 1966' (Vol. 3, Allen & Unwin, 1969).

When this Tribunal met, Bertrand Russell stressed to the attendees that there was no historical precedent. PT lack enforcement, state backing, and funding. All this seems true. But they do not lack of moral conscience. They do not lack historical vigilance. They do not lack civil society participation.[28] To this end, PT deliver a call for justice from the bottom to the top and urge for global justice of the people than of states.

The TWAIL critique

What, in the end, is the view of TWAIL to PT? European international law is inherently power based, while extending its imperial reach to Latin America, Asia and Africa. The uniform rules, since tested and proven in the developed states, shall bring prosperity and development to all people.[29]

However, this narrative has to be countered with new justice-based principles, which a Third World scholar needs to employ with energetic rigour. Is the term Third World derogatory in this context? Bernard W. Greene decisively explains that:

> [T]hird World nations are also characterised as being opposed to the power blocs, having a colonial past and being resentful of the former colonial powers and of imperialism, being underdeveloped economically, and suffering from illiteracy and domination of political life by small western-oriented and educated elites. While to a significant degree these are oversimplifications, they are sufficiently true to justify citing these factors as attributes of Third World nations for present purposes. It is no wonder, therefore, as Henry Kissinger has said, that the "Third World" is increasingly organized around calls for a "totally new economic order founded on ideology and national interests . . . stimulated by the view that the current system is loaded against the interests of the developing nations."

As this last quote suggests, the "Third World" is often perceived as a political organising force for what has been characterised as a New International Economic Order.[30]

The right to self-determination is one example to create a new (economic) order. The quest for people-centred justice mechanisms, such as the PT, could be new visions of justice-based mechanisms, deriving from the right to fair trial which is enshrined in art. 14.1 of the International Covenant on Civil and Political Rights: "[A]ll persons shall be equal before the courts and tribunals."[31]

28 see also Tor Krever, 'Remembering the Russell Tribunal' [2017] 5(3) London Review of International Law 483–492.

29 see also: M. Sornarajah, 'On Fighting for Global Justice: The Role of a Third World International Lawyer' [2016] 37(11) Third World Quarterly 1972–1989.

30 Bernard W. Greene, 'Toward a Definition of the Term Third World' [1980] 1 Boston College Third World Law Journal 13, 17.

31 International Covenant on Civil and Political Rights <www.ohchr.org/en/professionalinterest/pages/ccpr.aspx> accessed 1 May 2019.

Often it was argued that TWAIL is looking into the past, as it is constantly dwelling on the past and what colonialism has done to the Third World.[32] This can become a long and futile wail if new prescriptions are not advanced to counter the instrumental use of international law by hegemonic powers. Obviously, imperialism is an important aspect in the discourse. It needs to be accepted that the current power structure in the world needs to be contributed to the colonial power relations of the past, while the continuation of laws developed during the imperial times are continue being used.[33] Legal devices and tactics are deployed with new means, methods, and ruses: "[W]hile in the past, gunboat diplomacy was used to protect European investments, in modern times, instead of soldiers in fatigues, arbitrators in well-tailored suits protect foreign investments with conveniently crafted rules."[34] Wolfgang Kaleck writes to this end that:

> [U]niversalizing the existing practice of global criminal justice cannot be achieved without engaging with the current political reality. This reality is determined by the political framework in which powerful actors, such as the veto powers, states and regional elites, pursue their own political interests. Yet the power relations within this political field are not set in stone; non-state actors and social movements have a substantial role to play in the struggle for the law and political influence. Crucially, an imagined overly strict separation between the spheres of law and politics which is championed by many advocates will not solve the problem posed by political interests.[35]

Rule of law has replaced the rule of power. Simple exchange of words is the new justification for the exertion of hegemonic power to make new laws in the field of investment and trade.[36] The United Nations itself has often failed to realise the goal of a just system where hegemonic power dominates.[37] Sornarajah correctly asserts that:

> [M]uch international law making in the modern world has been transferred to international institutions and international tribunals. Both are non-representative and are capable of being manipulated to serve the interests of the alliance between the hegemonic public power of First World states and the private power of multinational corporations.[38]

32 S. G. Sreejith, 'An Auto-Critique of TWAIL's Historical Fallacy: Sketching an Alternative Manifesto' [2017] 38(7) Third World Quarterly, 2016, 1511–1512.
33 For more background: Thamil Venthan Ananthavinayagan, 'Uniting the Nations or Dividing and Conquering? The United Nations' Multilateralism Questioned—A Third World Scholar's Perspective' [2018] 29 Irish Studies in International Affairs 1–17.
34 Sornarajah, (note 29).
35 Kaleck, (note 23), 119.
36 Sornarajah, (note 29).
37 Ananthavinayagan, (note 33), 5.
38 Sornarajah, (note 29).

PT could transfer the power back to people, as Ronald Rogo has pointed out in the third chapter. They can give voice to grassroots movements, set up a counter-hegemonic narrative, decentralise the state-centric narrative and empower the Third World peoples in particular. To this end, PT become the guardians of moral justice which can develop groundbreaking norms for international law, with more relevance: customary international law. As Judge Trindade held with regards to the aspect of opinio juris that

> [O]pinio juris became a key element in the formation itself of international law, a law of conscience. This diminished the unilateral influence of the most powerful States, fostering international law-making in fulfilment of the public interest and in pursuance of the common good of the international community as a whole. . . . The foundations of the international legal order came to be reckoned as independent from, and transcending, the "will" of individual States; opinio juris communis came to give expression to the "juridical conscience," no longer only of nations and peoples – sustained in the past by the "historical school" – but of the international community as a whole, heading towards the universalization of international law.[39]

Hence, are PT a contribution towards a new facet of the formation of *opinio juris communis*? It is strongly affirmed. To echo B.S. Chimni, the formation of customary international law can be linked to "[p]rogressive ideas, beliefs, and practices in the global civil society. Increasingly, non-governmental organisations (NGOs) have become agents of lawmaking in the international legal order."[40] PT should be considered also as those transformative agents of change.

Universalisation of European principles and norms, the spread of human rights which grow out of Western liberalism and jurisprudence, have been hallmarks of the United Nations architecture.[41] Western states fomented their philosophy of human rights on the rest of the world "[b]ecause it dominated the United Nations at its inception."[42] It needs to be understood that the principal focus of international law at large was to strengthen, legitimize, and export the liberal democratic state to non-Western societies.[43] Makau Mutua, however, believes that human rights corpus and perception of justice is moving away from the paradigmatic Western

39 Obligations concerning Negotiations relating to Cessation of the Nuclear Arms Race and to Nuclear Disarmament (Marshall Islands v. India), Jurisdiction and Admissibility, Judgment, I.C.J. Reports 2016, Dissenting Opinion Judge Cançado Trindade, paras. 304–305.

40 B. S. Chimni, 'Customary International Law' [2016] 112(1) American Journal of International Law 42.

41 Antony Anghie, 'The Evolution of International Law: Colonial and Postcolonial Realities' [2006] 27(5) Third World Quarterly 739, 749.

42 Larissa Ramina, 'TWAIL – "Third World Approaches to International Law" and Human Rights: Some Considerations' [2018] 5(1) Revista de Investigações Constitucionais, Curitiba, 261, 267.

43 Ibid.

orientation, and slowly stops been seen as a "gift of the West to the 'rest' of the world," towards the construction of a truly universal project.[44] In his words, "[a] truly legitimate human rights movement cannot be cabined by powerful states and elites. It must be material for battle in the hands of the powerless. This, however, will not be possible unless the movement is purged of its Eurocentric, racist, free-market biases."[45] B.S. Chimni speaks of three different, yet interconnected claims for establishing a global law of welfare in the matrix of international human rights law, namely redistribution, claims for recognition and claims for representation.[46]

International criminal law, however, has never picked up on the ideas of redistribution, recognition or representation. Instead, speaking with Makau Mutua again, international criminal law was arriving as a "[m]orality comes from the West as a civilizing agent against lower forms of civilization."[47] Think of the images of the former ICC prosecutor Moreno Ocampo stepping from his private helicopter out to the area of the alleged savages. The West has far too often produced and reproduced the metaphors of the savages-saviour dichotomy. International criminal helped reproducing,

> [l]ike the very idiom of international criminal law and humanitarianism, the racialized metaphor of savages, victims and saviours: the violence of international crimes lies outside the civilized West; its victims are powerless, in need of saving by NATO intervention or us-trained human-rights lawyers.[48]

In the era of globalisation, the need of local spaces and indigenous cultures to be preserved is increasingly dependent on notions of sovereignty, which remains a cardinal doctrine in international law. Local spaces, the role of social movements in international law, are now imperative to reverse the current bias which favours the global over the local. Finally, speaking with Balakrishnan Rajagopal,

> [t]he fact remains that various social movements organized around multiple identities such as gender, environment, ethnicity, and class are the most potent popular mobilizations in the world today, and the question is in what ways international law has shaped and been shaped by these movements. Telling their story is a simple process of narrating a "history from below."[49]

44 Ibid.
45 Makau Mutua, 'Change in the Human Rights Universe' [2007] 20 Harvard Human Rights Journal 3.
46 B. S. Chimni, 'A Just World Under Law: A View From the South' [2007] 22(2) American University International Law Review 199, 213.
47 Makau Mutua, *Human Rights: A Political and Cultural Critique* (1st edition, Philadelphia, 2002).
48 Tor Krever, 'Dispensing Global Justice' [2014] 85 New Left Review 67, 94.
49 Balakrishnan Rajagopal, 'From Resistance to Renewal: The Third World, Social Movements, and the Expansion of International Institutions' [2000] 41 Harvard International Law Journal 529, 536–537.

TWAIL will and must encourage shared commonalities and solidarities to encounter the global hegemon and universalise justice. To this end, it is worth recalling the words of the United Nations Independent Expert on International Solidarity, Mr. Obiora C. Okafor:

> [T]he significant role played by civil society as agents of sociopolitical and economic change within both States and the international system is now very well acknowledged. These actors help to shape public opinion, drive policies, legitimize or delegitimize certain agents and forms of governance and push for social reform. They also tend to express solidarity with each other, and with individuals, groups and communities, both within and across the boundaries of the States in which they are located. . . . Against this background, the Independent Expert considers that it is important to study, comment on and report on the normative framework and conceptual apparatus that undergirds such expressions of human rights-based international solidarity by civil society groups; the ways in which civil society groups express human rights-based international solidarity; and the means through which this is done.[50]

Conclusion

PT gives voice to the struggles of people. TWAIL's focus is to empower the people. PT are postmodern mechanisms to dismantle dominant Western state power and empower subaltern voices in civil society of the Global South to harness counter-hegemonic potentials. Divisions created by contemporary world structure can be overcome through a sense of solidarity. To this end, it is necessary to stress the view of B.S. Chimini, who articulated that a unity needs be achieved,

> [b]ased on solidarity that understands the alienation and pain of victims of fragmented international law. But the flaw within the current celebration of fragmentation and its criticism is that both perspectives reify the concepts of fragmentation and unity. The concepts of fragmentation and unity are perceived as things and not part of a historical process that can be reconciled at a different site. Formal logic, to put it differently, rules out the unity of opposites. It helps disregard the fact that the future may see a fragmented international law reunite to reflect the interests of the transnational capitalist class. In other words, the earlier unity has necessarily to split to create a new unity. The nostalgia for a lost world blinkers a generation of international lawyers to the new configuration of global social forces that drives both fragmentation and unity. If a new unified international law that is responsive to

50 United Nations General Assembly, Report of the Independent Expert on Human Rights and International Solidarity, A/HRC/38/4, paras. 41–42.

> the fate of global subalterns is to be created, it is imperative to imagine suitable alternative futures.[51]

These kind of tribunals cannot be financed by the state. Their goal is the analysis, the recognition and the denunciation (political condemnation, awareness-raising, information, media coverage) of massive human rights violations that are yet unpunished. Their specificity lies in their purpose that is mainly recognitive, independent from all sentencing or revenge. The sessions are always public, except in those cases in which the protection of the victims supposes closed proceedings. As for deliberations, they take place in closed sessions. The responsibility denounced is that of states, being noted that the PT also rules on the responsibility of companies and multinationals; for example, the creation of alternative approaches to justice enables the civil society and overcomes the inaction of the international and domestic legal infrastructure, which is propounded by legal and political bias. The civil society tribunals, in this power vacuum, step in as "[a] sort of bottom-up resistance, generated by the impulse of civil society; in other terms, a counterpower. Such mechanisms offer another voice – a voice supposed to be that of the people."[52] PT must "brush history against the grain," in the words of Walter Benjamin.[53] PT not only derive from the aspect of fair trial as mentioned previously, but can be complemented with a new human right to truth. To this end, the United Nations Human Rights Commission, in one of its last reports issued, stated that:

> [a]s international law on the right to the truth has evolved to apply in all situations of serious violations of human rights, the material scope of the right to the truth has also expanded to include other elements. These may be summarized as the entitlement to seek and obtain information on: the causes leading to the person's victimization; the causes and conditions pertaining to the gross violations of international human rights law and serious violations of international humanitarian law; the progress and results of the investigation; the circumstances and reasons for the perpetration of crimes under international law and gross human rights violations; the circumstances in which violations took place; in the event of death, missing or enforced disappearance, the fate and whereabouts of the victims; and the identity of perpetrators.[54]

51 See B. S. Chimni, 'The Past, Present and Future of International Law' [2007] 8 Melbourne Journal of International Law.

52 Sévane Garibian, 'From Punishment to Acknowledgement: Tribunals of Opinion in Contexts of Impunity' *Open Democracy* (12 May 2015) <www.opendemocracy.net/en/opensecurity/from-punishment-to-acknowledgment-tribunals-of-opinion-in-contexts-of-i/> accessed 1 May 2019.

53 Walter Benjamin, *Illuminations* (1st edition, London, Collins/Fontana book, 1973), 248.

54 United Nations Economic and Social Council, Promotion and Protection of Human Rights, Study on the Right to the Truth Report of the Office of the United Nations High Commissioner for Human Rights, E/CN.4/2006/91, para. 38.

More crucially:

> [I]nternational criminal tribunals, truth commissions, commissions of inquiry, national criminal tribunals, national human rights institutions and other administrative bodies and proceedings may constitute important tools for ensuring the right to the truth. Judicial criminal proceedings, with a broad legal standing in the judicial process for any wronged party and to any person or non-governmental organization having a legitimate interest therein, are essential to ensuring the right to the truth. Judicial remedies, such as habeas corpus, are also important mechanisms to protect the right to the truth.[55]

In light of this, PT are vehicles for change, demanding the development of new norms, while reinforcing or rethinking the legitimacy of truth-seeking processes. A number of important developments at the United Nations contribute towards the right to the truth in international law, for example the report on impunity from 2005, the Convention on Enforced Disappearance from 2006, various resolutions of the Human Rights Council and the Human Rights Commission, and reports issued by the UN High Commissioner.[56] All are instruments that define the right to the truth broadly, as a right that is autonomous and both individual and collective societal. All contend that protection of this right can be ensured by multiple national and international mechanisms, judicial or not, retributive or restorative.

Against this background, it is necessary that TWAIL addresses the past and ongoing violations of the rights of people from the Global South through mechanisms that can provide the basis for restorative and empowering justice. PT are certainly one of those mechanisms to be deployed to create the counter-hegemonic and anti-hierarchical resistance, while paving the way for opinio juris communis. As Makau Mutua holds:

> [t]he harm or injury that the Third World would likely have suffered as a result of the unjust international legal, political, and economic order. Such scholarship or political action will be concerned with justice or the fairness of norms, institutions, processes, and practices in the transnational arena. Its overriding purpose must be the elimination of an aspect of Third World powerlessness. At a minimum, the author or political actor exposes, attacks, or unpacks a particular phenomenon that is inimical to the Third World. This is the most fundamental characteristic of TWAIL scholarship and political action.[57]

International law is driven by superiority complexes, since classical international law was based on the supremacy of white European peoples over non-Europeans,

55 Ibid., para. 61.

56 Garibian, (note 52).

57 Makau Mutua, 'What Is Twail?' [2000] 94 American Society of International Law, Proceedings of the 94th Annual Meeting, 31, 36.

while the one civilised and controlled the latter. European hegemony has a manifest pattern, which penetrates contemporary times.[58] Makau Mutua, gain poignantly holds that: "[T]he pattern is the long queue of the colonial administrator, the Bible-carrying missionary come to save the heathens, the commercial profiteer, the exporter of political democracy, and now the human rights crusader."[59] To this end, international law, the idea of the legal standards that permeate all parts of the law, is inherently a product of the West and has perhaps been the most important weapon in the spread of Eurocentrism. TWAIL, however, wants to "[a]ssume the moral equivalency of cultures and peoples and rejects "othering," the creation of dumb copies of the original."[60] TWAIL refutes the universalisation of specific cultures under the guise of promoting global order, peace and security, but embraces dialogic manoeuvres across cultures to establish, where necessary, the content of universally acceptable norms.[61] In consequence, PT are the platform with the moral and legal power of persuasion and persistence.

PT try overcome the liberal orthodoxy in Eurocentric lawmaking and procedural lithurgy. Vasuki Nesiah writes that:

> [L]ooked at in this way, we may be in a better position to develop a critical practice that recognizes how regressive policies can be couched in liberalisms's orthodoxies-for instance, regime change may be justified in the name of democracy and liberal values such as secularism; the denial of redistributive measures such as affirmative action may be justified in terms of formal justice and equality before the law (notwithstanding substantive injustice and entrenched inequalities); and reparations for slavery may be defeated on the basis of statute of limitations norms notwithstanding continued injustices.[62]

PT is about speaking truth to power. In the wake of this evolution and the ongoing debates surrounding the consecration of a new right to the truth, the UN General Assembly proclaimed the 24th of March International Day for the Right to the Truth concerning Gross Human Rights Violations and for the Dignity of Victims.[63] Moreover, the Human Rights Council adopted a resolution, in which it decided to appoint, for a period of three years, a Special Rapporteur on the promotion of truth, justice, reparation, and guarantees of non-recurrence.[64]

58 Ibid.

59 Ibid.

60 Ibid.

61 Ibid.

62 Vasuki Nesiah, 'Discussion Lines on Gender and Transitional Justice: An Introductory Essay Reflecting on the ICTJ Bellagio Workshop on Gender and Transitional Justice' [2006] 15(3) Columbia Journal of Gender & Law 799, 810.

63 United Nations, International Day for the Right to the Truth Concerning Gross Human Rights Violations and for the Dignity of Victims (24 March) <www.un.org/en/events/righttotruthday/> accessed 1 May 2019.

64 United Nations Human Rights Council, Special Rapporteur on the Promotion of Truth, Justice, Reparation and Guarantees of Non-Recurrence, A/HRC/RES/18/7.

However, these developments can be only seen as safeguarding the anti-hierarchical approach taken by PT, multifunctional, diverse and multi-faceted as they are. Apart of their specificities and differences, all these processes constitute a privileged, but poorly explored reserved space of civil society mobilisation on human rights issues concerning their own livelihood, involving a certain degree of creative transformation of the law and primarily expressing the recognitive function of justice – from punishment to acknowledgement.[65] In this vein, TWAIL presents a distinctive voice in the field of international law. But seen in a larger perspective, TWAIL does no more than to make real the promise of international law to transform itself into a system based not on power, but justice. It is supposed to hand back international law to the many, not the powerful few.

In a letter on the 19th of April 1967, addressed to Jean-Paul Sartre, Charles de Gaulle, President of France at that time wrote that: "*Toute justice, dans son principe comme dans son exécution, n'appartient qu'à l'Etat.*"[66] He has to be corrected: all the justice belongs to the people.

References

Books

Benjamin, Walter, *Illuminations* (1st edition, London, Collins/Fontana book, 1973).

Kaleck, Wolfgang, *Double Standards: International Criminal Law and the West* (1st edition, Oslo, Torkel Opsahl Academic EPublisher, 2015).

Mutua, Makau, *Human Rights: A Political and Cultural Critique* (1st edition, Philadelphia, University of Pennsylvania Press, 2008).

Russell, Bertrand, *Autobiography, Bertrand Russell – Speech to the First Meeting of Members of the War Crimes Tribunal, London, 13 November 1966* (Vol. 3, Australia, Allen & Unwin, 1969).

Articles

Ananthavinayagan, Thamil Venthan, 'Uniting the Nations or Dividing and Conquering? The United Nations' Multilateralism Questioned—A Third World Scholar's Perspective' [2018] 29 Irish Studies in International Affairs 1.

Anghie, Antony, 'The Evolution of International Law: Colonial and Postcolonial Realities' [2006] 27(5) Third World Quarterly 739.

Ba, Oumar, 'International Justice and the Postcolonial Condition' [2017] 63(4) Africa Today 44.

Badaru, Opeoluwa Adetoro, 'Examining the Utility of Third World Approaches to International Law for International Human Rights Law' [2008] 10 International Community Law Review 379.

65 Gariban, (note 52).

66 Edmond Jouve, 'Du Tribunal de Nuremberg ay Tribunal Permanent des Peuples' [1981] 46(3) Politique étrangère 669–670.

Boyle, Mark and Kobayashi, Audrey, 'In the Face of Epistemic Injustices? On the Meaning of People-Led War Crimes Tribunals' [2015] 33 Environment and Planning D: Society and Space 697.
Chimni, B. S., 'A Just World Under Law: A View from the South' [2007] 22(2) American University International Law Review 199.
Chimni, B. S., 'The Past, Present and Future of International Law' [2007] 8 Melbourne Journal of International Law.
Chimni, B. S., 'Customary International Law' [2016] 112(1) American Journal of International Law 1.
Chinkin, Christine, 'People's Tribunals: Legitimate or Rough Justice' [2006] 24 Windsor Y. B. Access Justice 201.
Greene, Bernard W., 'Toward a Definition of the Term Third World' [1980] 1 Boston College Third World Law Journal 13, 17.
Holmes, Stephen, 'Why International Justice Limps' [2002] 69(4) Social Research 1061.
Icaza, Rosalba, 'The Permanent People's Tribunals and Indigenous People's Struggles in Mexico: Between Coloniality and Epistemic Justice?' [2015] 1(15020) Palgrave Communications 1.
Jeffrey, Alex and Jakala, Michaelina, 'The Hybrid Legal Geographies of a War Crimes Court' [2014] 104 Annals of the Association of American Geographers 652.
Jouve, Edmond, 'Du Tribunal de Nuremberg ay Tribunal Permanent des Peuples' [1981] 46(3) Politique étrangère 669.
Krever, Tor, 'Dispensing Global Justice' [2014] 85 New Left Review 67.
Krever, Tor, 'Remembering the Russell Tribunal' [2017] 5(3) London Review of International Law 483.
Manfredi, Zachary, 'Sharpening the Vigilance of the World: Reconsidering the Russell Tribunal as Ritual, Humanity: An International Journal of Human Rights' [2018] 9(1) Humanitarianism and Development 75.
McNeill, William H., 'What We Mean by the West' [1997] 41(4) Orbis 514.
Mutua, Makau, 'What Is Twail?' [2000] 94 American Society of International Law, Proceedings of the 94th Annual Meeting 31.
Mutua, Makau, 'Change in the Human Rights Universe' [2007] 20 Harvard Human Rights Journal 3.
Mutua, Makau and Anghie, Antony, 'Proceedings of the Annual Meeting' [2000] 94 American Society of International Law 31.
Natarajan, Usha, Reynolds, John, Bhatia, Amar and Xavier, Sujith, 'Introduction: TWAIL – on Praxis and the Intellectual' [2016] 37(11) Third World Quarterly 1946.
Nesiah, Vasuki, 'Discussion Lines on Gender and Transitional Justice: An Introductory Essay Reflecting on the ICTJ Bellagio Workshop on Gender and Transitional Justice' [2006] 15(3) Columbia Journal of Gender & Law 799, 810.
Rajagopal, Balakrishnan, 'From Resistance to Renewal: The Third World, Social Movements, and the Expansion of International Institutions' [2000] 41 Harvard International Law Journal 529, 536.
Ramina, Larissa, 'TWAIL – "Third World Approaches to International Law" and Human Rights: Some Considerations' [2018] 5(1) Revista de Investigações Constitucionais, Curitiba 261.
Reynolds, John and Xavier, Sujith, '"The Dark Corners of the World": TWAIL and International Criminal Justice' [2016] 14 Journal of International Criminal Justice 959.

Schwoebel, Christine E. J., 'The Comfort of International Criminal Law' [2013] 24(2) Law and Critique 169.

Simm, Gabrielle and Byrnes, Andrew, 'International Peoples' Tribunals in Asia: Political Theatre, Juridical Farce, or Meaningful Intervention?' [2014] 4 Asian Journal of International Law 103.

Sornarajah, M., 'On Fighting for Global Justice: The Role of a Third World International Lawyer' [2016] 37(11) Third World Quarterly 1972.

Sreejith, S. G., 'An Auto-Critique of TWAIL's Historical Fallacy: Sketching an Alternative Manifesto' [2017] 38(7) Third World Quarterly 2016, 1511.

Tosa, Hiroyuki, 'Global Constitutional Order and the Deviant Other: Reflections on the Dualistic Nature of the ICC Process' [2018] 18(1) International Relations of the Asia-Pacific 45.

Websites

Chapman, Terrence and Chaudoin, Stephen, 'People Like the International Criminal Court – as Long as It Targets Other Problems in Other Countries' (*Washington Post*, 20 January 2011) <www.washingtonpost.com/news/monkey-cage/wp/2017/01/20/people-like-the-international-criminal-court-as-long-as-it-targets-other-problems-in-other-countries/> accessed 11 August 2019.

Garibian, Sévane, 'From Punishment to Acknowledgment: Tribunals of Opinion in Contexts of Impunity' (*OpenDemocracy*, 12 May 2015) <www.opendemocracy.net/en/opensecurity/from-punishment-to-acknowledgment-tribunals-of-opinion-in-contexts-of-i/> accessed 11 August 2019.

Murphy, Ray, 'Many Criticisms of International Criminal Court Have Validity' (*Irish Times*, 6 June 2013) <www.irishtimes.com/opinion/many-criticisms-of-international-criminal-court-have-validity-1.1418128> accessed 11 August 2019.

United Nations, International Day for the Right to the Truth Concerning Gross Human Rights Violations and for the Dignity of Victims (24 March) <www.un.org/en/events/righttotruthday/> accessed 1 May 2019.

Cases and documents

ICC Pre-Trial Chamber, ICC-02/17.

International Covenant on Civil and Political Rights <www.ohchr.org/en/professionalinterest/pages/ccpr.aspx> accessed 1 May 2019.

Obligations Concerning Negotiations Relating to Cessation of the Nuclear Arms Race and to Nuclear Disarmament (Marshall Islands v. India), Jurisdiction and Admissibility, Judgment, I.C.J. Reports 2016, Dissenting Opinion Judge Cansado Trindade.

United Nations Declaration on the Rights of Indigenous Peoples 2007.

United Nations Human Rights Council, Special Rapporteur on the Promotion of Truth, Justice, Reparation and Guarantees of Non-Recurrence, A/HRC/RES/18/7.

United Nations Economic and Social Council, Promotion and Protection of Human Rights, Study on the right to the truth Report of the Office of the United Nations High Commissioner for Human Rights, E/CN.4/2006/91.

United Nations General Assembly, Report of the Independent Expert on Human Rights and International Solidarity, A/HRC/38/4.

5 The right to tell

The Sarajevo Women Court in search for a feminist approach to justice

Nevenka Tromp

Introduction

This chapter will argue that in conflict and post-conflict societies where a robust international and national retributive justice system has been at place, such as was the case with the mechanisms at place to address the crimes committed during the wars in the former Yugoslavia, victims[1] still find it necessary to seek alternative ways to have their voices be heard. In the literature on transitional justice mechanisms, the international criminal justice has been considered for over two decades as a desired model. Now after two *ad hoc* tribunals, the ICTR and the ICTY closed their doors, and there has been a re-assessment of the sufficiency of the retributive justice in addressing the needs for justice in the societies that struggle to find a way forward after years and sometimes decades of violence. This led to re-opening the "tool box" of transitional justice mechanisms for several reasons: 1) there is a trend among the world's most powerful states that dominate global politics not to support the current International Criminal Court regime, which means that the recent or the still ongoing mass atrocities will never be prosecuted at international or national courts; 2) the measure of justice produced at the international criminal tribunals so far did not satisfy the victims, who continue seeking justice in the form of truth-seeking, restitution or other restorative justice mechanism; 3) the recognition of the "right to the truth" has led to the recognition of the "right to tell" claimed by different groups of participants of the justice-seeking victims, but also by those belonging to a blurred "grey-zone," i.e. the individuals who went from being a victim to becoming a perpetrator or the other way around. How could they tell their truth without self-incriminating themselves?

1 The UN defines victims as "persons who individually or collectively suffered harm, including physical or mental injury, emotional suffering, economic loss or substantial impairment of their fundamental rights through acts or omissions that constitute gross violations of international human rights law, or serious violations of international humanitarian law. The term 'victim' can also be applied to the immediate family or dependents of the direct victim and persons who have suffered harm in intervening to assist victims in distress or to prevent victimisation."

This chapter will investigate the SWC, an alternative model that has been created to supplement the existing transitional justice repertoire. The SWC has introduced a feminist approach to justice as a supplement to the transitional justice mechanisms that have been established in the post-conflict societies of the former Yugoslavia. The preparatory work for this PT took five years and the event itself took place from 7 to 10 May 2015 in Sarajevo. During the proceedings, 36 women claimed their right to tell the truth – on their own terms. Did this Court meet the expectation of its participants and its creators; what experience did it create among those attending; and how did it contribute to the best practices of alternative justice mechanisms?

In one of the first academic assessments of the SWC, transitional justice scholar Janine Clark argued that the feminist approach to justice as applied at the SWC justice could be seen as a form of "justice as recognition," which she defines as "the kind of justice that is involved in giving due recognition to the pain and humiliation experienced by victims of collective violence."[2]

The conceptual framework for this analysis of the SWC will be based on the concept known as the "right to the truth." This concept has recently entered the realm of international law by jurisprudential precedent and by the establishment of various truth-seeking mechanisms in the societies after the period of serious human rights abuses or armed conflicts. The right to the truth has become an objective of justice process – in both "hard" justice mechanism (retributive justice models) "soft" justice mechanism (such as truth commissions and PT).

Scholars place PT somewhere in between the criminal trials and truth commissions: they use the format of a criminal trial, not to prosecute the alleged perpetrators, but to solicit the testimonies from the victims, i.e. to record victims' experience of human suffering.[3] However, unlike the truth commission they do hold the alleged perpetrators to account and every judgement in the PT will likely name the wrongdoers, but unlike the criminal trials that deal only with the individual criminal responsibility, PT have mandate and power to identify as wrongdoers the states, state organs and other national and international organisations.[4]

This chapter will investigate: 1) the mandate, structure, legitimacy, and objective of the SWC; 2) the importance of emotions, empathy, and solidarity as a

2 Clark, (note 1), 67–87, 68. Clark quotes Frank Haldemann, and his article 'Another Kind of Justice: Transitional Justice as Recognition' [2008] 41(2) Cornell International Law Journal 678.

3 Shadi Sadr, "In other words, drawing on elements of truth and justice throughout the process up to their final products, tribunals stand somewhere between the realms of right to truth and right to justice, or somewhere between truth commissions and criminal trials. They achieve measures of both but deliver neither completely, as they issue a verdict without sentencing the accused," as quoted in "From Painkillers to the Cure: Challenges and Future of People's Tribunals" in Chapter 12.

4 See for example the Iran Tribunal Judgment, the Indonesia Tribunal Judgement and the China Tribunal Judgment. In all three cases the states have been condamned as criminal states. Further Ronald Rogo discusses earlier in this volume the distinction between truth commissions and People's Tribunals and why People's Tribunals may have a larger advantage over truth commissions. See also Ronald Rogo "People's Tribunals And Truth Commissions" Chapter 3.

driving force for victims when telling their stories at women (peoples') courts; 3) the different roles of the victims in the truth-telling process at a criminal trial and at a women (people's) courts; and 4) the transformative process from a victim to a feminist activist, by transforming personal experience to advance social changes by spreading the feminist message across the region.

Feminist approach to justice: mandate, legitimacy, and objectives of the Sarajevo Women Court

Feminist approach to justice

The feminist approach to justice has been seen as a reaction to the liberal philosophy of justice rooted in the influential social contract theory. In the feminist approach to justice – the core concept is injustice. In his seminal work, *Theory of Justice*, John Rawls claims that "justice is the first virtue of social institutions." Rawls's concept of justice is based on the social contract and on distributive justice, i.e. the model of justice that advances fairness of how rewards and costs are distributed across group members. This model is exactly where the feminist thinkers see the gender-based injustice arising: the law treats women more or less equal, while "custom, workplace discrimination, and the still conventional division of labor within the family" make women unequal. Based on this line of argumentation, the family becomes the first and the earliest experience of systematic injustice, which does not represent just private, but also social and political injustice. Feminists argue that injustice stemming from the traditional family is fundamental, for individuals that form a family are conditioned from early on to become accustomed to and accept injustice.

Critical assessments of the modern-day social contract theory come from feminist scholars and activists by questioning how seriously it takes women. The tests by which feminists evaluate the impact of social contract on women are, for example, to explore the relation between the contract and women's subordination to men, the so-called sexual contract; feminist arguments concerning the nature of the liberal individual; and the care argument.[5] How specific and different are the injustices against women? Are the existing national and international judicial systems adequate to deal with injustices suffered by women?

Philosopher and feminist scholar Daša Duhaček argues that all feminist theories basically originate in the experiences of injustice. Duhaček explores feminist justice and its place in existing models of justice, citing three models of relevance of Women Courts: mainstream justice that is concerned with the courts and their function to

> administer justice; feminist justice that address injustices; and transitional justice that deals with the alternative mechanism as response to mass atrocities

5 See: Carole Patman, *The Sexual Contract* (Stanford, Sandford University Press, 1986), 1–4.

> and human rights abuses.[6] The core characteristic of justice model adopted by SWC is that it does not adopt a (abstract) concept of justice, but instead it addresses (concrete) injustice. Feminist scholar Iris Marion Yung sums up the feminist approach to justice as a process that "weaves together the personal, the political, and the affective.[7]

This is premised on the feminist notion that seeking justice is always preceded by experience of injustice that is represented in suffering or distress of others or oneself.

Women courts in practice

The feminist approach to justice is a novel concept that challenges the mainstream justice based on the social contract approach. Although it has been around for some time now, its practical implementation has been of a more recent date. In 1976 the first Women Court was held in Brussels in 1976. The agenda of the Brussels court covered the widespread crimes against women such as rape, torture, slavery, pornography and forced sterilisation as well as social and economic injustices that exposed women to existential vulnerabilities and institutionalised inequality in different forms and intensity across all political systems of the world. With more than 2,000 women from 40 different countries participating in the event, the Brussels Court was deemed a great success.[8] It raised the expectation that similar courts would continue to address these injustices at national and international forums. In reality, it took over 15 years for The World Court of Women (WCW) to emerge. The revival of the idea of the women tribunals came in 1992 when the first women court was held in Lahore, Pakistan. About 40 women's courts were held since 1992 – mostly in South and Central America, Asia, and Africa. The relevance of the alternative justice models has been demonstrated by the proceedings held at the Women's International War Crimes Tribunal, also known as the "Comfort Women Tribunal." It was held in Tokyo in 2000, and it addressed Japan's military sexual slavery practices, i.e. the systemic abuse of women in the Pacific Asia territories occupied by the Japanese military before and during WWII. Its judgement resonated worldwide, giving the validation to this type of justice that served as an inspiration and encouragement for other women whose particular experiences of injustice would not otherwise be known to public.

6 See: Daša Duhaček, 'The Women's Court: A Feminist Approach to Justice' [May 2015] 2(2) European Journal of Women's Studies 159–176, 168.

7 Ibid., 175. Duhaček quotes Young.

8 See: Diana Russels (ed), *Crimes Against Women: Proceedings of the International Tribunal* (Berkeley, Russel Publications, 1990) <>www.dianarussell.com/f/Crimes_Against_Women_Tribunal.pdf>

The Sarajevo Women Court

The SWC focused on the experiences of women across the region, before, during and after the violent disintegration of Yugoslavia that took place in the 1990s. The first idea of a women court for the region of successor states for the former Yugoslavia was born during an international conference on new paradigms of justice and creation of alternative space for women's testimonies that was held in Sarajevo in 2000. But it was in 2006 the idea was picked up again with a new sort of urgency. The immediate reason for this urgency was the death of the former President Slobodan Milošević of Serbia and Federal Republic of Yugoslavia (FRY), who was the only president indicted and tried at the ICTY. Milošević was held by many as the politician who was responsible for the violent disintegration of Yugoslavia and thus for more than 130,000 war-related deaths, millions of displaced persons and devastated towns and industrial infrastructure during three wars that lasted from 1991 to 1999. His ICTY trial ended without a judgement as he died in his prison cell some four weeks before the trial was to be concluded. This left many of the victims and human rights activists deprived of a long-awaited ICTY judgement. It also exposed the fragility of the retributive justice system as the dominant justice paradigm that everyone looked up to.[9]

The initiative for a court came from the Women in Black, a feminist anti-war and pacifist NGO from Serbia. The first step was to mobilise NGOs from all Yugoslav successor in order to create a broad platform of support of women from the region, regardless whether they were directly involved in the war violence. Moreover, the initiators did underline and recognise the very different nature of experiences in the war-affected regions in which women were victims of war-related crimes (such as in Bosnia and Herzegovina and Kosovo) and the regions such as Serbia, which started the war and was the major perpetrator in four wars that marked the disintegration of Yugoslavia that went on from 1991–1995 (Slovenia, Croatia and Bosnia-Herzegovina wars) and from 1998–1999 (Kosovo war).[10] Despite the efforts to include as many as possible organisations, some victims' organisations have not been included and some were not even aware of the SWC taking place.[11] For example, Bakira Hasečić from the "Association of Women Victims of War," with headquarters in Sarajevo did not attend the hearings, as a protest for not being included in the initiative from the beginning. They

9 See: Nevenka Tromp, *Prosecuting Slobodan Milošević: The Unfinished Trial* (London, Routledge, 2016).

10 The facts on history of the SWC come from Zajović's 'The Women's Court – a Feminist Approach to Justice: Review of the Process of Organizing of the Women's Court' [2015] Women's Court: About the Process 6–67; Zajović, *Ženski sud: o događaju u Sarajevu i nastavku procesa*, 13–68.

11 Clark, (note 1), 82. Clark writes: "According to Zajović, one problem was that NGOs in BiH were not as professional and organised as they should have been in finding potential witnesses.".

threatened to stage protests in front of the court. After a long exchange of letters and emails, they gave up on a demonstration and sent an observer to follow the procedings.[12]

The official start of the court was October 2010 when the Initiative Board was formed. Initially, the initiative was called "The Women's Court for Former Yugoslavia" but soon it was renamed into "The Women's Court – Feminist Approach to Justice." As of 2013, the Initiative Board grew into the Organisation Committee of Women's Court – Feminist Approach to Justice, consisting of ten organisations.[13] Women in Black remained in charge of programme activities and coordination of the activities of the Organisation Committee (OC).[14]

In the months to come, the meetings were held all over the region and a long list of grievances was compiled. The grievances included, *inter alia*: persecution of those who are different (ethnic, ideological, sexual), forced conscription, poverty, corruption, sex trafficking, prostitution, hate speech, war propaganda, war mongering but also using the educational system as an instrument of war, undermining of physical, emotional and moral integrity of women raped in war, and many more.[15]

Searching for a feminist modus operandi

Staša Zajović from Women in Black, who was the *spiritus movens* behind the initiative, created in order to: galvanise women's contributions to the processes of transitional justice; increase the visibility of women in the transitional justice processes; reverse marginalisation of women by reducing them to objects of violence by stressing the continuity of women's contribution that started before the war, continued during the war and persisted in the period after the war.[16] According to Zajović, the women movements were active in opposing the war, advocating non-violent resistance, contributing to the confidence-building, peace-building and reconciliation processes, and yet their activities did not get the public prominence or political importance they deserved.[17] The feminist approach to justice in an organisational sense also meant that participants in the process were not simply adopting feminist principles of work, but they were also learning about feminist theories of justice. The feminist ethics included a consensus-based approach

12 A Telephone Interview with Bakira Hasečić, 13 August 2019.

13 The Movement of Mothers of Žepa and Srebrenica Enclaves, Foundation CURE, Sarajevo (Bosnia and Herzegovina); Anima – Center for Women's and Peace Education from Kotor (Montenegro); Center for Women's Studies and Center for Women Victims of War, Zagreb (Croatia); Kosova Women's Network (Kosovo); National Council for Gender Equality, Skopje, Macedonia; Women's Lobby of Slovenia, Maribor (Slovenia); and Center for Women's Studies and Women in Black, Belgrade (Serbia). See Zajović, "The Women's Court – a Feminist Approach to Justice . . .": 10.

14 Ibid.

15 Duhaček, (note 7), 165.

16 Zajović, 'The Women's Court – a Feminist Approach to Justice. . .' 12–13.

17 Ibid.

and to that purpose many educational and training workshops were held as well legal team meetings, consultations, and regular operational working meetings.[18]

The work of the SWC consists of three stages: a preparatory stage (2011–2015); the SWC proceedings in Sarajevo (7 to 10 May 2015); and post-Sarajevo outreach activism stage, 2015–to date and counting.

The preparatory work for the SWC took almost five years. One of the reasons for such a long preparatory stage was shoestring funding that was in part a consequence of the rejection of the founders of the SWC to accept any imposition of conditions by donors. The preparatory stage consisted of ten training sessions during which the local communities were targeted with the aim to include and train as many women (and men) as possible in order to prepare them for the SWC. The trainings were in the countries of the former Yugoslavia, primarily in Serbia and Bosnia and Herzegovina, while the activists from Kosovo and Slovenia participated in trainings in Macedonia and Croatia.[19]

Additionally, 16 regional seminars were held. In three days' time the participants were exposed to an intensive interactive and interdisciplinary informative and educational programme, learning about the international institutions of justice and institutions of justice at a national level; rape as war crime; Hannah Arendt's ethics of responsibility; alternative models of justice, and specifically the women's courts and tribunals; and about the process of creation of the SWC for former Yugoslavia.[20]

In order to inform and mobilise public about the SWC, 136 public presentations were held in the period from 2011 to 2014, covering some hundred towns throughout the region, jointly organised by the members of the Organisation Committee of the SWC in cooperation with the local civil society organisations. In order to create a more secure environment for women to come forward with their stories, the organisers also initiated feminist discussion circles (FDC), which were held 16 times in the period 2012 to 2014. For each session there was a reader prepared, intended to encourage the discussion between those who directly suffered violence, the activist and academics. The sort of exchange during the FDCs laid the foundation for the feminist ethics of care for the SWC witnesses.[21]

The outcome of the preparatory meetings were analysed and evaluated at the consultative meetings of the Organisational Committee. The assessment highlighted the unfavourable circumstances in which the NGOs generally – and the women organisations in particular – functioned, as consequence of a negative impact of "projectisation" or "NGO-isation" present in the post-conflict societies in the post-Yugoslav states. The NGO-isation of the civil society initiatives inevitably incited rivalry and competitiveness among various groups, as the activists compete in procuring the funds for the similar projects at the same donor organisations.

18 Ibid., 13–17.
19 Ibid., 18–21.
20 Ibid., 19.
21 Ibid., 19–20.

This problem affected many women organisations in the region and those with no success in fundraising became marginalised and disappointed. Additionally the organisers argued that women active though NGOs showed to be less critical and more compliant with the state authorities and the donors. That made many of them dominantly pro-government and indifferent to issues of transitional justice.[22] The women who were not part of an NGO and thus independent seemed more outspoken, critical and rebellious towards the centres of powers – i.e. the national governments, international community and other institutions of power and influence. The challenge was how to mobilise women outside the NGO space. Eventually, women activists (and men to a lesser extent) from around 200 civil society organisations took part in the process of organisation of the SWC.[23]

The SWC took place in Sarajevo[24] because of what it symbolised. Before the war that started in 1992, Sarajevo was a symbol of multi-ethnic, multi-confessional and multi-cultural tolerance; during the war it became a symbol of suffering of civilians as a consequence of the three and a half years of siege by the Serb armed forces; after the war it became a symbol of difficulties in working on the reconciliation processes in the post-conflict societies. Of all wars that accompanied the disintegration of Yugoslavia (in Croatia 1991–1992 and 1995; in Bosnia-Herzegovina 1992–1995; and Kosovo 1998–1999), the war in Bosnia-Herzegovina lasted the longest period of time and produced the biggest number of victims, of which an overwhelming majority were the Bosnian Muslims. It was also in the Bosnian war that the violence against women and the widespread and systematic nature of rapes led to inclusion of rapes in the already existing repertoire of crimes against humanity.

Right to tell: the testimonies

When asked what they expected from a justice process, most of the participants put truth in first place, followed by justice. That of course meant to learn who was responsible for the injustice and suffering that happened to them, but also to understand why it happened. The initiative to offer a public space for women to focus on their experience of pain, suffering and injustices created an opportunity for a truth-telling where personal stories are told by conveying the emotions of anxiety, fear and despair. In the existing transitional justice approach, there is a significant validity to focus on injustice and how it makes the victim feel, which according to Clark is "a more constructive approach than focusing on harms done to women as women."[25] Clark argues that "the emphasis on a meta 'woman's experience' potentially detracts from and dilutes the micro specifics of women's individual experiences." By applying the concept of "justice as recognition" Clark argues that "to overemphasize the common factor of gender is deeply discordant with the heterogeneity (in terms of ethnic belonging, religious convictions,

22 Ibid., 20–21.
23 Ibid., 22.
24 Ibid., 29.
25 Clark, (note 1), 76.

socioeconomic backgrounds, age, etc.) of the women who testified." She argues that it might have been more constructive to spotlight "the women's personal stories rather than simply their common identity as women." Clark also questions the feminist approach to justice and its emphasis on women as victims of patriarchy, which she argues contributes to "de-individualizing them, depersonalizing their specific stories and essentializing them as victims." She joins here the critics of feminist approach to justice, who argue that singling out the women as victims affirms stereotypes that can undercut arguments that women should be treated "as fully engaged actors with independent, crosscutting and competing needs."[26]

This chapter will argue that the SWC contributed to the truth-seeking process by creating the space for women who suffered to tell their own story on their own terms. Despite all official proclamations of importance of the "right to the truth," there is no protocol or guidance for truth-seeking methodology. Many victims of the violence in the former Yugoslavia have suffered – and many still suffer – in silence because there was no public space offered to them to tell their personal story in public. That led to a diffused plethora of many individual and collective initiatives that are difficult to locate, collect, and archive. The SWC is the only PT that deals with the direct and indirect consequences of violence in the former Yugoslavia. The court events were held from 7 to 10 May 2015, with the testimonies lasting two days, from 8 to 9 May. In two days 36 women testified in front of an audience consisting of 500 people, mostly women from the region and the representatives of women organisations from abroad. The panel of seven judges listened to the testimonies. It is significant that the composition of the panel was in favour of non-lawyers.[27] The audience was receptive and reacted by laughs, worry and tears that were expressions of support and empathy. After each of thematic session, a panel of experts would contextualise each story by analysing the political, historical, cultural and socio-economic processes that made violence possible. This was part of feminist approach to justice methodology by which a subjective story was connected with an objective analysis.[28] The women victims of the crimes committed by the Serb forces in Croatia, Bosnia-Herzegovina and Kosovo were very supportive of

26 Ibid., 75.

27 The panel of seven judges was chaired by Charlotte Bunch (Center for Women's Global Leadership, Rutgers University, SAD). The members of the panel were: Prof.dr. Vesna Rakić-Vodinelić (Belgrade, Serbia), Dr. Kirsten Campbell (Goldsmiths College, London, UK) Gorana Mlinarević (Sarajevo, Bosnia-Herzegovina) Prof. dr. Dianne Otto (Melbourne Law School, Australija) Dr. Latinka Perović (Beograd, Serbia), Vesna Teršelič (Zagreb, Croatia). The Advisory Board comprised of: Marta Drury (SAD), Monika Hauser (Switzerland/Germany), Mariemme H. Lucas (Algeria).

28 See the expert analyses prepared after each of the thematic blocs and published in the SWC proceedings: Vjollca Krasniqi, Rada Iveković, Renata J. Kirin, Miroslava Malešević, Snježana Milivojević "Banalnost zla: orodnjeno nasilje protiv civila"; Marijana Senjak, "Žensko tijelo kao bojno polje"; Bojan Aleksov, Snežana Obrenović, Staša Zajović: "Militarističko nasilje i otpor žena"; Renata J Kirin, Vjollca Krasniqi, Rada Iveković, Snježana Milivojević, Miroslava Malešević: "Ubiti „drugog": etničko nasilje u ratu"; Tatjana Đurić Kuzmanović i Senka Rastoder: "Ekonomsko nasilje nad ženama" in Zajović, *Ženski sud: o događaju u Sarajevu i nastavku procesa*.

the witnesses from Serbia. Some of them did not know about the resistance by women against forced mobilisation of their husbands, fathers, brothers and sons.[29] They recognised the emotions in their stories: a grieving mother who lost her son in the Srebrenica genocide in 1995 could relate easily to the mother whose son was killed in 2004 in Serbia by his own colleagues while serving a compulsory military service in the national army.[30]

Testimonies

The testimonies were distributed over five topic-based panels: war against the civilian population – militaristic, ethnic, gender-based violence; woman's body – a battlefield (sexual violence in war zones); militaristic violence and women's resistance; persecution of those who are different – in war and peace (ethnic violence); and an undeclared war (social and economic violence, women's resistance).[31]

War against the civilian population – militaristic, ethnic, gender-based violence

Jelena Baketa lived with her husband a small place called Lovas in the east of Croatia, at the very border close to the border with Serbia. She recalled how she lost one son at the very beginning of the Serbia's occupation of the area and how she did everything she could to locate his dead body and bury it with due respect in the family grave at the local graveyard. The war intensified in the summer of 1991 and Jelena left her home in a refugee convoy that brought her to the Croatian capital Zagreb. She left her husband and two other sons in the war-stricken area. After Vukovar fell under the control of Serbia in November 1991, Jelena was reunited with her husband and the second son, who both joined her in Zagreb. The third son – Goran – went missing and despite the fact that the whole area was reintegrated in Croatia in November 1995 and the Serb occupying forces left, there has been no information available about the fate of the missing persons. She testified:

> My middle son disappeared in Vukovar, he was taken from Vukovar hospital and today I know nothing about him. When they were driven to Ovčara, one

29 "Now that a mother from Serbia is speaking openly, it is a lot easier for me. We are victims, but I don't blame your son or your husband. They were forced, this was the case in BiH, too." (a witness from Tuzla, BiH); "I didn't know that the mothers in Serbia protested, wanting their children to be returned from the war zone" (a witness from Sarajevo). In Zajović (ed), *The Women's Court: About the Process*, 55.

30 See: "Now that a mother from Serbia is speaking openly, it is a lot easier for me. We are victims, but I don't blame your son or your husband. They were forced, this was the case in BiH, too" (a witness from Tuzla, BiH); "I didn't know that the mothers in Serbia protested, wanting their children to be returned from the war zone" (a witness from Sarajevo).

31 Zajović, *Ženski sud: o događaju u Sarajevu i nastavku procesa*, 142–147.

> bus disappeared. It is not true that nothing is known about that bus, but to this day that bus has not been found, nor have people who were in it. What did happen, I don't know. Did he end up in the Danube river? Was he killed? I had all kinds of information, but I don't know the truth even today.[32]

Together with the association Mothers of Lovas, Jelena is still hoping to find out what happened to her son. She testified in Sarajevo about her personal struggle to balance her feeling from a despair that Goran was killed in the most awful way and that she will never be able to bid him a proper farewell, to an ever living hope that he is still alive, unable all these years to contact her. But Jelena is aware of the reality: if Goran is still alive – there is no way he would not find a way to get in touch with his mother. Jelena is unable to give up her investigation and find out what had happened to Goran. For example, she contacted Serb doctor, now living in Serbia, but he denied even being in Vukovar at all. Jelena knows that he did not speak the truth but has not power to compel him to. Once she heard an accused at a criminal trial talking about a mass grave and when the victims were listed she heard Goran's name. The defendant refused any contact with Jelena. Jelena finished her testimony with a request to those in power in Serbia to open the files where she could find the information about her son. To have a grave with his name would make such a huge difference to her.

Female body as a battlefield (sexual crimes in war)

Edina Karić was 15 years old when the war started in the spring of 1992. She recalled how she was detained with her fellow Bosnian Muslims by the Serb forces. She testified:

> They called out me and two other girls. They took us to an empty house in Bratunac. We were raped that night. They would take us to special rooms. That night a soldier raped me, while those two girls were raped by another two soldiers. They left the next day, and another one came to guard us. The night fell, when a group of soldiers barged in. I know a lot of them, they were my neighbours. They gathered us and took us to rooms. Several soldiers raped each of us throughout the night.[33]

She managed to survive the war and married a man of the same ethnic group, hoping that she had found safety. Her marriage was abusive and despite the fact that she had two children, no education and no job she left. She struggled but managed to raise her children on her own. However, she could not avoid the breaking point and she sought help. The therapy helped her and she got her high school diploma, got a driving licence and a job. The fact that she can take care

32 Ibid., 70–73.
33 Ibid., 119–121.

of herself and her children empowered her but the consequences of the multiple traumas she went through never completely disappeared. She copes by being active in a women organisation where women with similar background help her by sharing their own experience and supporting her when things get rough again.

The stigma about the sexual crimes has been very hard on women from Kosovo. One of them Nurija Tolaj,[34] a mother of three children, from Dečane in Kosovo testified how the Kosovo Albanians were first expelled from their homes in March 1998 by the Serb security forces to come back again in September that same year. But the real ordeal was to start after the NATO intervention in Kosovo and Serbia in March 1999. The local Serbs from Dečane were engaged in maltreatment of the Kosovo Albanian civilians, keeping them on different locations. Women suffered a lot: Serbs from Dečane sexually abused women from 13 to 80 years, often in front of their family members. Nurija enjoys support and affection of her family, but many women that went through the similar ordeal have been encouraged by families to remain silent and have been suffering in solitude. Yet, despite the support Nurija was receiving, she contemplated suicide twice. Nurija and her children receive counselling for the trauma they suffered. The Serbs from Dečane, whom they all know by name and surname, have never been held to the account for the crimes they committed. Some of them hold positions in the public administration at the Serb territories in the north of Kosovo.

Militaristic violence and resistance by women

Rosa Jakovljević comes from Bela Reka, a small place in Serbia. She testified:

> My son was killed during peacetime. I lost him while he was doing his regular military service in Topčider. Two soldiers were killed in the army barracks in Topčider, and the killer hasn't been found yet. I don't know why they killed them. Have they seen something they weren't supposed to see? Did they see something they weren't supposed to? They were locked up in the military court three days before they were killed.[35]

She lost her son Dragan in 2004 while he was serving a compulsory military service in the army of Serbia (or more precisely *Vojska Jugoslavije*/Army of Yugoslavia) then still a part of a loose federation called Serbia-Montenegro. She got her son back in a body bag with the incredible explanation by the army authorities he and his fellow conscript and friends – Dražen Milovanović from a town of Paraćina – killed each other with their own guns. The bodies of the two young men were found in vicinity of a secret bunker called Karaš 150 metres below the ground level the premise of the Topčider barrack in Belgrade. The official version

34 Ibid., 121–123.
35 Ibid., 142–147.

was that the two friends had killed each other. The bullets fired from their guns inflicted the fatal wounds. In disbelief, the grieved families started their own quest for truth and an independent commission concluded that the young men could not kill each other in the way the army presented it to the families. There was a third person involved. The army never provided the name of this third person. During their investigation Rosa testified that many stories reached the family – one was that the two friends were involved in guns and drugs traffic; that they were mentally unfit to serve in the elite military guard; or that they had to be eliminated because they saw General Ratko Mladić while on guard duty. General Ratko Mladić was since 1995 one of the world's most wanted fugitives. Serbian authorities persistently denied to the ICTY any involvement of hiding the world's most wanted fugitive with a bounty money on his head worth 6 million EUR. The young conscripts – Dragan and his friend Dražen – could not but recognise the general as his photos were all over the media. The third mysterious death was of a young soldier, whose duty was to drive general Mladić. Rosa and her family have been suing the army. But instead of truth and justice they have been exposed to denial and obstruction. Despite the independent commission report (the FBI contributed to it) that conclusively stated that the two young men could not kill each other, this has been ignored by the Serbian army. The army lawyers keep repeating the same story, i.e. that the two friends killed each other. Rosa will not and cannot give up. She still remembers vividly Dragan's funeral when she addressed the all mothers present "Mothers do not send your sons to the army!" To Rosa's despair, justice is not to be expected any time soon. In spite of the decision reached by Serbia's Supreme Court to speed up the investigation, the relevant judicial authorities did not act upon it and the case remains stuck at the preliminary stage of criminal investigation with no charges pressed and no indictees named.

Persecution of the "other" in the time of war and peace

Marija Lovrić had a husband and two children when they moved in the summer of 1991 to a new house at the outskirts of Osijek, a Croatian town in the eastern Slavonia, close to the border between Croatia and Serbia.[36] Marija's happiness lasted three months. In September 1991 the war started. The Yugoslav Army tanks, when leaving their barracks in Osijek, turned towards the city and fired at all houses on the outskirts. It also damaged their new house, but not so much that they could not live in it. Her husband urged Marija to take her children – of whom one had cerebral palsy – to friends' house in the northwest of Croatia. Her husband, who was director of the central post office in Osijek, stayed behind. He would call every morning from his office. One Friday in November 1991 he failed to call. She got worried. They talked on Monday and he told he that he was sent on a leave, but he was not allowed to leave the town. That was their last

36 Ibid., 190–194.

conversation. The only information she got about that fateful date came from a woman tenant who lived in their house and who observed the coming and leaving of two men and a woman in uniforms with insignia of the Army of Croatia. They took Branko with them and he never came back.

Marija returned to Osijek immediately after Croatia's independence was internationally recognised and the peace returned to Osijek. She testified:

> We returned home on 17 January 1992 and then our golgotha began. I went to my work organisation and asked to start working again, because there was a rule that those who had sick or handicapped children could leave the town until that madness subsides. I came to the firm and asked to be returned to work. One of them said, 'Marija, we are not going to feed Chetnik children.' And I was questioned at the MUP. And there someone asked me what I was by nationality. I said I was Croatian. Where was I born? In Osijek. My parents are Croats from Vrbovec. What kind of Croatian are you when you married a Serb? 'And I said," Sir, you are mistaken: I did not marry a Serb, I married a man!'[37]

She was hopeful that she would find Branko. Marija went back to her old workplace but was turned back. There was no empathy for her. Her former colleague refused to give her job back saying that they would not feed Chetniks (a term denoting a Serb nationalist extremist, op.a.) children. The most substantial help she got was from her friends, and particularly from one woman friend who would buy food, clothes and schoolbooks for her children. In the times of want, Marija succeeded because of kindness of people around her. Her children finished school, but she feels that the wartime stigma follows them. Her younger son is a qualified lawyer but back in Osijek he could never find a job. Marija feels that there is no end to her struggles in sight – ever.

(Un)declared war: socio-economic crimes against women and women resistance

Anka Vukićević is a physiotherapist. She got her first job in December 1992 in the General Hospital in Nikšić, a town in the north of Montenegro. It was a fixed-time contract. Anka's job description did not differ from her colleagues with a permanent contract, but her working conditions were much more severe. She had no rights: no annual leave, no sick leave, no meals or transportation subsidies. Anka was young and prepared to endure it, hoping that everything would change for better. After she got married and she decided to get pregnant, but it appeared that she needed to follow a fertility treatment. It was tough and demanding and she opened a sick leave. There was pressure from the hospital management to

37 Ibid., 230–233.

break the sick leave but Anka persisted and in 2004 she had a daughter. When her daughter was 17 days old, Anka was fired. She testified:

> I asked for the right I had as a mother – the right to maternity leave. An employee in the public health institution where I worked gave me an ultimatum saying: 'You'll either work or be fired.' Between the work and the child, I chose to be with the child. And since 2004 until today, . . ., my trial with the institution still lasts. And now the case is with the Strasbourg court against the state of Montenegro.[38]

She sued the hospital and in the process she lost many friends. Her colleagues avoided her as much as they could because they did not want to be associated with her as it could have ruined their prospects at work. The trial isolated her and her husband even more. She did not fight only her employer but the whole system. All state institutions by default closed their ranks and stuck to each other. The position of her employer was that she never handed over her sick leave papers. She found the papers in the hospital archive thanks to a friend who worked there. She was allowed back but only for a six month period. Then the hospital fired her again. After that Anka mobilised media. She explained what happened to after she got pregnant and how the system deprives women of their basic rights – the right to have a child. She filed a lawsuit against her employer at the European Court of Human Rights in Strasbourg. Anka experienced her fighting for her rights as empowerment. People on street recognise her now and profess their support for her struggle against the system. She feels empowered by the support.

Victims and the truth-telling at the criminal court and women court

The UN definition of the right to the truth stipulates that it is an "an inalienable and autonomous right, linked to the duty and obligation of the State to protect and guarantee human rights, to conduct effective investigations and to guarantee effective remedy and reparations."[39] The UN definition emphasises the importance of states in guaranteeing human rights and to remedy the breaches. In reality, states are very often also the wrongdoer and when states are facilitating the investigation and prosecution, some states will do it strictly because of formal obligation and not as a duty towards the victims to learn the truth. The truth-seeking process at national and International Criminal Courts would allow

38 See: Geoffrey Nice and Nevenka Tromp, 'International Criminal Tribunals and Cooperation with States: Serbia and the Provision of Evidence for the Slobodan Milošević Trial at the ICTY' in Margaret de Guzman and Diane Amann (eds), *Arcs of Global Justice; Essays in Honor of William A. Schabas* (Oxford, Oxford University Press, 2018) 445–465.

39 "The Basic Principles and Guidelines on the Right to a Remedy and Reparation for Victims of Gross Violations of International Human Rights Law and Serious Violations of International Humanitarian Law" a UN document adopted in December 2005, para. 7.

for some truth to emerge as long as it does not hurt the national interests of the state. The state that directly or indirectly participated in the armed conflict or human rights abuses will control how much truth is enough to satisfy the legal process without hurting the national and vital state interest.[40] This makes society-driven truth-seeking initiatives welcome and necessary. The involvement of as many different groups in the process of truth-seeking also means that many different methods will contribute to a "liberalisation" of truth-telling, with no model being superior or better.

During the process of organising the SWC the majority of participants from across the region praised the ICTY as the relevant and efficient legal institution with the capacity to deal with crimes committed in the region of the former Yugoslavia. The first serious blow to the retributive justice system exercised in The Hague came with the death of Slobodan Milošević before the end of his ICTY trial. With no judgement reached and no verdict rendered, many victims felt deprived of justice. In 2012 women active in the SWC initiative started expressing their mistrust in institutions of justice at the national and international level. This radical change of heart among the ICTY's most devoted supporters was triggered by some long-awaited judgements that turned out to be hugely disappointing.[41] The ICTY's acquittals of the indictees from Serbia left many victims disappointed, as those acquitted reflected the legal, political and historical evaluation of the criminal regime of Slobodan Milošević – in a way it exonerated Serbia from responsibility for the crimes committed in Croatia and Bosnia-Herzegovina in the 1990s wars.[42] The witnesses who testified at the ICTY trials saw their considerable effort to contribute to the criminal trial disappear in the oblivion. Their distrust in the institutions reflected also the level of regional war crime courts. The victims saw how the indictees before the Special Court for War Crimes in Serbia were released while waiting the start of the trial; that the number of trials drastically decreased; and that the local prosecutors relied too much on the verdicts of the ICTY. The SWC participants expressed the opinion that the political elites and authorities see local war crime trials as an obligation imposed by the international community. They are not interested in administrating justice but to simulate the justice process while using it to achieve concrete political and

40 Nice and Tromp, (note 39), 446, 455.

41 The participants said: "The international justice system has collapsed. The judgments in The Hague confirm this (Radovan Karadzic and Vojislav Seselj)." and "In discussions about the impact of recent judgments (March and April 2016) at The Hague tribunal (Radovan Karadzic, sentenced to 40 years in prison and Vojislav Seselj, acquitted), the participants said that the verdicts had many negative consequences." Further the participants said: "Instead of condemning the criminals, he resulted in the victims being convicted and the criminals being rewarded"; "The Hague Tribunal is a political court through which they dictate world politics"; "I have been an ardent supporter of The Hague tribunal since its inception. To me, that court is a big disappointment now." See: Zajović, ***Ženski sud: o događaju u Sarajevu i nastavku procesa***, 55–56.

42 See: Nevenka Tromp, 'In Search for Truth at Mass Atrocities Trials: Will Judges and Lawyers Have the Last Word?' [June 2018] XII(1) The Journal of Comparative Law 65–67.

economic gains. The victims saw despite the robust retributive justice mechanisms – international and national – no public acknowledgement of wrongdoings and crimes; no reparations; no truth; no respect for the dignity of victims; no the change of value system and moral order.[43] One woman who participated at the SWC said that

> at state institutions no one hears you as a victim, you are nothing. We learned at the SWC to listen to each other and hear what that other story was, the SWC put the victim at the forefront. It is the first and basic thing that, I think, has given every woman the strength to take on the hardship she has been through since the war.[44]

Hard justice: victims and the truth telling at a criminal trial

Retributive justice as an institutionalised legal response to mass atrocities is a perpetrator-centered justice that puts perpetrators in the centre of the judicial process. Success or failure of a criminal trial is often measured by its judgement. Judgments represent a form of justice in which the judges decide how successful the prosecution was in proving beyond reasonable doubt the crimes as charged in the indictment against an individual or a group of individuals. A judgement can bring a conviction or an acquittal. In the case of a conviction, perpetrators will most likely be sentenced to serve time in a prison. In the case of an acquittal, victims will protest but once all legal avenues are exhausted, their voices outside of the courtroom will not count. What can victims expect from retributive justice? A selected number of victims will be called as witnesses at a criminal trial in order to help establish the facts when, where and how the crimes were committed and by whom. Victim witnesses will be carefully selected and even the victims very much willing to testify will never be called as witnesses. It is certainly true for victims of mass atrocities, given the fact that mass atrocities left behind a great number of victims. The prosecution decides on its own discretion how much evidence to put before judges to prove a charge from the indictment beyond reasonable doubt. The forensic process for investigation and prosecution of mass atrocities at a criminal trial is based on strict rules and procedures. This rule driven forensic format is there to guarantee authority and integrity of due process, within which administration of justice for victims and fair trial for a defendant have to be achieved. Before, during and after the testimony, victim witnesses will be treated according the rules and procedures of the respective court. Some victim witnesses often feel that they did not tell their own story in court. Their narratives are interrupted; they are asked to give shortest possible "yes" and "no" answers; they feel that they need to control their emotions in an environment full

43 Zajović, *Women's Court: About the Process*, 24–25.
44 Zajović, *Ženski sud: o događaju u Sarajevu i nastavku procesa*, 36.

of strangers; and they worry that any sign of emotion could impact the credibility of their story before the judges. Very often it means that there would be no space available within the forensic process where victim witnesses can talk about their emotions, traumas and anxieties. The witnesses in the courtroom have to answer the fact-based questions that are deemed relevant by the prosecution or defence. If a victim witness is cross-examined by the other side – often the defence – in which the accuracy of the testimony or credibility of the victim is challenged, the experience of the testimony might not bring an emotional relief but trigger an additional trauma.[45]

Success or failure of a criminal trial is often measured by its judgement. Judgments represent a form of justice in which the judges decide on how successful the prosecution was in proving beyond reasonable doubt the crimes as charged in the indictment against an individual of a group of individuals. A judgement can bring a conviction or an acquittal. In the case of a conviction, an accused will most likely be sentenced to serve time in a prison. In the case of an acquittal – victims might protest but their voices outside of the courtroom will not have any effect on the judgement. Only those who participate in the criminal trial can make difference. Some of them will be called to testify, but many willing to testify might in the end never be called as witnesses.

In the case of self-representation in the court, the uncomfortable and adverse questions can come from the accused whom the witness holds responsible for the crimes. But sometimes a witness facing the wrongdoer creates an opportunity to appeal to the judges for permission to speak, and if granted the permission at the end of the testimony, the witness could plead to the accused to reveal the details of her child's fate. Even the most compassionate and emphatic of judges could not help because there is no protocol or mechanism available to them to compel the accused to volunteer any information outside of the realm of his defence. Moreover, the strict rules of a fair trial guarantee to the accused a wide range of rights – right against self-incrimination being a very important one.

45 The UN stipulates that:

> Victims should be treated with humanity and respect for their dignity and human rights, and appropriate measures should be taken to ensure their safety, physical and psychological well-being and privacy, as well as those of their families. The State should ensure that its domestic laws, to the extent possible, provide that a victim who has suffered violence or trauma should benefit from special consideration and care to avoid his or her re-traumatization in the course of legal and administrative procedures designed to provide justice and reparation.

See: "Basic Principles and Guidelines on the Right to a Remedy and Reparation for Victims of Gross Violations of International Human Rights Law and Serious Violations of International Humanitarian Law," Chapter VI/10. Adopted and proclaimed by General Assembly resolution 60/147 of 16 December 2005 <>www.ohchr.org/EN/ProfessionalInterest/Pages/RemedyAndReparation.aspx>

Soft justice: women courts as a metaphor of justice?

Attempting to position women courts in the existing of justice mechanisms, Daša Duhaček argues that they are structured as legal proceedings, but they are a metaphor for the court-based retributive justice. Yet, the metaphor is misleading as PT, in this case women courts, will produce a judgement but that will not be legally binding, i.e. there will be no punishment and no jail sentence to serve. Not only because PT are not part of the executive punitive (state) power and thus even if they would like to, would not be able enforce sentences they impose. For that reason alone the women courts will not be bound to observe all the rules that constitute a fair trial in the way that would be necessary at a criminal trial, where the stakes for the accused are much higher: if found guilty a defendant at a criminal trial would be sentenced most probably to serve time in prison. So, for example, the Women Court did not need to follow the strict rules on disclosure of the evidence that might be favourable to the persons named by witnesses as perpetrators. The emphasis was not on individual wrongdoers like it is the case in a criminal trial but on the social, political, economic and cultural forces which made the human rights abuses and injustices against women take place in such a systematic way. The intended objective was not to punish states or individuals, but to initiate a change in the behaviour of individuals and effectuate the transformation of dominate socio-economic, political and cultural paradigm.

The truth-telling coming from the victims will add to pluralism of narratives and cannot be treated as the definitive and absolute truth of the events. The heroic national historiography that glorifies the national struggles and wars of its male heroes needs to be complemented with the experiences of suffering people, who have been exposed to political violence and wars. The SWC introduced the emotional narrative into the truth-telling: a grieving mother or a struggling widow talked about personal loss, which has in their personal emotional experience been more important than any geopolitical and geostrategic designs of their respective states and the political leaders.

Transformative power of the Women Court: from victim to survivor and from witness to activist

After the court hearing the SWC continued with organising meetings across the region. Following the events in Sarajevo, seven regional meetings were held from 2015 to 2016. The events were attended by about 230 people.[46]

46 Women in Black, Belgrade, coordinated the continuation of the Women's Court process programme and other activities with the support – Anima, Kotor (Montenegro), Center for Women Victims of War, Zagreb (Croatia), Cure Foundation, Sarajevo; some members of the former Women's Court Organising Committee who operated until the events in Sarajevo participate occasionally (Gender Equality Council, Skopje, Macedonia) – while other members provided support, but without active participation in joint activities.

All the meetings were attended by witnesses, but also by the organisers of the SWC, as well as local, regional and international activists involved in the process. The meeting agendas dealt with the personal reflections and evaluations of the Sarajevo events; preparations of the texts of the testimonies; writing a report on activities; planning the continuation of the SWC process; and providing legal and psychological support for witnesses who needed it. The post-testimony meetings were considered to be part of the feminist approach to justice as the support and solidarity continued. The effects of the testimonies on the women were assessed and also in outreach events. Some women felt that giving a voice to their experience of suffering transformed them from a victim to a survivor.

Proponents of the "justice of recognition" argue that the public recognition of the harm done can serve an important purpose in facilitating connection between the harm inflicted and needs of those who were affected by it precisely because it does not treat those who have suffered injustice simply as victims. From some 200 women involved in the SWC initiative, only 36 women eventually testified, but because of the intensive preparatory stage, many women who joined in went through a transformative process: they shared their stories during the regional preparatory meeting; they re-told their stories many times and through the interaction of others they are able to change their perspective about their own understanding of what happened to them and how to deal with their own pain.[47] This change of perspective helped them to re-channel their energy and move from a survivor to a motivator and an activist.

Many other women who testified at the SWC were already activists. For example, Nadežda Kostić from Serbia who testified at the SWC was a weathered anti-war activist since 1999. She testified how her two sons were mobilised by the Yugoslav Army (VJ – *Vojska Jugoslavije*) during the Kosovo war in 1999. She described the ordeal she went through, fearing to lose both of them in a senseless war that the Serbia's political leaders led them to. After she heard from a neighbour that in the case that two sons from a family were mobilised, there is a rule that allows a waiver for one of the sons. The family conferred which of the two will go to the war and which will stay at home. Her older son took the decision and went to the war to save his younger sibling. In her memory, the Kosovo war was not about the territory and which side will win or lose Kosovo – for her the war was about keeping her family safe. She joined the other mothers in demonstrations in their hometown of Kruševac, demanding the return of thier sons from the Kosovo battlefileds. Their sons heard about the protests and decided to leave Kosovo in a convoy of military vehicles. They reached Kruševac and were reunited with their families. To avoid the punishment as deserters they eventually returned to Kosovo. Nadežda's son came back, but the war experience took its toll on his health. He told how alcohol, drugs and pills were provided to the soldiers. Shortly after the war Nadežda was diagnosed with the cancer. She survived

47 Clark quotes Marijana Senjak. See: Clark, (note 1), 75.

and decided to become an activist so that no more mothers would have to go through the same ordeal of seeing off their children to war.[48]

Conclusion

The conclusion of every court should be a judgement. Only two of seven judges had a law degree, but neither of them had experience in the criminal justice system as a lawyer or a judge. Also the mandate of the SWC was not such that it wanted to compete with the international legal concept as exercised at the ICTY. The qualification of crimes was applied very broadly and included injustices, suffering and trauma caused by political and socio-economic structures of inequality. The SWC produced a preliminary judgement that – unlike similar people's court judgements – did not name the names of wrongdoers. Instead it provided a huge list of cases for violence and consequences of violence; and instead of individual names it produced a long list of state institutions that were – and still are – considered major wrongdoers. The state that was – based on the testimonies – singled out as the major wrongdoer is Serbia. The judgement reads more as a political, military and socio-economic analysis of the conflicts than a legal document. It also issued the list of eight recommendations in which one reads:

> States and other social institutions (private and public), such as the media, education systems, religious communities, families, as well as individuals – all share responsibility for ending patriarchal, hetero-normative and militaristic views that perpetuate and feed all forms of violence and discrimination against women.[49]

The SWC's paramount importance was to empower the witnesses to tell their version of the truth. The application of the "right to the truth" as exercised by the SWC showed that 1) the "right to the truth" should not be limited to a process in which victims are passive recipients of someone else's truth (perpetrators' accounts, criminal trial judgements, the archives of states, international organisations or other public or private institutions). Victims should be allowed and encouraged to actively participate in the truth-seeking process; 2) the "right to tell" should be an integral part of the "right to the truth" and should be exercised by offering the victims platforms to tell their own account on their own terms; 3) the "right to tell" should include emotional, ethical and moral narratives to be part of the truth-telling process and thus allow for emotions to be also included in the realm of historical and collective narrative; and 4) the truth-telling at PT has a transformative potential when it encourages its participants to move on from being a "victim" to feel as a "survivor" and ideally to become an "activist."

48 Zajović, *Ženski sud: o događaju u Sarajevu i nastavku procesa* 157–162.
49 Ibid., 254. There are in total eight recommendations.

The application of feminist model of justice offered an interesting approach where the truth-telling included emotions, compassion and empathy in an interactive way. The critics who expressed a caution of the trap of feminist driven court to reinforce the stereotype of women as objects of violence might be proven wrong. The most innovative feature of this court that it aimed at empowering the women to take an active role in giving a form to their story and encouraging them to become agents of change by becoming motivators, activists and advocates of change. The challenge for the SWC will now be how to articulate the post-Sarajevo common purpose and how to keep the existing network of women organisations active while in the same time expanding it with new activists who will keep spreading the message.

References

Basic Principles and Guidelines on the Right to a Remedy and Reparation for Victims of Gross Violations of International Human Rights Law and Serious Violations of International Humanitarian Law (Chapter VI/10, 16 December 2005) <www.ohchr.org/EN/ProfessionalInterest/Pages/RemedyAndReparation.aspx>

Clark, Janine, 'Transitional Justice as Recognition: An Analysis of the Women Court in Sarajevo' [2016] International Journal of Transitional Justice 67–87.

Tromp, Nevenka, 'In Search for Truth at Mass Atrocities Trials: Will Judges and Lawyers Have the Last Word?' [June 2018] XII(1) The Journal of Comparative Law 65–67.

Zajović, Staša, 'Svedokinje na Ženskom sudu: akterke pravde' in *Ženski sud: o događaju u Sarajevu i o nastavku proces* (Belgrade, Žene u crnom, 2017), pp. 13–68.

Zajović, Staša (ed), *Women's Court: About the Process* (Belgrade, Women in Black & Centre for Women Studies, 2015).

Zajović, Staša, *Ženski sud: o događaju u Sarajevu i nastavku proces* (Belgrade, Žene u crnom, 2017).

6 The Iran Tribunal

An international People's Tribunal for the promotion of truth and justice

Geoffrey Nice, Hamid Sabi, Shokoufeh Sakhi and Roya Ghiasi

Introduction

The Iran Tribunal documented breaches of human rights against political prisoners in Iran in the 1980s and organised a quasi-judicial process by which the Islamic Republic of Iran (IRI) was found guilty of gross violations of human tights and the commission of crimes against humanity.

The founders of the Iran Tribunal advanced this process over seven years from 2007 to 2013. They maintain that the process had established irrefutable evidence of the atrocities committed by the state of the IRI against its own civilian population. It also provided substantial benefits to the victims (and their families) by allowing their grievances to be aired and recorded.

This process may now be a precedent, or exemplar, for how informal tribunals, operated according to strict judicial standards, can be established at low financial cost by victims of state-sponsored atrocities and others. In this case it was victims, those close to victims, the bereaved of those killed in the atrocities and other interested citizens of the state concerned together with international human rights lawyers and activists who drove the process. They came to be served (*pro bono*) by independent, impartial lawyers and judges who created a record of evidence and an authoritative judgement on a ruling system that is still in power.

Background

The Iranian Revolution of February 1979 (which later was named the "Islamic" Revolution) witnessed a massive uprising across all social and political groupings in Iranian society of those opposed the monarchy of Mohammad Reza Shah Pahlavi. The supporters of the revolution were, first and foremost, ordinary people, regardless of their class, religion, ethnicity or political group affiliation. In the final days of the Revolution the military also joined the movement and made the success of the Revolution inevitable.

Revolutionary fervour was propelled by anti-dictatorship and anti-imperialist agendas, focused and united on the overthrow of the ruling system of the Shah. However, there was no commonly shared revolutionary vision detailing a programme to replace the Pahlavi Monarchy. Nevertheless, regardless of the presence of religion as part of the revolutionary forces, there was a "shared" assumption that the autocratic rule of the Shah would be succeeded by a democratic one, one that would bring some kind of socio-economic distributive justice[1] as well as political freedom,[2] i.e. freedom of expression and belief.

Ayatollah Ruhollah Khomeini became the unquestioned leader of the Revolution by public acclaim. His arrival on 1 February 1979 brought millions of people to the streets of Tehran to welcome him and he virtually took over control of the government upon his arrival. On 11 February 1979 the revolution became triumphant.

The pro-Khomeini religious groupings, organised through neighbourhood mosques, established a militia, the "Islamic Revolution Committees" which took control over the public space by setting up check points within the cities. Within one week after the victory over the Pahlavi monarchy, on the direct orders of Khomeini, "Islamic revolutionary courts" were established which issued death sentences for the Shah's supporters, army leaders[3] and, later, those accused of "corruption on earth."

The new state-sanctioned violence under the sentiment of "revolutionary wrath" was supported by the public (if largely passively), as well as by other political groups which had no share in the power. Very soon some independent newspapers and journalists, supporters of civil liberties as well as democratic and leftist groups, began distancing themselves from the new government under the leadership of Khomeini and the Islamic Republic Party. They openly criticised the state's organised and widespread attacks on the newly won liberties. The leaders of various political and civil organisations became targets of persecution and – later – prosecution by the "Islamic revolutionary courts."

In mid-March 1979 the war against Kurdish people began; in August 1979 Khomeini issued a *fatwa* against Kurdish political leaders and organisations. Between 1979 and 1983 thousands of Kurdish people were killed and more than 1,200 Kurdish prisoners were executed.[4]

On 18 April 1980, after Friday prayers, Khomeini gave a speech which formally initiated the Islamic "Cultural Revolution," calling for an attack on the country's universities and colleges by "Hezbollah," the Islamic Committees and the Islamic

1 A much-repeated saying of Khomeini was his promise, after his return from exile, that Iranian citizens would get equal share of the oil revenue, that low-income people would have access to free housing, water, electricity and public transit. (Khomeini's speeches in February and March 1979, in *Sahife Noor*, (صحیفه نور), Vol. VI, 262, 273, 297).

2 Before his arrival in Tehran, Khomeini famously promised that Iranians would have political freedom, where even communists would have freedom of expression (Khomeini's interview with *De Volkskrant* (7 November 1978), in *Sahife Noor*, (صحیفه نور) Vol. IV, 364.

3 The first group, four of the Shah's army generals, was put on trial and executed on February 16, 1979 <>www.iranchamber.com/history/islamic_revolution/revolution_and_iran_after1979_1.php>

4 Steven Ward, *Immortal: A Military History of Iran and Its Armed Forces* (Washington, DC, Georgetown University Press, 2009).

Revolutionary Guards.[5] For two months the country's university and college campuses remained under siege until their fall in June 1980. They remained shut for three years, under the supervision of the "Supreme Cultural Revolution Council" which was tasked with purging the students, academics and administrative staffs from every non–pro-government political group and critical individuals.

In September 1980, hostilities between Iran and Iraq turned into an all-out war, allowing the IRI to introduce even harsher measures in the pretext of national security. In February 1981, the plain-clothed militia, Hezbollah, started systematic violent attacks on the leftists' public rallies and gatherings, accompanied with bombing their offices and leftist bookstores. From March 1981, the line of attack spread against the Islamic group, Mujahedin Khalq Organisation (MKO) as well as against the then-president Mr. Bani-Sadr. Soon other national-liberal groups were targeted.

Finally, on 20 June 1981, the MKO which had initially supported the Revolution and Khomeini, openly broke away from the latter's camp, calling a mass rally (estimated participation: between 200,000 to 500,000, depending on the source) in support of president Bani-Sadr and against Khomeini and his supporters. The demonstration was attacked violently by the government's militia (plain clothes thugs and revolutionary guards). Thousands of MKO supporters and bystanders were arrested; many of them were schoolchildren in their teenage years, and some were as young as ten years old. On 27 September 1981, under the slogan "long-live freedom, death to Khomeini," the MKO called for an armed uprising against the IRI.

During the weeks that followed, tens of thousands of people were arrested on political charges and every day tens of prisoners, and some days more than a hundred were executed, some of them in their early teens. The revolutionary courts responsible for the executions did not follow any standard process. The trials were summary, lasting a few minutes.[6] In most cases the identities of the victims were not even established. Daily newspapers carried pictures of those who had been executed the night before and called on relatives to come forward and identify them.[7]

5 The final declaration of war against the left came in the April 18, 1980 Friday Prayer of Tehran in which Khamene'i officially announced the "holy war" *(jehad)* against the university. . . . The state-controlled press of Iran reported clashes between government-organized armed gangs (known as *chumdq-adrdn,* 'club-wielders') and students throughout the country. . . . Four hundred students were injured and two killed in Shiraz; in Tehran University, three were killed and over 160 wounded; some 350 persons were wounded, and one killed in Mashhad all on April 23. On April 22, at least ten were killed on the campuses of Ahvaz and Gilan universities. (Shahrzad Mojab, *The State and University: The 'Islamic Cultural Revolution' in the Institution of Higher Education of Iran, 1980–1987.* PhD, Department of Educational Policy Studies, University of Illinois at Urbana-Champaign (1991), 84.

6 See *Findings of the Truth Commission,* 26–29 <http://irantribunal.com/index.php/en/sessions/truth-commission/306-findings-truth-commission>

7 See an image of the front page of a main evening newspapers, *Etelat* (24 June 1980) <http://1.bp.blogspot.com/-reiJjMD8llg/Tm25St8_IBI/AAAAAAAAAv8/zpW664TNcYU/s1600/165114_179711655384566_116049491750783_503806_147480_n.jpg>

The IRI did not limit its repression to the Mujahedin and their supporters. In the summer of 1981, a concerted attack on most leftist groups and parties was organised and by 1983 almost all political organisations and individuals suspected of being anti-IRI, whether of the left, liberal or right, became the targets of the state's violence and prisons across the country were filled with hundreds of thousands of political prisoners.

June 1981 marks the beginning of a decade of terror and repression that is known as the "bloody decade." During the 1980s thousands of civil rights and political activists were arrested and tortured and large numbers were executed. The decade culminated in the 1988 mass killing of political prisoners. In accordance with a *fatwa* of Ayatollah Khomeini, thousands of remaining political prisoners were brought before Khomeini's especial committee later known as "the death committee." Between five to seven thousand prisoners were executed in the summer of 1988 following this *fatwa*.[8]

The campaign for the Iran Tribunal (the campaign)

In the early 1980s the executions were widely publicised by the state-controlled media; the names of those executed the night before were read by the state-run radio station and their pictures were printed in daily papers.[9] However, the 1988 mass executions were carried out in complete secrecy. In the summer of 1988 political prisons across Iran were locked down weeks before the executions. Family visits to prisoners were cancelled. The bodies of victims were dumped in unmarked mass graves and the families of victims were not notified of the executions for some time and even when they were, they were warned not to inform anyone of the executions.[10]

The families of victims and survivors of the 1980s bloody decade informed international bodies and human rights activists of the events that had occurred in Iran in the 1980s and of the fate of political prisoners. Although it was widely acknowledged that the Islamic Republic paid little attention to human rights and had grossly violated the rights of its civilian citizens, all relevant NGOs – *except* Amnesty International – showed little interest in engaging with Iran on issues of human rights.

The United Nations Human Rights Commission appointed special rapporteurs on human rights for Iran but neither Reynaldo Galindo Pohl (the first

8 See Amnesty International Report, *Iran: Violations of Human Rights 1987–1990*, MDE 13/21/90 <>www.amnesty.org/en/library/asset/MDE13/021/1990/en/5c32759d-ee5e-11dd-9381-bdd29f83d3a8/mde130211990en.html>. Also see Iran Tribunal's collation of the names of over 5000 victims in this period. <>www.irantribunal.com/index.php/en/resourses/documents/27-list-of-political-mass-executions-in-1980s>; and see list of over ten thousands executed men and women (in Farsi) prepared by "Committee in Defence of Human Rights in Iran – Sweden" <>www.komitedefa.org/text/edamha.pdf>

9 See (note 8).

10 See *The Findings of the Truth Commission*, supra 90 ff.

rapporteur) nor his successor, Maurice Copithorne, paid much attention to the fate of political prisoners in Iran. Galindo Pohl visited Iran several times during his mission and Maurice Copithorne was only allowed in once. Both held numerous interviews with the families of the victims and survivors of the massacre. However they were both unable to verify the massacre of political prisoners in their reports and merely acknowledged that torture and mistreatment of prisoners were rampant in Iran and that the judiciary failed to respect any aspect of the rule of law or Iran's obligations under the International Covenant on Civil and Political Rights (ICCPR) which had been ratified by Iran on 24 June 1975 without any reservation.[11]

The families of the victims and survivors had no choice but to organise their own campaign. In 2007, the families and survivors set up the Campaign for the Iran Tribunal in Sweden with branches in Germany, the United Kingdom, Canada, and the United States. The Campaign was a "grass roots" organisation initiated, participated in and funded by the survivors and families of the victims of the bloody decade. The aim of the Campaign was to establish a process that would allow the members of the families of the victims and the survivors to submit and record their evidence of the events in the 1980s and to establish an independent tribunal to review the facts and render a judgement as to the culpability of the Islamic Republic of Iran in the violation of the rights of its citizens, including its crimes against humanity.

The Campaign decided that the funding of the Tribunal process should be entirely shouldered by its members and refused, steadfastly, to accept funding from institutions and corporations. Members agreed to contribute a minimum of €10 per month. Further donations from individuals were accepted at a later stage. By the time that the Legal Steering Committee was established the Campaign had over €70,000 in its coffers.

The proceedings

In February 2011 the Campaign established an International Legal Steering committee chaired by Professor John Cooper QC and prominent Iranian and international lawyers consisting of Sir Geoffrey Nice QC; Professor Eric David; Professor Richard Falk; Professor Payam Akhavan; Professor Kader Asmal (died 2011); Doctor Nancy Hormachea; Doctor Matine Daftary and Mr. Hamid Sabi.

The Legal Steering Committee decided to establish a truth commission for hearing the evidence of the witnesses and an international tribunal to issue a judgement on this issue. The Campaign preferred two-stage proceedings, modelled on South

11 Under Article 2.1 of the ICCPR: Each State Party to the present Covenant undertakes to respect and to ensure to all individuals within its territory and subject to its jurisdiction the rights recognised in the present Covenant, without distinction of any kind, such as race, colour, sex, language, religion, political or other opinion, national or social origin, property, birth or other status. <>www.ohchr.org/EN/ProfessionalInterest/Pages/CCPR.aspx>

Africa's experience of "Truth and Reconciliation" for the first stage (excluding "reconciliation" as none of the perpetrators offered to participate) with the second stage being modelled on the Russell Tribunal. This process would allow the victims to relate their experiences during the Truth Commission stage without entering legal arguments as to the nature of crimes committed by the IRI.

The Steering Committee was concerned about the lack of representation by the Islamic Republic of Iran. It reviewed the possibilities of appointing a special counsel to represent the IRI or appointing an *amicus* to raise issues that the IRI would have raised. Eventually both considerations were rejected. Appointment of a special counsel or *amicus* would have adversely affected the process of the Tribunal. It would have substantially increased the costs of the proceedings which would have been beyond the means of the Campaign. At the same time the proceedings would have become much longer as a result of cross examination. Also, the members considered that exposing the witnesses to cross examination in an adversarial manner would expose the witnesses to combative process that may have seemed abusive to the witnesses and that could have been or seemed to be inappropriate for the Tribunal.

Instead it was agreed to formally invite the government of Islamic Republic to participate in the hearings of the Tribunal in The Hague.

The Steering Committee sent invitations to over 60 international judges, lawyers and human rights activists inviting them to serve as Truth Commissioners or Judges in the Iran Tribunal process. While the Campaign accepted to pay for the travel expenses and lodging of the Commissioners and Judges, it made it clear that no attendance fee would be payable. Those who responded and participated in the proceedings did so free of charge.

The Truth Commission was established in June 2012 consisting of six members headed by Professor Maurice Copithorne (former UN special rapporteur on human rights for Iran); Louise Asmal; Anne Burley; Eric David; William Schabas and Daniel Turp. The Commission held its hearings over five days (18–22 June 2012) at the Amnesty International Human Rights Action Centre in London.

The Campaign had circulated a questionnaire among its members (over 3,000 former political prisoners and families of victims) and selected over 100 witnesses for the process of the Truth Commission. The Campaign organised for the witnesses travel to London and their lodging and daily transport to the hearings. Almost all the witnesses paid for their own travel expenses. Families of the victims in London hosted the witnesses in their homes.

Each witness submitted a written statement in advance. Seventy-five witnesses were heard by the Commission over the five-day hearing. Those who could not participate in person were heard through Skype. The witnesses were not sworn in but were asked by the Chair to confirm the veracity of their statements. The witnesses were led by the Tribunal's Counsel[12] through their statements. The

12 Counsel to the Tribunal was Mr. Hamid Sabi. Nihonkoku Kenpo [Kenpo] [Constitution] art 9 para 2 (Japan).

Commissioners then posed their questions to the witnesses. The proceedings were broadcast via the internet and satellite television channels, including broadcasts direct into Iran where it was viewed by many thousands.

The Truth Commission's findings were published in July 2012.[13]

Over nearly 25 years since the massacre of political prisoners in the summer of 1988, IRI had been able to keep the massacre and treatment of the political prisoners as a secret. The massacre was not acknowledged officially and the state officials at every stage would dismiss the suggestions as "rumours" spread by the opposition groups to undermine the Islamic State.

The live broadcast of the proceedings of the Truth Commission forced the government to acknowledge the massacre but continued to defend it as justified for the security of the regime. The younger population in Iran was for the first time questioning the legitimacy of the state in the brutal massacre of the political prisoners which had been kept as a secret until then.

The Steering Committee then established the panel of international judges to preside over the Iran Tribunal. Six international judges accepted the commission: Judge Johan Kriegler, former President of South Africa's Constitutional Court during the transition (presiding); John Dugard SC; Margaret Ratner Kunstler; Michael Mansfield QC; Makau Mutua, and Patricia Sellers. The Steering Committee also invited the Islamic Republic of Iran (through its Embassy in The Hague) to participate in the Tribunal's process. The IRI did not respond to this invitation.

The Tribunal held its hearings in the Conference Centre at The Peace Palace in The Hague, between 25–27 October 2012. Nineteen witnesses and experts testified before the Tribunal. Again, the proceedings were broadcast directly into Iran with many thousands of viewings. The Tribunal was assisted by a team of prosecutors headed by Professor Payam Akhavan and assisted by Professor John Cooper QC, Professor Sir Geoffrey Nice QC, Ms. Mojdeh Shahriari, Mr. Kaveh Shahrouz, Dr. Nancy Hormachea and Ms. Gissou Nia. The Tribunal published its judgement on 5 February 2013.[14]

The Campaign raised further funds for the second stage of the proceedings from its members and supporters. Again all the judges and prosecutors provided their services free of charge.[15]

The findings of the Truth Commission

The Truth Commission's report which was published in July 2012 runs to over 400 pages. It consists of a 64-page body of the report followed by appendices,

13 *Findings of the Truth Commission* <http://irantribunal.com/index.php/en/sessions/truth-commission/306-findings-truth-commission>

14 Tribunal Judgment Can Be Located <http://irantribunal.com/images/PDF/Iran%20Tribunal%20Judgment.pdf>

15 The total costs of both proceedings in London and the Hague, including the rental of the Library of the Peace Palace, came to approximately €150,000.

in particular the testimony of the witnesses (summaries of both written and oral testimony). Some of the witness statements had been redacted at the witnesses' requests to ensure their safety.

The report reviews the treatment of political prisoners in six chapters dealing with:

- i Captivity;
- ii Execution;
- iii Prisons;
- iv Victims;
- v Families; and finally
- vi The perpetrators.

Every paragraph of the report is supported by references to the witness statements as listed in Part E of the report. Invariably the witnesses confirm that prisoners were tortured, gravely mistreated and subjected to mock trials and mock executions as well as to actual non-judicial execution of the worst kind. The witnesses testified to the harsh conditions of their incarceration and the lack of any due process. None of the witnesses had access to independent legal counsel. None of the prisoners were properly notified of their alleged crimes and the charges against them; the hearings took a few minutes each, without allowing the accused any right of defence; the court hearings were held mostly inside the prison compounds or in places where the general public had no access; the executions were extrajudicial and the entire process was in violation of the mandatory rules of the ICCPR and in violation of the Articles of the Universal Declaration of Human Rights.

The witnesses identified 32 prisons around Iran (Findings of the Truth Commission, *supra* Chapter 3) where political prisoners were incarcerated. Torture, mistreatment, flogging, mock executions, sham trials and finally executions in all prisons followed similar patterns. The Commission concluded (*ibid* page 64)

> The arrests, disappearance, methods of torture, "trials" and executions as attested by witnesses had the same characteristics in all prisons and detention centres in Iran, whether in Mashhad, Shiraz, Tehran or Mahabad. The witness testimonies disclosed a similar widespread pattern of brutality and disregard for basic human rights as well as extra-judicial executions throughout the country.
>
> The Commission concludes that these violations of human rights were devised, instigated and executed (or caused to be executed) by a single central authority, and as such the Government of the Islamic Republic of Iran is the only authority responsible for these acts. The facts reported by the Commission have been committed by state officials: "judges", "prosecutors", prison officials, torturers and interrogators (references omitted). Because they are state agents it follows that Iran itself bears international responsibility.

The entire proceedings of the Truth Commission were free from political agendas. The witnesses were from a wide range of political affiliation. As the Report confirms (*ibid* Section 4.5.1 page 46) the political affiliations related to some 15 organisations from religious groupings to various political groupings as well as a variety of ethnic minorities.

The verdict of the Tribunal

The Judgment of the Iran Tribunal, published on 5 February 2013, reviews the factual aspects of the case. It adopts the findings of the Truth Commission as a factual basis which has been corroborated by witnesses appearing before the Tribunal. The Judgment reviews the treatment of Baha'is, Arab Iranians, Kurdish Iranians, women, and other political prisoners; the Judgment also reviews the types of torture, the processes of the trials and executions. It concludes[16]

a There is overwhelming evidence in support of the allegation that substantial and widespread violations of human rights occurred in Iranian prisons between 1981 and 1988;
b The violations were committed by state officials, judges, prosecutors, prison officials, torturers and interrogators "within the walls of state institutions and on direct instruction of state officials";
c The violations were widespread and systematic and were committed against the civilian population in furtherance of the state policy; and
d As concluded by the Truth Commission, these violations of human rights were devised, instigated and executed (or caused to be executed) by a single central authority and as such the Islamic Republic of Iran is the only authority responsible for these acts.

The Tribunal then considered the applicable law. In doing so it briefly looked at the provisions of Iranian law. While Iranian law is not considered to be binding on the Tribunal, the Tribunal nevertheless noted that certain rights, such as freedom of assembly, freedom of expression, presumption of innocence, right to counsel and prohibition of torture were guaranteed by the Constitution, but nevertheless totally ignored by Iran's judiciary in dealing with political prisoners.[17]

The Tribunal then considered customary international law as it was in the 1980s and its further development. It also considers whether as a matter of customary international law a state can be held responsible for crimes against humanity. It concluded:[18]

> *In the present case, the control of the Islamic Republic of Iran over its agents, prosecutors, judges, prison officials, interrogators and other individuals involved in the commission of these crimes cannot be challenged. The Tribunal therefore holds that as a matter of international law, the Islamic Republic of Iran can*

16 Ibid., 29.
17 Ibid., para. 103, p. 30.
18 Ibid., para. 165.

> *be held responsible for crimes against humanity, committed at its behest by state officials and within the state establishments and prisons.*

Finally, the Tribunal concluded in its verdict:

I The Islamic Republic of Iran has committed crimes against humanity in the 1980–1989 periods against its own citizens in violation of applicable international laws;

II The Islamic Republic of Iran bears absolute responsibility for the gross violations of human rights against its citizens under the International Covenant of Civil and Political Rights; and,

III Customary International law holds the Islamic Republic of Iran fully accountable for its systematic and widespread commission of crimes against humanity in Iran in the 1980–1989 period.

Consequences of the publication of the Tribunal's Judgement

The process of the Iran Tribunal attracted responses from different angles.

The *émigré'* community, especially former political prisoners, their families and opposition groups were elated by the clear and convincing terms employed by the Tribunal in condemning the abuses by the IRI. The organisers were complemented for their achievement and many former prisoners of conscience who did not or could not participate in the process offered to provide further support and testimony for the Tribunal.

Inside Iran, substantial awareness was created, especially among the younger generation, as to the well-kept secret of the regime, namely the mass murder of the political prisoners in the summer of 1988. This was assisted by the footage broadcast regularly thereafter by international media and opposition groups showing the process of the Iran Tribunal. Live streaming of the hearings of the Truth Commission and the Tribunal attracted much interest in Iran. In the last day of the hearing in The Hague on 27 October 2012 the number of live streaming reached over 900,000; most viewers were in Iran.

The reaction from the government and state officials in Iran was muted. For 25 years the state policy had been to deny the existence of the massacre. The official version of the history was that some of the members of MKO were killed during the latter's incursion into west Iran in summer of 1988. The senior members of the regime now had to accept that political prisoners were murdered in cold blood and in their thousands in that period while in the custody of the government.

The first state reaction to the Iran Tribunal was an article, titled "What is happening behind the scene of Iran Tribunal 'show,'"[19] published in *Borhan*, a website affiliated to the Iranian state. Here for the first time the issue of the

19 سید محمدمهدی پیامبری ,پشت پرده‌ی دادگاه نمایشی "ایران تریبونال" چیست؟ <http://borhan.ir/NSite/FullStory/News/?Id=3809>, بخش مطلب: 3809, 13 July 2012.

1988 massacre of the prisoners is mentioned and defended by the author. Later *Baztab*, a website close to the leader of the IRI, Ayatollah Khamnei, claimed that he was instrumental in getting amnesty for the leftist groups, thereby effectively admitting the massacre.[20] Other semi-official websites explained the massacre as a necessity for national security as the prisoners were preparing to break out and join the armed struggle against the regime.

The debate about the massacre, long happening within the diaspora, became a public discourse in Iran during the presidential elections of 2013 when the apparently "moderate" candidate, Hassan Rouhani, accused the extremists of being involved in the murder of the prisoners. Mr. Rouhani won the elections in a landslide as a moderate. Bizarrely and ironically one of his first acts as the new president was to appoint Mustafa Pour-Mohammadi, the Prosecutor of Evin Prison and a most notorious member of the death committee, as the Minister of Justice.

During his confirmation hearing before the Parliament, Mr. Pour-Mohammadi acknowledged his role as a member of the death committee and defended his actions as necessary for the survival of the regime. The successor of Pour Mahammadi as the Minister of Justice, Alireza Avaie, has an even worse record than his predecessor. As the prosecutor (and member of death committee) in Dezful (South of Iran) he attempted to ensure that not a single political prisoner would survive the massacre. The only survivor, Mr. Mohammad Ashogh, though condemned to death, managed to escape before his execution. Finally, the present incumbent as head of judiciary, Ebrahim Raissi, was another member of the death committee in 1988.

A further reaction to the process of Iran Tribunal was the disclosure of audio tapes of Ayatollah Montazeri by his son Ahmad Montazeri in August 2016. Montazeri was named as the successor of Khomeini. However, in 1988 he raised serious objections to the ongoing massacre of political prisoners. He summoned Pour Mohammadi and Raissi and told them to stop this massacre.[21] Ayatollah Montazeri told Pour Mohammadi and Raissi that they would be considered as murderers and criminals by the Iranian people. The publication of the audio recording of this event created an uproar against Pour Mohammadi (who stepped down later from the Ministry of Justice). Mr. Raissi was criticised for his role during the presidential election of 2017, when he was running as the regime's favourite candidate but lost the election to the incumbent Hassan Rouhani. His recent appointment as the Head of Judiciary by the Leader has created internal and external opposition to the appointment.

The response by the international media and coverage of the Tribunal's process was weak. The story was *passé* and uninteresting for the readers. Nonetheless, *The Independent* in the UK published a full-page report on 8 February 2013 under

20 This article was republished at <http://news.gooya.com/politics/archives/2012/12/15>

21 Hossein Ali Montazeri, '1988 Executions of Prisoners in Iran' (11 August 2015) <www.bing.com/videos/search?q=ahmad+montazeri&&view=detail&mid=F92737C464542B298247F92737C464542B298247&&FORM=VRDGAR> accessed 20 March 2019.

the heading of "IRAN'S SERBERINCA – HOW AYATOLLAH KHOMEINI SANCTIONED DEATHS OF 20,000 ENEMIES OF THE STATE." *The Guardian* and *Al Jazeera* gave limited coverage to the story. BBC Persia and VOA Persian gave full coverage of the Tribunal's proceedings in London and the Hague and have continued to cover the story to this date.

Copies of the Judgment and the Report of the Truth Commission were submitted to the Secretary General of the United Nations, the Special Rapporteur on Human Rights for Iran; the Human Rights High Commissioner and the UN Special Rapporteur on the Promotion of Truth, Justice, Reparation, and Guarantees of Non-Recurrence. No reaction has been made to any of these submissions.

Conclusion

The international community and specialised organs of the United Nations are inherently incapable of responding to internal atrocities committed by the totalitarian governments against their own civilian citizens. The only exceptions are when the major powers decide to move the Security Council to engage in these events such as in the former Yugoslavia, Rwanda and the like. Even then such engagements are invariably too late to stop the atrocities and the process adopted for redress too complicated, overly expensive and overly time-consuming to provide meaningful redress for the victims. The experience of the Iran Tribunal may be a guide for the frustrated victims of internal atrocities who have no other recourse to justice. The experience demonstrates that an effective People's Tribunal may be able to set in motion changes in the public discourse that would force those in power to revise their policies.

Over the last 35 years since the establishment of the IRI, its state officials have had a free hand in carrying out these crimes without accountability. As a consequence, a culture of impunity is now well established in Iran and has become institutionalised. The state officials consider themselves above law, beyond reproach and immune from any prosecution or even criticism for the crimes they have committed.

As set out previously some of the perpetrators listed in the Truth Commission's Report were given prominent positions in the government. They openly boast about their past activities and the criminality of the means adopted. To date no prison official, no torturer and none of the interrogators who were involved in the "bloody decade" of 1980s has yet been the subject of disciplinary or other proceedings whereby their conduct in torturing and executing political prisoners could be questioned and there has not been a single case of reparations for the death or mistreatment of political prisoners.

Since the publication of the Judgment of Iran Tribunal, the regime has, without acknowledging the judgement, changed its narrative in relation to these crimes. The blanket denial of the past and attribution of the "rumours" of the massacre of political prisoners to Zionists and agents of imperialism is gone. Officials, if forced to discuss these issues, consider the massacre (or legal execution of a few prisoners who intended to carry out armed struggle – as the official version is now constructed) a necessity for national security.

Without acknowledging the injustice imposed by the state of the IRI on Iranian citizens and without punishing the perpetrators there is no guarantee of non-recurrence. Many of the perpetrators, whether listed in the report of the Truth Commission or not, have been rewarded with important political positions in the successive governments of the IRI.

What has made the Campaign for Iran Tribunal a unique undertaking is that it is a PT in true sense. It was conceived, funded, promoted and executed entirely by the victim community. Lawyers and judges were employed (on a *pro bono* basis) at a later stage to carry out the mandate of the Tribunal. In this way it is different from some of other People's Tribunals where the originator(s) were usually human rights activists seeking resolution for the suffering of others with whom's suffering the originators may have had no direct or personal connection. The Iran Tribunal – perhaps closest to the "Comfort Women Tribunal" of 2,000 among other such tribunals – reflected the interests of and responded to the needs of many victims. The organisers (the Campaign and its broad membership among the political prisoners in Iran) had a personal stake in promoting the tribunal to bring publicly pronounced justice for themselves and other hapless victims of state-sponsored gross atrocities.

The Iran Tribunal is therefore, an extraordinary process whereby those affected by the crimes against humanity have managed to establish an internationally acceptable process to verify and record the truth about the crimes committed against them, as well as finding the Islamic Republic of Iran responsible for commission of crimes against humanity and gross violation of human rights against its own civilian citizens.

The findings of the Truth Commission as well as the Iran Tribunal's Judgment has contributed to the furtherance and promotion of truth, accountability and justice in Iran, an indispensable step in the direction of preventing the continuous IRI state violence against its citizens.

The Iran Tribunal demonstrated that where international bodies fail to redress abuses committed by totalitarian regimes, it falls to ordinary citizens and those affected to organise redress. The Iran Tribunal has proved that the task can be undertaken with limited resources relying on the contributions of those affected and the good will of professionals and human rights activists.

References

De Volkskrant (7 November 1978) in IV *Sahife Noor* (صحيفه نور) 364).

Mojab, Shahrzad, *The State and University: The 'Islamic Cultural Revolution' in the Institution of Higher Education of Iran, 1980–1987*. PhD, Department of Educational Policy Studies, University of Illinois at Urbana-Champaign (1991), p. 84.

The Iran Tribunal Judgment, Prosecutor v. Islamic Republic of Iran (5 February 2013) <http://irantribunal.com/images/PDF/Iran%20Tribunal%20Judgment.pdf>

Ward, Steven, *Immortal: A Military History of Iran and Its Armed Forces* (Washington, DC, Georgetown University Press, 2009).

7 The role of the PPT in securing the rights of Rohingya and other minorities in Myanmar

Azril Mohd Amin

Background

Recognition of the inherent dignity and of the equal and inalienable rights of all humans is the foundation of freedom, justice and peace in the world no matter what creed or origin, and disregard and contempt for human rights have resulted in barbarous acts which have outraged the conscience of mankind. To this end, it is essential that human rights be protected by law. Such was the experience two world wars have collectively taught us all and it is to this end that the Universal Declaration of Human Rights (UDHR) was proclaimed, at least according to its first, second and third preambles. Article 1 of the same document also makes clear that all human beings are born free and equal in dignity and rights.

Yet it is also trite that not all peoples get to enjoy the rights and freedoms that have been conceived by this universal human rights instrument, made better in its application by complementing instruments such as the Cairo Declaration of Human Rights in Islam (CDHRI) which encapsulates Islamic teachings and the ASEAN Human Rights Declaration (AHRD) which includes Asian values.

For context, the former CDHRI declaration is an alternative relativist instrument proclaimed under the auspices of Foreign Ministers of Muslim nations acting in concert within the Organisation of Islamic Conference (OIC) meeting in Cairo, Egypt in 1990 and was adopted by the same meeting on 5 August of the same year in response to the UDHR's failure to take into account the cultural and religious context of Islamic nations, in what the then Iranian representative to the United Nations aptly characterised in 1982 as a secular understanding of the Judeo-Christian tradition that cannot be implemented without transgressing Islamic law.[1]

The latter AHRD declaration was adopted by the Foreign Ministers of ASEAN states meeting in Phnom Penh, Cambodia on 18 November 2012 and basically does the same for South East Asia what the CDHRI did for Muslim members of the OIC, which is to encapsulate and narrate human rights from the Asian perspective,

1 David Littman, 'Universal Human Rights and "Human Rights in Islam"' *Midstream* (New York, February–March 1999).

mainly by including therein a section on general principles mainly emphasising cultural context (such as contained in Article 7 thereof) and the need to balance rights with responsibility to the community (as contained in Article 6 thereof) from which the general interpretation of subsequent sections on civil and political as well as economic, social and cultural rights must be based upon.

The UDHR, together with the CDHRI and AHRD, collectively play a role in the articulation, promotion and safeguarding of general human rights principles embedded amongst the civilised nations of South East Asia and for this it is crucial that the rights afforded by all these documents be enshrined in the domestic laws of sundry ASEAN states. This must be so for where rights have not been respected nor protected by law, outrageous violations of the same have gone unabated and this is particularly true in respect of minorities residing in Myanmar, such as the Muslim Rohingyas and Kachins.

Muslim Rohingya in particular have had a presence in Burma since the conversion by Arab traders of early Indian kingdoms such as the Maurya Empire within Arakan since the 7th century when it was a centre of maritime trade and cultural exchange between Burma and the outside world[2], and have lived in peace within Burma with other ethnicities there up until Burmese independence in 1948 and thereafter until about 1982 when the Myanmar government passed a law stripping almost all Rohingya of their Burmese citizenship.[3] Since then, they have been subject to systematic discrimination including the denial of education, jobs, housing and even basic sanitation in conditions widely compared to apartheid.[4] Such discrimination has often been accompanied by state-sanctioned violence, most notably the latest which occurred around 2016 and is still ongoing, which is the basis for the inquiry commenced by the Permanent People's Tribunal (PPT) as discussed further ahead.

Kachin are another minority group in Myanmar subject to systematic discrimination and state-sponsored violence. Although unlike Rohingya they are a recognised minority group within the 1982 Burmese citizenship law and the Myanmar constitution due to their participation in the pre-independence Panglong Agreement between the disparate ethnic groups of Burma, their condition took a turn for the worse since 1961 when Buddhism was declared the state religion which was considered by them to be an affront to their Christian faith.[5] Since then they have experienced similar restrictions on their right to food, access to healthcare, housing, water and sanitation.[6] Largely in response to the Kachin situation operated

2 Syed Islam, *A Handbook of Terrorism and Insurgency in Southeast Asia*, Andrew T. H. Tan (ed) (Edward Elgar Publishing, 2009), 327.

3 Discrimination in Arakan, *Human Rights Watch* (May 2000) <>www.hrw.org/reports/2000/burma/burm005-02.htm>

4 Emanuel Stoakes, 'Myanmar's Rohingya Apartheid' *The Diplomat* (14 October 2014) <https://thediplomat.com/2014/10/myanmars-rohingya-apartheid/>

5 Kachin, 'World Directory of Minorities and Indigenous Peoples, Minority Rights Group International' <https://minorityrights.org/minorities/kachin/>

6 They Block Everything, *Fortify Rights* (August 2018), 55–58 <>www.fortifyrights.org/downloads/They_Block_Everything_EN_Fortify_Rights_August_2018.pdf>

Kachin Independence Organisation (KIO) has been waging a guerrilla war of autonomy against the Buddhist centric Burmese army.[7]

While both the Rohingya and Kachin minorities have been suffering discrimination and violence since at least the 1970s, the situation has become much worse especially for the Rohingya.[8] According to the global human rights organisation Human Rights Watch, Rohingya Muslims continue to be on the receiving end of grave human rights abuses by the security forces of the Burmese state. The military campaign of ethnic cleansing which began in August 2017 has seen more than 730,000 Rohingya flee to neighbouring Bangladesh in the same year, with more than 14,500 Rohingya having fled to Bangladesh between January and November 2018. For the estimated 500,000–600,000 Rohingya still in Myanmar, particularly Rakhine state, conditions remain dire. A total of 392 Rohingya villages have been destroyed by Burmese authorities as of March 2018 and more than 128,000 Muslims – about 125,000 Rohingya and 3,000 Kaman – have been arbitrarily deprived of their liberty by being detained in camps since 2012.[9]

Among some of the many crimes committed against the Rohingya are the close cooperation between the Burmese military apparatus and local vigilantes in the systematic burning down of hundreds of Rohingya villages across northern Rakhine state, with satellite imagery showing a pattern of burning that was deliberate, organised and consistent over time occurring across northern Rakhine State. These targeted Rohingya homes, mosques and other structures. In villages where people from different ethnic groups lived side by side, the Rohingya areas were typically burned to the ground, while the homes of their neighbours remained unscathed.[10] Other crimes included systematic torture including forced interrogations and beatings, deprivation of food and even deliberate burning of the skin. These gruesome atrocities in particular were committed by the Myanmar Border Guard Police to Rohingya of Rathedaung township at the Zay Di Pyin base in Myanmar.[11] There are also reports of widespread and systematic gang rape committed by soldiers in the Burmese army against Rohingya women.[12]

Kachin too have been subject to numerous atrocities by the Burmese state, although this must be appreciated within the context of the Burmese army's response to the activities of Kachin guerrilla activity. Members of that minority

7 Benedict Rogers, 'The Shocking Crimes Against Burma's Kachin People' *Catholic Herald* (6 September 2018) <https://catholicherald.co.uk/commentandblogs/2018/09/06/the-shocking-crimes-against-burmas-kachin-people/>

8 Eleanor Albert and Andrew Chatzky, 'The Rohingya Crisis, Council on Foreign Relations' (5 December 2018) <>www.cfr.org/backgrounder/rohingya-crisis>

9 Human Rights Watch, 'Myanmar Events of 2018, World Report 2019' <>www.hrw.org/world-report/2019/country-chapters/burma>

10 Sergio Pecanha and Jeremy White, 'Satellite Images Show More Than 200 Rohingya Villages Burned in Myanmar' *New York Times* (18 September 2017) <>www.nytimes.com/interactive/2017/09/18/world/asia/rohingya-villages.html>

11 'We Will Destroy Everything' (*Amnesty International*, 2018), 9 <>www.amnesty.org/download/Documents/ASA1686302018ENGLISH.PDF>

12 Ibid., 11.

ethnic group in particular have been known to suffer from explosions of detonating landmines being buried within and around Kachin state by both the army and the guerrillas, leading to loss of limb where they do not result in loss of life for Kachin civilians. The presence of these landmines also complicate relief efforts by humanitarian organisations and contribute towards a fear of returning home for many displaced Kachin due to the presence of these landmines.[13]

The Rohingya and Kachin PPT

It is in the context of the atrocities and crimes committed against both the Rohingya and Kachin that the PPT concluding session on Myanmar which had convened at the Faculty of Law, University of Malaya in Kuala Lumpur from the 18 to the 22 of September 2017 assumed extraordinary significance considering the UN Security Council's unanimous call to the Myanmar government to end its military campaign against the Rohingyas on 13 September 2017.

As introduced in Chapter 1, the PPT is an international opinion tribunal examining cases regarding violations of human rights and the rights of peoples founded in June 1979 in Bologna, Italy by a group of legal experts, writers and other cultural community leaders from 31 countries. The PPT is rooted in the historical experience of the Russell Tribunal on Vietnam (1966–67) and on dictatorships in Latin America (1974–1976) and has adopted as its governing statute the Universal Declaration of Peoples' Rights made in Algiers, Algeria in 1976. It operates when international courts and forums fail to do so due to geopolitical or other reasons.[14]

Hearings took place over three days, with 11 expert testimonies presented as well as 16 fact witnesses, including nine direct victims. In addition, over 1,000 pages of documentation were submitted by the Prosecution in evidence, including notarised testimony from 35 additional witnesses and over 30 minutes of audio-video footage.[15]

The arguments of the prosecution, the views of the expert witnesses and the testimonies of the victims were analysed by a panel of judges with exemplary credentials as we shall see going forward. They come from different countries and backgrounds and were of impeccable qualification and credibility. Noteworthy amongst them were Daniel Feierstein, a founder of the Centre for Genocide Studies in Argentina, who chaired the panel; Zulaiha Ismail, who is a trustee of the Perdana Global Peace Foundation, which is a non-governmental organisation dedicated to criminalising war in Malaysia; Helen Jarvis, who sits on the advisory

13 They Block Everything, (note 6).

14 Ibid., 3.

15 Permanent People's Tribunal, Final Judgment of the Session of the Permanent Peoples' Tribunal on State Crimes Allegedly Committed in Myanmar Against the Rohingyas, Kachins and Other Groups. <http://permanentpeoplestribunal.org/preliminary-judgment-of-the-final-session-of-the-permanent-peoples-tribunal-on-state-crimes-allegedly-committed-in-myanmar-against-the-kachin-rohingyas-and-other-myanmar-muslims/?lang=en>

board of the Centre for the Study of Genocide and Justice in Dhaka, Bangladesh but who is from Cambodia and Australia; and Nursyahbani Katjasungkana of Indonesia who served as the general coordinator of the International People's Tribunal on Crimes against Humanity against Genocide 1965–1966 with respect to her own country.[16]

Last but not least is Shadi Sadr who is a human rights lawyer from the Republic of Iran and the founder and director of Raahi, a legal centre for women that was closed by Iranian authorities in 2007 as well as the executive director of Justice for Iran (JFI), which oversees the creation and implementation of research projects on the rights of ethnic and religious minorities and also served as a member of the panel of judges for the International People's Tribunal on Crimes against Humanity and Genocide committed in 1965 to 1966 in Indonesia.[17] Such an experienced yet diverse panel were certainly well placed to make credible findings in respect of the nature of crimes committed against the Burmese minorities.

The PPT terms of reference included broadening the focus from the most acutely affected Rohingyas to the general policy of the Myanmar state on Kachins and other groups as well as documenting, in order to qualify, the historical and structural roots and causes of the events leading to the numerous atrocities, as opposed to merely focusing on the atrocities committed in 2017 and onwards. This was due to the fact that the PPT with respect to Myanmar had been mooted as early as 2013 considering the so-called constitutional reforms leading from military to civilian control in Myanmar and the subsequent release of Aung San Suu Kyi from house arrest and the holding of elections in Myanmar for the first time since 1990 in 2010. The PPT only acquired more urgency when atrocities against Rohingya continued to proliferate, leading to the genocide of 2017 and later.[18]

In proceeding with its terms of reference, it was crucial for the PPT to avoid considering the numerous crimes and atrocities as occasional incidents and strictly internal affairs of a still young and "fragile democracy," with no political, strategic or economic interactions with and impact on regional and global actors and interests, as the international pariah Aung San Syu Kyi would have the world believe. It was also important to qualify juridically the severity and the responsibility of the crimes not only in view of the most pertinent international criminal qualification but to stress and justify with the greatest emphasis the absolute priority for concrete responses to the urgency of the needs of the affected peoples.[19]

The prosecution was led by Doreen Chen from Australia, a human rights lawyer who is the co-founder and director of Destination Justice through which

16 Final Judgment on State Crimes Allegedly Committed in Myanmar Against the Rohingyas, Kachins and Other Groups, University of Malaya, Faculty of Law, 18–22 September 2017, Kuala Lumpur, Malaysia, 9 and Annex 1.

17 Ibid.

18 Ibid., 5.

19 Ibid., 7.

she supports persecuted human rights defenders, particularly in Southeast Asia. In her great effort she was aided by myself, Azril Mohd Amin of the Centre for Human Rights Research and Advocacy of Malaysia and the prosecution team, which included Dir Kheizwan Kamaruddin, Fahmi Abd. Moin, Luqman Mazlan, Dr. Mohd Afandi Salleh, Rafna Farin Abdul B. Ra'far and Dato' Rosal Azimin Ahmad, as well as Dr. Thomas McManus from the School of Law, Queen Mary University, London.[20] This has been the format chosen since the PPT is merely an opinion tribunal stepping in to give visibility and legitimacy to the authority of peoples when states and the international bodies fail to protect their rights, due to geopolitical reasons or other motivations.[21]

In accordance with the right of those accused of crimes to submit their defence in strict compliance with its governing statute, the Universal Declaration of Peoples' Rights which was declared in Algiers, Algeria in 1976, the PPT had also invited Myanmar State Counsellor, Aung San Suu Kyi, Vice-President Myint Swe and Commander in Chief of the Myanmar Armed Forces, Senior General Min Aung Hlaing to appear before the Tribunal or to make representations. They did not reply.[22]

As they did not reply no defence was constituted on their behalf, whether staffed by legal representatives or otherwise. The PPT made every effort necessary, reasonable and practicable to afford interested parties the right to their defence, such as noting the communication of the session to representatives of Myanmar civil and military authorities, noting the formal acknowledgement of the invitation by representatives of such authorities and even asking if any representative of the Myanmar Government was present each time a session commenced, but no response was ever received.[23]

The tribunal also extended invitations to various international agencies such as the United Nations and the European Union. Among them were António Guterres, Secretary-General of the United Nations, Zeid Ra'ad Al Hussein, United Nations High Commissioner for Human Rights, Professor Yanghee Lee, Special Rapporteur on the Human Rights Situation in Myanmar and Kofi Annan, former Secretary-General of the United Nations and the Chair of the Rakhine Commission. All these invitees did respond to the PPT invitation but were regretfully unable to attend.[24]

There were also renowned expert witnesses who had testified. Among them, Greg Stanton, Research Professor in Genocide Studies and Prevention at George Mason University in the United States of America. He is widely regarded internationally as one of the most authoritative voices on the crime of genocide. Dr. Chandra Muzaffar, who is a Malaysian intellectual and human rights activist

20 Ibid., 9 and Annex 2.
21 Ibid., 3.
22 Ibid., 10.
23 Ibid., 10–11.
24 Ibid.

who has actively campaigned on issues of human rights and intercivilisational dialogue, gave a speech on the last day of the Tribunal. Dr. Chandra founded various human rights NGOs such as Aliran in 1977, the International Movement for a Just World in 1991 and had won various prizes for his activism including the Rockefeller Social Science Fellowship in Development Studies for Southeast Asia in 1984 and 1985 and the Harry J. Benda Prize for distinguished scholarship on Southeast Asia in 1989.

Yet another renowned expert was Maung Zarni who as a student founded and led the Internet-based Free Burma Coalition out of Madison, Wisconsin in the United States of America from 1995 to 1998. He has written extensively on the Burmese affairs including democratic transition, peace process, transnational activism, Islamophobia and Rohingya genocide and recently with Alice Cowley co-authored various research dissertations into the slow genocide of the Rohingya in Myanmar.[25]

The crux of the PPT was to make findings in respect of the extent to which Rohingya and other minorities have suffered from the brutal human rights violations and indeed such findings make for very grim reading. The nature of the military campaign foisted upon the Rohingya and other minority groups of Myanmar and the horrendous consequences emanating from it were vividly described in the testimonies of its victims at the PPT. The findings generally indicate that it was not just the severely persecuted Muslim Rohingyas who suffered. Christian Kachins also presented serious evidence of war crimes, crimes against humanity and the crime of genocide.

Among the most harrowing were testimony from a Rohingya Imam stated eight people in his village were burned alive by the military. He stated that at least 1,000 were killed. There was also testimony from a 30-year-old Rohingya woman who had fled to Bangladesh for three months prior that the Myanmar Army took seven women from her village and raped them. Another ethnic Rohingya, Mumtaz Begum testified to the PPT that the Burmese military killed her husband and shot her son. The Tribunal also heard from a Rohingya rape victim who relayed the horrific testimony that eight other women besides her were raped and her husband was killed.[26]

Evidence by expert witnesses was no less chilling. Abdul Malik Mujahid, Chair of the Burma Task Force, testified and presented evidence of the use of rape as weapon of war by the Myanmar army and the mass scale of this atrocity. According to him, rape was the most common crime against humanity described in the day-long testimonies through videos and eyewitnesses at the PPT. Maung Zarni noted that the real players behind the scene were not the phantom "democratically-elected government of Suu Kyi" but rather that the Burmese junta is still in the driver's seat.

25 Ibid., Annex 2, p. 57.

26 Executive Summary, Opening Session on Myanmar's State Crimes against the Rohingya, Kachin and Other Groups, Queen Mary University, London, 6–7 March 2017, p. 1.

Penny Green, who moderated the Opening Session on Myanmar's State Crimes against the Rohingya, Kachin and Other Groups held at the Queen Mary University in London from 6 to 7 March 2017 concluded by noting the highpoint of the hearings, the fact that both Rohingya and Kachin have joined together in solidarity to learn from one another's suffering and persecution and to forge greater bonds of solidarity.[27]

The tribunal reached a conclusion, via consensus, that Myanmar intended to commit genocide against the Kachin people. Further, Myanmar is guilty of the crime of genocide against the Rohingya. Moreover, that genocide against the Rohingya was taking place with ongoing acts of genocide. The PPT also found a strong possibility that the number of casualties of that genocide will be even higher in the future if nothing is done to stop it. As for the other Myanmar Muslims and the Kachin, the PPT surmised that even if the implementation of the genocide is not yet taking place, it concluded that continuous persecution, together with the crimes against humanity and war crimes against them could amount to the implementation of genocide in the near future.

The PPT believed that all these crimes, which go yet unpunished, were committed with an intent to commit the same by the Burmese junta and by the pariah regime led by Aung San Su Kyi who holds power in Myanmar and seem to be part of a plan to deny every expression of autonomy and self-government of the people of Kachin state and, more generally, to humiliate and to destroy the ethnic and cultural identity of minorities living in the country.[28]

PPT afterwards

The findings of the judges of the PPT were then communicated to various UN Human Rights bodies including its Human Rights Council in Geneva. The Office of the Adviser on the Prevention of Genocide in New York also received the findings and are mulling over the next course of action to take. To date however, no official response has been received by the preceding organisations in respect to the findings of the PPT in this regard. This is also true with respect to other UN agencies or the Myanmar government.

It appears as there has also been no official communication of the findings of the PPT to the Rohingya or Kachin peoples or representatives. This is unfortunate, for it prevents action in response to the tribunal's findings. Indeed, action must be taken and the sooner this can be done the more lives can be saved and the human rights and dignity of the various ethnic minorities of Myanmar can be restored, allowing them to take their rightful place alongside other nations enjoying the rights and freedoms accorded them by the UDHR, CDHRI and AHRD.

27 Ibid., 1.

28 Final Judgment on State Crimes Allegedly Committed in Myanmar Against the Rohingyas, Kachins and Other Groups, University of Malaya, Faculty of Law, 18–22 September 2017, Kuala Lumpur, Malaysia, 48–49.

However, the quest for justice for Rohingya, Kachin and other minorities who might be suffering due to the impunity offered the Myanmar regime should not stop here. Civil society groups all over the world must also be brought into the picture and highlight the need for further and better measures to be taken, including lobbying the great powers of the United Nations Security Council, or bringing Myanmar before the ICC where it must answer charges of committing wanton genocide and crimes against humanity. The media also has a critical role to play in disseminating the findings of the Tribunal and must not keep silent in the face of wanton and systematic human rights violations by the murderous Burmese regime.

One ends with the hope that the media will emphasise the two principal goals of the Tribunal. One goal is exposing with incontrovertible evidence the true situation in Myanmar and using that as a basis for spreading public awareness. The second goal is strengthening international law and international institutions in our endeavour to ensure that justice is done to the Rohingya, Kachin and other minorities in Myanmar. It is only by the realisation of these goals that justice and dignity can be secured for the Rohingya, Kachin and other Burmese minorities, so that human rights can truly be universally realised and enjoyed by all.

References

Albert, Eleanor and Chatzky, Andrew, 'The Rohingya Crisis, Council on Foreign Relations' (5 December 2018) <www.cfr.org/backgrounder/rohingya-crisis>

Discrimination in Arakan, Human Rights Watch (May 2000) <www.hrw.org/reports/2000/burma/burm005-02.htm>

Executive Summary, Opening Session on Myanmar's State Crimes Against the Rohingya, Kachin and Other Groups, Queen Mary University, London, 6–7 March 2017.

Final Judgment on State Crimes Allegedly Committed in Myanmar Against the Rohingyas, Kachins and Other Groups, University of Malaya, Faculty of Law (18–22 September 2017), Kuala Lumpur, Malaysia.

Human Rights Watch, 'Myanmar Events of 2018, World Report 2019' <www.hrw.org/world-report/2019/country-chapters/burma>

Islam, Syed, *A Handbook of Terrorism and Insurgency in Southeast Asia* (Andrew T. H. Tan (ed), Edward Elgar Publishing, 2009).

Kachin, 'World Directory of Minorities and Indigenous Peoples' (Minority Rights Group International) <https://minorityrights.org/minorities/kachin/>

Littman, David, 'Universal Human Rights and Human Rights in Islam' [February–March, 1999] *Midstream*.

Pecanha, Sergio and White, Jeremy, 'Satellite Images Show More Than 200 Rohingya Villages Burned in Myanmar' *New York Times* (18 September 2017) <www.nytimes.com/interactive/2017/09/18/world/asia/rohingya-villages.html>

Permanent People's Tribunal, 'Final Judgment of the Session of the Permanent Peoples' Tribunal on State Crimes Allegedly Committed in Myanmar Against the Rohingyas, Kachins and Other Groups' <http://permanentpeoplestribunal.org/preliminary-judgment-of-the-final-session-of-the-permanent-peoples-tribunal-on-state-crimes-allegedly-committed-in-myanmar-against-the-kachin-rohingyas-and-other-myanmar-muslims/?lang=en>

Rogers, Benedict, 'The Shocking Crimes Against Burma's Kachin People' *Catholic Herald* (6 September 2018) <https://catholicherald.co.uk/commentandblogs/2018/09/06/the-shocking-crimes-against-burmas-kachin-people/>

Stoakes, Emanuel, 'Myanmar's Rohingya Apartheid' *The Diplomat* (14 October 2014) <https://thediplomat.com/2014/10/myanmars-rohingya-apartheid/>

They Block Everything (Fortify Rights, August 2018) <www.fortifyrights.org/downloads/They_Block_Everything_EN_Fortify_Rights_August_2018.pdf>

We Will Destroy Everything (Amnesty International, 2018) <www.amnesty.org/download/Documents/ASA1686302018ENGLISH.PDF>

8 People's Tribunals, law and ecological justice

The Australian contribution

Binoy Kampmark

Introduction

The degree of interest in ecological justice and laws protecting nature in Australia has developed traction in recent years. This is much in line with international developments elevating the environment within the context of a legal framework where action can be initiated to redress abuses and harms against ecology. Law, in other words, has met ecology, a "rocky courtship between a couple that has matured into a kind of marriage . . . that settled around developments in environmental law."[1] This consummation also fits within the broader milieu of community and social campaigns to modify human conduct in terms of green living and more environmentally amenable, sustainable options in the face of climate change. But advocates cannot help but note that Australian domestic law lags in the environmental field, being limited in terms of effective jurisprudence and broad reaching legislation. An acknowledged gap in the vision of seeking a protective regime for the rights of nature, and the structure of change, has been slow in coming.

Activists remain hampered by a range of legal restrictions and state-centric attitudes that has yet to recognise the importance of rights of nature, along with any entrenched notions of environmental protection. Legislators and bureaucrats find themselves playing permanent, sometimes intentional catch-up, obstructing moves towards an understanding about what has been termed the Great Law or Wild Law of human affairs. (Such a law, as designated by Father Thomas Berry and Cormack Cullinan, suggested such a principle as organisational and spiritual, an ecological rule to enable a flourishing of the Earth community).[2] Given that

1 Jamie Murray, 'Placing the Animal in the Dialogue Between Law and Ecology' [July 2018] 39(1–2) Liverpool Law Review 9–27; Richard Brooks, Ross Jones and Ross Virginia, *Law and Ecology: The Rise of the Ecosystem Regime* (Aldershot, Ashgate, 2002).

2 T. Berry, *The Great Work: Our Way into the Future* (London, Random House, 1999); C. Cullinan, *Wild Law: A Manifesto for Earth Justice* (2nd ed., Totnes, Green Books, 2011); N. Rogers and M. Maloney (eds), *Law as if the Earth Really Mattered: The Wild Law Judgment Project* (Abingdon, Routledge, 2017).

the country retains one of the world's most powerful commodity resources lobbies, and insists on the here and now rather than the existentially challenged future, the challenge is not surprising.[3] Australian politicians have been consistently attracted to the fossil fuel industry or have hired advisors with such experience to advance their political campaigns and fortunes. Such moves have seen the country slip down the international corruption index given, in the words of Transparency International, "inappropriate industry lobbying in large-scale projects such as mining," a "revolving doors" policy an "a culture of mateship."[4] Australia remains an example of what sociologist Karie Marie Norgaard sees as an example of lag in understanding the severity of environmental crisis, notably in terms of climate change, the "gap between the severity of the problem and its lack of public salience."[5]

The approach to existential environmental threats on the part of the human species has resembled, according to Norgaard, the absurdity of a double life; there is awareness about global warming, for instance, but little inclination to "integrate this knowledge into everyday life."[6] This, in turn, has sparked a range of traditional protests and marches. It has also led to the formation of such specific organisations such as Earth Rights International (ERI), which combines "the power of law and the power of people in defense of human rights and the environment." This necessarily entails an understanding of the intersection of the environment with human rights, duly defined as "earth rights."[7]

This is not to say that Australia is a minnow in the history of environmental activism. In a broader sense, a targeted activism assisted by legal and practical expertise has developed. Extra-curial involvement by legal voices has become more common, much in contrast with the more traditional appraisal of lawyers as maintainers of, in the words of Gill H. Boehringer and Stuart Russell, "state authority and the hegemonic domination of successive ruling classes."[8] The emergence of lawyer resistance movements, contend the authors, is an important part of a global development that can also see fruition in extra-curial involvement through the establishment of such bodies as peoples' tribunals.

3 See, for instance, Paul Karp and Nick Evershed, 'Coal Lobby Ads Biggest Third-Party Political Expenditure in Australia' *The Guardian* (1 February 2018); Matthew Rose, 'Connections Between Australian Politics and Coal Lobby Run Deep' *SBS News* (16 September 2015).

4 Cited in Adam Lucas, 'Revealed: The Extent of Job-Swapping Between Public Servants and Fossil Fuel Lobbyists' *The Conversation* (5 March 2018).

5 Kari Marie Norgaard, 'The Everyday Denial of Climate Change' [5 July 2012] The Bulletin of Atomic Scientists <https://thebulletin.org/2012/07/the-everyday-denial-of-climate-change/>

6 Ibid.

7 ESCR-Net, 'EarthRights International (ERI)' EarthRights International <>www.escr-net.org/member/earthrights-international-eri>

8 Gill H. Boehringer and Stuart Russell, 'Globalisation, Lawyers and the State' [September 2008] 33(3) Alternative Law Journal 169–172.

This has also been supplemented by advances in ecological jurisprudence, featuring the re-envisaging of judicial decisions from an "Earth-centred point."[9] As Michelle Maloney of the Australian Earth Laws Alliance explains, "right of nature" and "legal personhood for nature" laws seek to "shift the legal status of the natural world from being human property, or merely objects in the law, to being recognised as living entities in their own right and subjects of the law."[10]

The PPT as environmental formula

In 2018, an editorial in the *Journal of Energy & Natural Resources Law* confidently observed that there had been a veritable global "explosion" of tribunals and courts hearing lawsuits involving environmental issues.[11] Two figures have been key to this field: George (Rock) Pring and Cathering Pring. According to the Prings, this development has "dramatically" changed the "playing field for environmental justice around the world."[12] Legal practitioners have been urged to take such bodies seriously. "If these legal professionals are not familiar with ECTs, from both procedural and substantive perspectives, they risk not responsibly representing their clients' interests."[13] Old legal procedures are being revised, with ECTs engaged with ideas of sustainability as articulated by the United Nations and multi-level bodies.

This chapter, however, goes beyond the positive law dimension of such legal positivism, considering the history of ecological activism in the Australian context and efforts to protect the particular biodiversity of the Australian environment through community efforts. Of specific interest is the formula of PT as part of a broader protest and activist agenda. The international background inspiring and motivating Australian efforts with respect to such efforts is also considered, including the impediments of positive law and the traditional legal process. It considers efforts made by collective groups through the prism of ecological justice, viewed through a popular, people's lenses. The philosophy, agenda, and constitution of such bodies as the Rights of Nature Tribunal for Australia (RONA) in attempting to formulate and implement nature laws at the legislative, constitutional, and local level are also documented. Reflections on the influence and

9 N. Rogers and M. Maloney (eds), *Law as If Earth Really Mattered: The World Law Judgment Project* (1st Edition, Abingdon, Routledge, 2018).

10 Michelle Maloney, 'Rights of Nature 2018 – Information for Australian Communities, Australian Earth Laws Alliance' (20 June 2018), 3 <https://rightsofnature.org.au/wp-content/uploads/2018/06/Rights-of-Nature-2018_Information-for-Australian-communities_20-June-2018.pdf>

11 Don C. Smith, 'Environmental Courts and Tribunals: Changing Environmental and Natural Resources Law Around the Globe' [2018] 36(2) Journal of Energy & Natural Resources Law 137–140.

12 George (Rock) Pring and Cathering Pring, *Environmental Courts & Tribunals: A Guide to Policy Makers* (UN Environment Programme, 2016), 1.

13 Smith, (note 11).

findings made by such bodies in influencing the environment debate in Australia are also discussed.

The tribunal system, or more accurately the peoples' tribunal or inquiry, has become a mechanism to overcome, at least to some degree, the obstacles placed in the way of environmental reform and the limitations of positive law. These processes do not lessen the gravity of the alleged offences or depredations upon the environment but suggest alternative justice approaches in the field that refocus the language of legitimacy towards a popular means of redress. The source of legitimacy, in other words, is relocated, fashioned as a statement outside traditional norms of power and deliberation. As will be discussed in this chapter, established legal bodies such as the Australian High Court continue to demonstrate a latent conservatism, preferring parliament to legislate on more solid protections. To that end, peoples' tribunals on environmental protection become important and significant in addressing and publicising various lacunae in environmental-ecological regulations.

This is not all. Such tribunals are commonly associated with the experiments of the Russell Tribunal held in response to holding the United States and its allies to account for their conduct in the Vietnam War.[14] The PT functions as a response outside the customary positive law of states.[15] As the PT on Afghanistan acknowledged, its legitimacy does not derive from the legitimacy of states but from the opinions of the people themselves.[16] Their role has been significant in politicising community action in the popular judicial sphere in the face of perceived impotence: the broader public, not connected directly to the state, as judges, duly became gatherers of evidence and formulators of an approach more commonly associated with the inquisitorial method.

Historically, this technique of poking fun, and yet appropriating the power of its repudiation, has an extensive lineage going back to the 1930s when disempowered and fearful populaces pondered the emergence of the all-powerful totalitarian state.[17] Redress for injustices in such environments would have been, in a de jure sense, impossible, given the legitimising propensities of the state. During

14 Gabrielle Simm and Andrew Byrnes, 'International Peoples' Tribunals in Asia: Political Theatre, Juridical Farce or Meaningful Intervention?' [2014] 4 Asian Journal of International Law 103. For a broader discussion, see Andrew Byrnes and Gabrielle Simm (eds), *Peoples' Tribunals and International Law* (Cambridge: Cambridge University Press, 2018).

15 See Tribunale Permanente dei Popoli [Permanent Peoples' Tribunal], Afghanistan, Prime Sessionae, Stoccolma 1–3 Maggio 1981 [Afghanistan, First Session, Stockholm, 1–3 May 1981], Fondazione Internaziolane Lelio Basso per Il Dirrito e la Liberazione dei Popoli [Lelio Basso International Foundation for the Rights for the Rights and Liberation of Peoples], noted in Andrew Byrnes and Gabrielle Simm, 'Peoples' Tribunals, International Law and the Use of Force' [2013] 36(2) University of New South Wales Law Journal 711, fn. 83.

16 Noted in Byrnes and Simm, 'Peoples' Tribunals, International Law and the Use of Force' fn. 83.

17 See Louis Anthes, 'Public Deliberative Drama: The 1934 Mock Trial of Adolf Hitler for "Crimes Against Civilization"' [1998] 42 American Journal of Legal History 391; American Jewish Congress, *The Case of Civilization Against Hitlerism* (R.O. Ballou, 1934).

the Cold War, the PT format became a common form of address to abuses of power. As has been accurately noted,

> Whatever its problems, the Russell Tribunal did, however, provide inspiration, a model and theoretical justification for the holding of such tribunals – in which the actions of governments and others were subjected to legal scrutiny against international legal standards, as well as against other legal and non-legal norms.[18]

The issue of seeking environmental justice is a feature of the praxis behind PT. Organisations such as the Australian Earth Laws Alliance openly embrace a community driven philosophy of ecological protection, one which "advocates for Earth centred law, governance and ethics" which requires a "rethink [of] our legal, political, economic and governance systems so they support, rather than undermine the integrity and health of the Earth."[19] To that end, the alliance established a Tribunal Panel in assessing the application of such jurisprudence to the Australian context.[20]

Originally developed as a response to abuses of power, such tribunals have become varied and heterogenous entities. These have developed further authority, if not urgency, in light of the climate change debate and the threats posed by environmental calamities. These informal bodies can also be seen as incorporating ecological integrity into illegal instruments, one that, in the words of Prue Taylor,

> acknowledges human need to use natural resources, but goes further to recognise that humanity is an integral part of ecological systems. . . . A sense of moral responsibility towards nature will be an essential component of this endeavour." What Taylor insists upon here is recognising such ecological human rights that "give legal effect to moral obligations by expressing them in term of responsibilities to protect and enhance ecological systems, in acknowledgement of a range of values.[21]

Reasons for PT

The emerging attractions of environmental PT and bodies of inquiry in Australia must be seen within the broader social and environmental movements that have shaped the background of debates on environmental degradation. To understand

18 Byrnes and Simm, 'International Peoples' Tribunals: Their Nature, Practice and Significance' in Peoples' Tribunals and International Law, 13.

19 Australian Earth Laws Alliance, 'How We Work' <>www.earthlaws.org.au/how-we-work/>

20 Australian Earth Laws Alliance, 'Tribunal Panel' 2018 <>www.earthlaws.org.au/events/tribunal2018/panel/>

21 Prue Taylor, *An Ecological Approach to International Law: Responding to the Challenges of Climate Change* (Abingdon, Oxon, Routledge,1998), 106.

this approach requires an appraisal of the history of such ecological and environmental protest, one characterised by the mixed legacy of at times improbable legal victories and reactive legislation passed by the Commonwealth Parliament. Ecological attitudes, to that end, have been complex and mixed. "Australians," it has been noted, "tend to take a perverse pride in the harshness of their landscape and its challenging environments."[22] Juridical and legislative advances in Australia on the concept of environmental and ecological justice have often been tardy, lagging behind the position taken by advocates for the Rights of Nature that "the non-human world has just as much right to exist as humans do."[23] Efforts towards that vision have tended to be disparate. The Environmental Defenders of North Queensland, by way of example, launched a campaign in March 2013 "aimed at bestowing legal personality on the Great Barrier Reef World Heritage Area." To attain such a goal would result in vesting rights and duties including "the right to be free from lawful interference, and the rights to exist, persist and reproduce."[24]

Rights to nature and rights *of* nature are concepts far more in advance in the legislative settings of New Zealand. The concept of legal personhood, by way of example, has been extended to the Whanganui River. In accordance with New Zealand legal regulation, "rights and interests" have vested it with juridical character. In 2017, the local battle of the Maori tribe of Whanganui in the North Island to seek recognition of the river as an ancestor was recognised. Gerrard Albert, a lead negotiator behind the campaign, articulated the philosophy as such:

> We have fought to find an approximation in law so that all others can understand that from our perspective treating the river as living entity is the correct way to approach it, as in indivisible whole, instead of the traditional model for the last 100 year treating it from a perspective of ownership and management.[25]

In Australia, similar suggestions have been made about the Great Barrier Reef. As the Green Institute poses, "If BHP Billiton has rights, and can act as a legal person, why shouldn't the Great Barrier Reef?"[26]

22 Donald Stuart Green, *Australia, New Zealand and the Pacific: An Environmental History* (Santa Barbara, CA, ABC-CLIO, 2005), 1.

23 Maloney, (note 10), 4.

24 Friends of the Earth, 'Legal Personality for Great Barrier Reef' Environmental Defenders Office of North Queensland, Chain Reaction #120 (March 2013) <>www.foe.org.au/legal-personality-great-barrier-reef>

25 Eleanor Ainge Roy, 'New Zealand River Granted Same Legal Rights as Human Being' *The Guardian* (16 March 2017).

26 The Green Institute, *Rebalancing Rights: Communities, Corporations and Nature* (The Green Institute, 2019) <>www.greeninstitute.org.au/wp-content/uploads/2019/03/Green-Institute-Publication-Rebalancing-Rights.pdf>

Environmental courts vary in constitution, ensconced within "fully developed independent judicial branch bodies with highly trained staffs and large budgets all the way to simple, underfunded village ECs that handle environmental cases one day a month with rotating judges."[27] In the Australian context, they have been driven by community advocates, academics and practitioners, often motivated by interdisciplinary considerations.[28] They tend to know that influence is, at first instance, limited. Strong lobbies and influences friendly to coal and non-renewables feature in the struggle. Evidentiary and regulatory frameworks made claims difficult to succeed. That said, ecological advancements in Australia have also been given encouragement through court battles featuring the implied constitutional right to freedom of communication on political subjects.[29] But an understanding as to why PT have an invaluable role to play in the Australian context can be gathered by the limitations of High Court jurisprudence.

In 2017, former Greens Senator Bob Brown and Jessica Hoyt won a High Court case which invalidated the *Workplace (Protection from Protesters) Act 2014 (Tas)*.[30] The act criminalised forms of protest construed as interfering with any "business activity," "business premises" or business access areas. The ambit of this was broad enough to cover forestry and other industrial activities taking place on public or private land. Despite finding those provisions of the act criminalising protest invalid, the limitations of legal action in Australia favouring environmental protection were also exposed. The High Court, for instance, found that the aims of the Act were legitimate; it failed, rather, on the issue of "structured proportionality."[31] Laws might still single out protesters in a legitimate way, even though the Tasmanian law in question was "enacted against a background where protesters, or at least some of them, were perceived to be those persons, or groups, who would cause damage or disrupt economic activities during protests of particular kinds." The Act itself was simply disproportionate, vague, broad, a "blunt instrument to achieve" the purpose of imposing sanctions. To presume, however, an actual right to engage in environmental protest would be a long bow to draw indeed.

The efforts by environmental groups to seek redress through the court process haven been patchy in terms of success, suggesting the need for other avenues for environmental conservation. The Australian Conservation Foundation's efforts to invalidate decisions concerning the proposed establishment of a resort in central Queensland in the late 1970s failed in the High Court for want of legal standing. The ACF, in other words, could not demonstrate sufficiently that it had a special interest in the matter above that of other members of the public to warrant proceeding with the action. Environmental administrative acts in of

27 Pring and Pring, (note 12), 13.
28 See, for instance, the NSW Land and Environment Court <>www.lec.justice.nsw.gov.au/>
29 *Lange v Australian Broadcasting Corporation* (1997) 145 ALR 96.
30 *Brown v Tasmania* [2017] HCA 43 (13 October 2017).
31 For problems in this approach, see *Clubb v Edwards; Preston v Avery* [2019] HCA 11.

their own did not create enforceable rights for private individuals.[32] It was also acknowledged that other jurisdictions (the United States and Canada), tended to be more flexible in determining what constituted a "real concern" for those seeking legal redress in environmental cases.[33]

Australia has, admittedly, progressed in a fashion since the late 1970s. The Franklin River Dam project in Tasmania stands a highpoint, featuring boycotts, embargoes, trespass, and general acts of mass civil disobedience culminating in actual political change.[34] "The proposed dam was halted," recalls activist Michael Connors. "It was a victory enabled by protest, politics and law. . . . It bruised a working class convinced that cheap energy was the key to jobs – and I know that such feelings remain today."[35] In 1983, Launceston resident Kathleen Maxwell would note in a letter to Fairfax Press about the ample and extensive resistance of some 1,300 people charged with offences associated with treading on the land of the Hydro Electric Commission in South-West Tasmania. "The Apple Isle and the Banana State now have similar images in eyes of the rest of Australians – a fruity disregard for the rights of individuals."[36] The police, however, were left in a bind on how best to proceed with them, dropping many prosecutions as a result. The point, however, had been made: outcomes were possible in the Australian political process using protest.

The High Court case with respect to environmental protection was the culmination of such activism.[37] That said, the validity of such laws did not derive from locally enshrined protections specific to environmental protection but the external affairs power relevant to making and enforcing treaties in Australian law. The 1983 decision was hardly an enlightened decision; it simply affirmed that the Commonwealth could pass legislation protecting the Tasmanian Wilderness World Heritage Area pursuant to the external affairs power of the Australian Constitution. The content of the law was less relevant than the link to international conventions. The Tasmanian state government's attempt to continue the dam failed by a single vote. There was, on the judicial bench, no environmental awakening, per se.

Since then, Australian laws, and broader regulations on the subject have been passed to ensure the protection of biodiversity and the environment, covering world heritage and national heritage properties.[38] Included in this

32 *Australian Conservation Foundation v Commonwealth* [1979] HCA 1; (1980) 146 CLR 493, per J. Per Gibbs, para. 8.

33 *Baker v Carr* (1962) US 186; *Sierra Club v Morton* (1972) 405 US 727, 731–740; noted in *Australian Conservation Foundation*, at para. 41, per J. Aickin.

34 Clive Hamilton, *What Do We Want? The Story of Protest in Australia* (Australia, NLA Publishing, 2016); K. Pink, *Through Hells Gates* (Burnie, Advocate Newspaper, 1984); 'Franklin Dam Protest Cycle' *The Canberra Times* (17 December 1982), 9.

35 Michael Connors, 'How the Franklin Protesters Won the Fight' *New Matilda* (9 December 2012).

36 Kathleen Maxwell, 'The Franklin Dam Issue' Letter to the Editor, *Canberra Times* (28 May 1982), 2.

37 *Commonwealth v Tasmania* ("Tasmanian Dam case") [1983] HCA 21; (1983) 158 CLR 1.

38 *Environment Protection and Biodiversity Conservation Act 1999* (Cth).

are various listed wetlands under the Ramsar Convention, threated species and ecological communities, marine areas, the Great Barrier Reef Marine Park and migratory species. These items of legislation tend to betray a fundamental bias: they do not vest rights in members of the public or groups to conduct challenges, but rather place the onus here on entities keen to undertake actions that might be detrimental to the environment; they must seek approval through the relevant Australian environment minister, a process that is dogged by political interest and consideration.[39] Structural limitations, in other words, remain in asserting legal grounds for challenging abusive environmental practices.

Other notable legal cases testing the legal application of Australian environmental laws have been specifically significant. The Flying Fox Case involved the efforts of conservationist Dr. Carol Booth to use the *Environment Protection and Biodiversity Conservation Act 1999* (Cth) to prevent the killing of thousands of Spectacled Flying Foxes (*Pteropus conspicillatus*) on a North Queensland lychee farm.[40] State and Commonwealth regulators refused to prevent the killings caused by electric grids running down the lines of lychee trees. Branson J of the Federal Court did grant an injunction at trial, satisfied that the operation of the grid on an annual basis would halve the population of Spectacled Flying Foxes in less than five years. "Such an impact would be sufficient to render the species endangered within that time frame."[41]

While such curial examples demonstrate inroads into conventional legal conservatism, the scope for change remains narrow, necessitating other, more diverse efforts to ensure preservation and conservation of environmental systems. If anything, such instances of active environmental consciousness as the Franklin Dam protest have caused despondence on the part of observers claiming that Australians are now reluctant to engage in civil disobedience when it comes to protecting Nature.[42] Such a view might be unduly pessimistic. Broader, more generalised community activism has culminated in the establishment of various informal bodies which have sought to test the existing legal and jurisprudential nature of environmental justice. As former Australian High Court justice Michael Kirby explains, albeit in the context of how human rights abuses are dealt with more broadly,

> Humble people, in countries that cannot secure the action of their governments, which are often the perpetrators of terrible wrongs and human rights

39 Australian Government, Department of Environment, Matters of National Significance, Significant impact guidelines 1.1, Environment Protection and Biodiversity Conservation Act 1999 (Canberra, Commonwealth of Australia, 2013) <>www.environment.gov.au/system/files/resources/42f84df4-720b-4dcf-b262-48679a3aba58/files/nes-guidelines_1.pdf>

40 *Booth v Bosworth* [2001] FCA 1453 (17 October 2001).

41 Ibid., per J. Branson.

42 Connors, (note 35).

abuses . . . they can't get action but they have not lost their voice, they have not lost the dignity of their voice.[43]

Australian community groups have tapped into a broader international movement such as the Global Environmental Justice Project. The Jesuit Social Services, by way of example, has expressed an interest in ecological justice approaches since 2008. The organisation makes a specific point of linking domains of engagement. "In an increasingly complex era of climate crisis, environmental degradation and rising social equality, new challenges towards building a just society are appearing."[44] Special attention is given to the position of indigenous populations, their dispossession. "Viewing the circumstances of Aboriginal and Torres Strait Islander people through an ecological lens highlights how social disadvantage and marginalisation are caused by the loss of relationships with country."[45]

The Australian Centre for the Rights of Nature has spearheaded a campaign to acknowledge the importance of recognising the legal rights of the Great Barrier Reef.[46] This supplements the expertise in environmental law outlining a range of potential reforms to environmental laws.[47] The "goal of environmental law," insists the Australian Panel of Experts on Environmental Law (APEEL), "should be derived from a broader societal goal."[48] Principles yet to carry weight in Australia – that of environmental governance being flexible and responsive, environmental restoration and the principle of non-regression, should be taken seriously.[49] One technical paper by APEEL stresses the value of environmental democracy, requiring the involvement of a participating, informed citizenry in government processes and governance of the environmental commons. Along with this comes the necessary "enforceable right to a clean and healthy environment." As such, Australian laws remained in of themselves patchwork matters, and of "limited effectiveness."[50] There was, as yet, no firm legally based concept of the "commons" in Australian environmental governance, one covering biodiversity, water, air, minerals, climate and ecological systems.

43 Australian Human Rights Institute, 'New Book Documents Peoples' Tribunals as Avenue for Activism and Justice' (16 May 2018) <>www.humanrights.unsw.edu.au/news/new-book-documents-peoples-tribunals-avenue-activism-and-justice>

44 Jesuit Social Services, 'Ecological Justice: Expanding the Conversation' (February 2018) <http://jss.org.au/wp-content/uploads/2018/02/Ecological-Justice-Expanding-the-Conversation.pdf>

45 Ibid., 6.

46 Interview with AELA convenor, Michelle Maloney, ABC Drive (North Queensland) (22 August 2018) <>www.abc.net.au/radio/programs/north-qld-drive/drive/10125168>

47 The Australian Panel of Experts on Environmental Law (APEEL), *The Foundations of Environmental Law: Goals, Objects, Principles and Norms* (Technical Paper, 2017) <https://static1.squarespace.com/static/56401dfde4b090fd5510d622/t/58e5f852d1758eb801c117d8/1491466330447/APEEL_Foundations_for_environmental_law.pdf>

48 Ibid., 3.

49 Ibid., Recommendation 1.3, 4.

50 Ibid. See specifically Recommendation 8.1.

Such movements in Australian ecological activism have set the scene for the establishment of PT with a specific ecological-environmental focus. What follows is an overview of some of these bodies, their constitution and broader contribution to the body of ecological deliberations. These are of recent vintage and consider various heterogenous experiments in the field. Some, such as the People's Nuclear Tribunal from 2016, are directed to the implications to ecological law and justice arising from the conduct of states in war and peace. Others, such as RONA, deal and have directly dealt with environmental matters as their specific concern.

The People's Nuclear Tribunal

In 2016, the International People's Tribunal on Nuclear Weapons and the Destruction of Human Civilisation held at the University of Sydney and co-sponsored by the Centre for Peace and Conflict Studies as part of its Human Survival Project, the Sydney Centre for International Law, People for Nuclear Disarmament and Aotearoa Lawyers for Peace (New Zealand), handed down a judgement affirming that that using or threatening to use nuclear weapons was illegal. The Tribunal was also convinced by the gravity of the submissions to "convict" leaders of the nine nuclear-armed States for war crimes, crimes against humanity, crimes against peace, crimes of threatening, planning and preparing acts which would constitute genocide, ecocide and omnicide.[51] The entire tribunal process – the adducing of evidence by community experts, broader community participation, and the decision reached by members – showed the significance of the PT format not merely in trying states more broadly over the issue of possessing and potentially using nuclear weapons, but the environmental consequences of doing so.

The proceedings were also significant in attempting to identify a firmer basis from which environmental law and principles of accountability for degrading ecological systems in war could be determined. The judgement is cognisant not merely of the humanitarian dimension of nuclear weapons, but their broader, irreversibly destructive impact on the environment. The tribunal's reasoning provides an important community effort in seeking to clarify, and logically extend the commentary and opinions of international jurisprudence into a broader civic setting. In the words of Keith Suter, one of the tribunal members, the 1996 International Court of Justice ruling "generally" found that the threat or use of nuclear weapons was illegal.[52] "Since then, the increased awareness of the catastrophic impact of any use of nuclear weapons, and the strengthening of international humanitarian, human rights and environmental law, render any threat or use of nuclear weapons illegal."[53]

51 Unfold Zero, 'People's Tribunal on Nuclear Weapons Convicts Leaders – Tribute to Tribunal Visionary' (17 August 2016) <>www.unfoldzero.org/peoples-tribunal-on-nuclear-weapons-convicts-leaders-tribute-to-tribunal-visionary/>

52 See ICJ Advisory Opinion, 'Legality of the Threat or Use of Nuclear Weapons' [1996] ICJ 2, para. 35: "Ionizing radiation has the potential to damage the future environment, food and marine ecosystem, and to cause genetic defects and illness in future generations."

53 Quoted in Unfold Zero, (note 51).

The destructive nature of such weapons was unequivocally accepted; deploying them in any theatre would lead to the destruction of whole species, not to mention the elimination of the human species itself. The 2016 judgement also acknowledged the dangers of fallout effects and the prolongation of suffering to species caused by nuclear winter. The necessity for environmental protection under international law, drawing from evidence submitted by prosecution expert witness Steven Starr, Director of the Clinical Laboratory Science Programme, was accepted as essential.[54] "The research," summarised Starr,

> predicts that immense firestorms, produced by nuclear war fought with these weapons could lift 150 million tons of smoke into the stratosphere. There it rapidly would block the 70 percent of sunlight from reaching the Northern Hemisphere and 35 percent of sunlight from reaching the Southern Hemisphere.[55]

The prosecution also noted in its case that such weapons, even if used in a localised or regional conflict, were also in breach of the "precautionary principle" evident in the World Charter for Nature adopted by the UN General Assembly in 1982, namely, that

> Activities which are likely to pose a significant risk to nature shall be preceded by an exhaustive examination; their proponents shall demonstrate that expected benefits outweigh potential damage to nature, and where potential adverse effects are not fully understood, the activities should not proceed.[56]

The material on emerging frameworks of international environmental law was also noted in the evidence of Professor Emilie Gaillard of the University of Caen, Normandy, taking cognisance of the principle of ecocide, and along with that the emergence of such concepts as ecoviolence and ecocriminality.[57] Gaillard's valuable amicus submission proved expansive, noting the genealogy of the term across a range of international legal instruments.[58]

54 International Peoples Tribunal on Nuclear Powers and the Destruction of Human Civilisation, University of Sydney, Australia (7–8 July 2016) Tribunal Decision, para. 108 <>www.global-directions.com/ipt.pdf>

55 Tribunal Decision, para. 110.

56 Ibid., para. 112. Further documents affirming the precautionary principle can also be found in the Montreal Protocol, the Rio Declaration and the Kyoto Protocol.

57 L. Westra, *Globalization, Violence and World Governance* (Brill, 2011); J. P. Stoett, *Global Ecopolitics: Crisis, Governance and Justice* (Toronto, University of Toronto Press, 2012); T. F. Homer-Dixon and J Blitt, *Ecoviolence: Links Among Environment, Population and Security* (Rowman & Littlefield, 1998); Emilie Gaillard, Amicus submission to the International Peoples' Tribunal on the Nuclear Powers and the Destruction of Human Civilisation, Emerging International Law: Future Generations and Ecocide, Hearings (7 July 2016) <>www.unfoldzero.org/wp-content/uploads/Emerging-law-.EGAILLARD.pdf>

58 See, for instance, the Convention on the Prohibition of Military or Any Other Hostile Use of Environmental Modification Techniques (ENDMOD), 1976, Article 1; Rio Declaration, Principle 24; ICJ Advisory Opinion, para. 30.

People's Tribunals and Earth laws

More specific tribunals have directed attention to the idea of Earth Laws as practice and critique in Australian environmental practice, some of which feature Australia as a subject of broader inquiry.[59] But a few local efforts are worth enumerating, notably those doing what Maloney describes as exploring "how ancient and emerging ecological law and governance systems are working in the 21st century."[60] The Rights of Nature Tribunal constitutes the Regional Chamber of the International Rights of Nature Tribunal, deliberating over issues specific to its remit. Proceedings have involved, amongst other things, hearings touching on recognising the legal rights of the Great Barrier Reef in Brisbane on 22 October 2016 involving "citizens and Earth lawyers."[61] The aim of the tribunal was to

> provide an important forum for citizens of Australia to speak on behalf of the Earth community; to challenge the current legal system's failure to protect the health of the natural world; to highlight the role that government agencies and corporations play a part in destroying the Earth community and to recommend that citizens would like to see happen, to protect and restore Australia's precious ecosystems and wider Earth community.[62]

Its format was patterned on rules developed by the Global Alliance for the Rights of Nature, with panel judges making recommendations drawn from citizenry, legal and scientific expertise.

The body of deliberations in these sessions resort, significantly, to the legitimising grounding of the Universal Declaration of Rights of Mother Earth formulated at Cochabamba, Bolivia in 2010.[63] The tribunal structure was much in keeping with the international push in seeing nature as having, in of itself, immutable rights, of which the International Tribunal for the Rights of Nature was its offshoot. Such bodies were, in accordance with their spirit, "created to provide systemic Rights of Nature based alternatives to the false solutions and failed negotiations of governing Nation States."[64]

59 For instance, the Permanent Peoples' Tribunal on Human Rights, Fracking, and Climate Change (14–18 May 2018) <www.peoplestribunalongas.org/2018/01/25/media-release-re-ppt/> See also Michelle Maloney, 'Building an Alternative Jurisprudence for the Earth: The International Rights of Nature Tribunal' [Fall 2016] 41 Vermont Law Review 129–142.

60 Maloney, (note 10), 3.

61 Australian Peoples' Tribunal for Community and Nature's Rights, 'Cases Heart at the 2016 Rights of Nature Tribunal Australia' <https://tribunal.org.au/aptribunal/2016-tribunal/> Tribunal rulings, to date, have yet to be published.

62 Rights of Nature Tribunal Australia 2016 (22 October 2016), Banco Court, Brisbane. Overview available at <http://majala.com.au/news/2016-rights-of-nature-tribunal-australia>

63 Universal Declaration of Rights of Mother Earth, Formulated at the World People's Congress on Climate Change and the Rights of Mother Earth, Cochahamba, Bolivia (22 April 2010) <https://therightsofnature.org/universal-declaration/>

64 Global Alliance for the Rights of Nature, 'What Is an International Rights of Nature Tribunal?' <http://therightsofnature.org/rights-of-nature-tribunal/>

Other environmental hearings have also featured, variously, the Mardoowarra/ Fitzroy River (Western Australia); Australian forests (with waterways and connected systems); the Great Artesian Basin and its contamination and depletion of groundwater, the Atmospheric Commons and the Great Barrier Reef. The countering parties have been, in turn, the Federal and Western Australian governments, the coal seam gas industry and the fossil fuel industry. In the Mardoowarra/Fitzroy River case, as with others reviewed by RONA, was stressed that participants were drawing their legitimacy form "their rights, and the rights of the natural world as set out in the Universal Declarations of Rights of Mother Earth."

The RONA sessions of 2016 considered the calamitous implications of Australian mistreatment of specific areas of the Australian environment, stressing threats to biodiversity and ecology in each of the hearings. Environmentalist Sarah Moles warned about the depletion of the Great Artesian Basin, Australia's only reliable source of constant water.[65] Environmental engineer Gavin Mudd encouraged the taking of steps to protect unique biodiversity in the water systems of the Basin.[66] Discussions before the tribunal also pondered methods of changing environmental laws, be it through street protest or an actual change in the politics of Canberra proper.[67]

On October 27, 2018, another cognate body of the PPT environmental movement considered ecological degradation arising from industrial scale agriculture. The Australian People's Tribunal for Community and Nature's Rights, as with RONA's previous hearings, held an open session to the public in Banco Court on George Street in Brisbane. The Tribunal itself was constituted in a hybrid manner typical in seeking a broader, holistic perspective on justice. Legally trained individuals and indigenous figures were present: legal representatives Gwynn MacCarrick, Gill Boehringer and Michelle Maloney, Ross Williams of the Bindal/Juru First Nations, and Mary Graham, a representative of the Kombumerri First Nations people.[68]

The 2018 session placed strong emphasis on the detrimental impacts of agriculture "on the living world" with a view of focusing on community opinions.[69] The APTCNR was gloomy about the severity of ecological effects wrought by climate change, insisting, in advertising for submissions, about the dangers it posed.

> As climate change increases the severity of droughts, heat waves and water shortages, we need to examine the real cost of current agricultural practices and find effective ways to grow food and fibre in Australia, which don't destroy the foundations of our ecosystems and communities.[70]

65 Presentation available at <>www.youtube.com/watch?v=3HflZUL0U_4>

66 Presentation available at <https://youtu.be/D0Np_xVd7lE>

67 Discussion with Jo Bragg, presentation at <https://youtu.be/D0Np_xVd7lE>

68 Australian Peoples' Tribunal for Community and Nature's Rights, 'Citizen's Inquiry: The Impacts of Industrial Scale Agriculture on Community and Nature's Rights' (27 October) Banco Court, Brisbane <>www.earthlaws.org.au/events/tribunal2018/>

69 Ibid., Closing Remarks <>www.youtube.com/watch?time_continue=47&v=MN-O6L4jDJk>

70 Australian Peoples' Tribunal for Community and Nature's Rights, <https://tribunal.org.au/a-p-tribunals/2018-tribunal/>

The Australian example is particularly problematic, given continued, and intense efforts in land clearing deemed some of the most intense on the planet. Previously functioning food systems were subsequently disrupted by the introduction agricultural features: fencing, cattle, sheep and impacts on water systems.[71] Aggressive instances of soil erosion had resulted. The judging committee found instances of ecocide on the Brigalow belt bioregion, an area characterised by diverse combination of geological, soil and landform patterns.[72]

Tribunal members acknowledged the global economic system and the detrimental interactions between capitalism and the environment. Australia, claimed the World Wildlife Fund for Nature, ranks along with the Amazon, Borneo, the Congo Basin and other "threatened regions" in that regard.[73] "In Australia, land clearing for grazing has led to significant ecological impacts and largescale irrigation for crops has had a devastating impact on many of our water systems – rivers, streams and groundwater."[74]

Following traditional evidentiary and informal formulae, case studies adduced by expert witnesses focused on the detrimental effects on the water systems, with invitees asked to delve into specific details of environmental degradation. Dr. Bruce Lindsay of Environmental Justice Australia was keen to focus on the issue of water governance in the Murray Darling Basin. Industrialisation of the basin (weirs, damns, irrigation extraction, drainage schemes) and the broader "engineering of the landscape" had led to modifications of the eco-hydrological nature of the system.[75]

In this current year (2019), work continues in another incarnation of the Citizens' Inquiry into the Health of the Darling River and Menindee Lakes. This effort is a further example of community participation and tribunal work in action, the outcome of a petition to the Australian People's Tribunal in early 2018 to consider supporting "communities affected by the declining health of the Darling River."[76] The hearings are scheduled as a special annex of the Australian

71 Ibid., Closing Remarks.

72 For information on the region, see Queensland Government, Brigalow Belt (BRB) Region, WetlandInfo (2017) <https://wetlandinfo.des.qld.gov.au/wetlands/facts-maps/bioregion-brigalow-belt-brb/>; Paul S. Sattler and Rebecca Williams (eds), *The Conservation Status of Queensland's Bioregional Ecosystems* (Brisbane, Environmental Protection Agency, Queensland Government, 1999).

73 The claim is made in WWF, 'Tree-Clearing in Australia' Fact Sheet (May 2017) <>www.wwf.org.au/ArticleDocuments/355/pub-fact-sheet-tree-clearing-in-australia-23may17.pdf.aspx>

74 About the 2018 Tribunal Session <https://tribunal.org.au/aptribunal/2018-tribunal/#about>

75 Bruce Lindsay, 'Case Study 2: The Impacts of the Industrial Scale Agriculture on the Murray Darling Basin, with a Focus on the Darling River and Menindee Lakes' Presentation to Australian Peoples' Tribunal for Community and Nature's Rights (27 October 2018) <https://youtu.be/PAhNNCbd-vU>

76 Australian Peoples' Tribunal for Community and Nature's Rights, 'More Details About the 2019 Citizens' Inquiry into the Health or the Daring River and Menindee Lakes' 2019 <https://tribunal.org.au/aptribunal/darling-menindee/more-info/#why-created>

People's Tribunal for Community and Nature's Rights.[77] The formula here, as with previous examples discussed, involves discussions and submissions in the presence of an "unbiased forum" to share stories of community members about the Darling River. Such proceedings further the ecological project and continue to publicise breaches of earth laws and misdemeanours against the environment.

The influence of Australia's peoples' tribunals

Australian environmental consciousness, ranging from classic protest methods to legal action in traditional juridical forums, has been piqued. Recent initiatives include such public campaigns as a "war against plastic" instituted by various groups, including the national broadcaster, the ABC.[78] Climate change marches featuring campaigns with protesting school children have also stimulated spirited, and in some cases aggressive debate.[79] In late 2018, thousands went on strike, propelled by the actions of Greta Thunberg in Sweden, who insisted on taking time off to spend time in front of the Swedish parliament in an effort to stir action.[80]

The PT system can be considered a vital part of this galvanising movement, providing an essential, public mechanism by which convictions can be aired and conduct of the powerful examined in the Australian context. Despite lacking the traditional bite of enforcement, the urgings suggested at such gatherings – an acknowledgement of ecological devastation, a call to cease such activities with accompanying restorative measures, and possible compensation – provide their own variant of justice for the environment.[81]

The idea of such PT, powered by less rigid and restrictive mechanisms offered by the state, has offered Australian activists and advocates for environmental justice an avenue that has proliferated. It features a series of interrelated and connected approaches to ecological justice, a point deemed ever more pressing given the depredations of climate change and environmental decline. The challenges posed by governments sympathetic to the mineral resource sector and sceptical of climate change have given such approaches an even greater urgency.

77 2019 Citizens' Inquiry into the Health of the Darling River and Menindee Lakes, A Special Hearing of the Australian Peoples' Tribunal for Community and Nature's Rights (30 January–30 April 2019) <https://tribunal.org.au/aptribunal/darling-menindee/>

78 Dom Knight, 'Australia: The Country That Went to War Over Plastic Bags' *The Guardian* (4 August 2018); ABC, War on Waste <>www.abc.net.au/ourfocus/waronwaste/>

79 Nick Baker, 'Australia's Young Climate Change Activists to Strike Again – and People Are Listening' *SBS News* (12 March 2019).

80 ABC News, 'Students Strike for Climate Change Protests, Defying Calls to Stay in School' (1 November 2018).

81 See Lisa J. Mead, Michelle Maloney, Phoebe Bishop and Cassie Heaslip, 'In the Permanent Peoples' Tribunal Session on Human Rights, Fracking and Climate Change, On Petition for an Advisory Opinion on the Question of the Impacts of Fracking and Climate Change' (31 March 2018), 15 <http://earthlawyers.org/wp-content/uploads/2018/04/PPT-Natures-Rights-Final-Submission-31.03.18.pdf>

The push towards enshrining principles of rights of nature in Australian law has not fallen on deaf ears. Such efforts have received modest representative support from legislators in the Australian federal parliament. Greens Senator Marheen Faraqi, on 21 August 2018, told the Senate that Australia should recognise the concept of Rights of Nature in law.

> Nature has an intrinsic value, it is not a commodity to be used and abused. Let's enshrine the rights of nature in law to protect Australia's natural wonders like the Great Barrier Reef, the Great Artesian Basin and the Murray Darling system from greedy exploitation.[82]

Politicians at the state level, notably Michael Berkman, a member of the Queensland parliament, have lamented the deficiencies in his state regarding the recently passed *Human Rights Act* in not recognising an explicit right to a safe and healthy environment.[83] Despite such regret, the aims of the PT formula to focus on earth-centred jurisprudence, with its emphasis on active citizens marshalled against the limitations of positive law, are being gradually realised.

82 Mehreen Faruqi, Speech, Australian Senate (21 August 2018) <https://rightsofnature.org.au/2018/08/24/greens-senator-rights-of-nature/>

83 Discussion in Benedict Coyne, 'A Day of Celebration: The Human Rights Act' *Independent Australia* (10 March 2019).

9 People's Tribunals and how they examine childhood sexual abuse

Alan Collins

Introduction

The United Kingdom Child Sex Abuse People's Tribunal ("UKCSAPT")[1] was established by survivors of childhood sexual abuse[2] and their supporters.

UKCSAPT was an independent body that emerged from the need of survivors to be heard and in response to their determination to secure government and parliamentary acknowledgement of the extent of sexual abuse of children in the UK.

There was a widespread perception in the survivor community, and in society generally, that successive UK governments had failed to properly address and investigate child sexual abuse in institutional contexts, both because of political expediency as well as cultural attitudes and misconceptions about its extent. There had been a series of high-profile sexual abuse cases which exposed serious offending by individuals in the public eye, and this resulted in serious concern that they had been effectively allowed to commit offences because of their perceived position in society. Consequentially there was considerable distrust of the "establishment," which, whether this was ill-founded or justified, meant that the UK government's attempt to establish its own inquiry *viz* Independent Inquiry into Child Sexual Abuse (IICSA) was problematic.[3] The IICSA was established to examine how the country's institutions handled their duty of care to protect children from sexual abuse. It was set up after investigations into high-profile sexual abuse scandals revealed widespread abuse, with allegations stretching back over decades, concerning prominent media and political figures, and inadequate safeguarding by institutions and organisations responsible for child welfare. Originally IICSA was intended to be a panel inquiry supported by experts, similar to the Hillsborough Independent Panel.[4] However, after strenuous objec-

1 The official website of the UKCSAPT can be found at <https://ukcsapt.wordpress.com/>

2 A child is sexually abused when they are forced or persuaded to take part in sexual activities (they need not be physically forced for sexual abuse to occur).

3 The official website of the Independent Inquiry into Child Sex Abuse can be found at <>www.iicsa.org.uk/>

4 The Report of the Hillsborough Independent Panel can be found at <>www.gov.uk/government/publications/the-report-of-the-hillsborough-independent-panel>

tions related to the panel's scope and its independence from those being investigated, and the resignation of its first two intended chairs, it was reconstituted in February 2015 as a statutory inquiry under the Inquiries Act 2005, giving it greatly increased powers to compel sworn testimony and to examine classified information. Nevertheless it was dogged by ongoing controversy which impeded the ability to attract survivor participation.[5]

In September 2014, a meeting was called among a group of survivors, lawyers, and activists to discuss an independent movement to address child sex abuse. Given the distrust of government and the lack of confidence in the IICSA, it was suggested that a PT with a popular mandate be established to address the needs and realities of survivors with a view to identifying comprehensive and sustainable solutions to the scourge against children and society.

UKCSAPT was officially launched in December 2014 with an initial awareness campaign aimed at publicising its establishment and mandate among the survivor community. Its steering committee decided that in view of limited resources, the focus should be on allegations of complicity and cover-up of child sexual abuse by institutions and the responsibility of those in authority for these failings. The mandate was defined as follows:

- Independently raise potential avenues of inquiry related to the context, nature, and depth of institutional child sex abuse;
- Provide a safe space free from interference and scrutiny to allow survivors, supporters, and witnesses to speak freely regarding institutional child sex abuse;
- Independently establish how institutional policies and judicial systems have failed survivors and failed to protect the best interests of the child; and
- Independently determine and discuss which constructive remedies could best address institutional child sexual abuse and the allegations brought forth.

It was pursued in the expectation that an independent panel of experts would sit as a tribunal and hear the survivors' accounts and concerns about the sexual abuse that has afflicted their lives, produce an objective report that articulated its findings, and make recommendations to government in line with the mandate.

The steering committee appointed four experts to sit as an independent panel to examine the evidence and apply the terms of the mandate and produce a report.[6] The panel would sit as a tribunal ("Tribunal") and was assisted by two lawyers.[7]

5 Tom Parmenter, 'Abuse Survivors Lose Faith in Goddard Inquiry' *Sky News* (25 May 2015) <https://news.sky.com/story/abuse-survivors-lose-faith-in-goddard-inquiry-10358187>

6 Payam Akhavan LLB (York University), LLM, SJD Professor of International Law at McGill University; Heather Bacon Chartered Clinical Psychologist (retired); Catherine McCall, a Licenced Marriage and Family Therapist and Clinical Fellow in the American Association for Marriage and Family Therapy; and Basia Spalek, BSc (Hons), MA, PhD. Professor of Conflict Transformation at the University of Derby.

7 Alan Collins solicitor-advocate and partner Hugh James, London; and Regina Paulose JD LLM.

The resulting report was delivered to the UK parliament and government bodies in March 2016.[8]

Methodology for the gathering of facts

The most pressing challenge was to obtain evidence from survivors who would need to be convinced that providing testimony would be worthwhile. In February 2015 there was an open call made for confidential submissions by survivors and others through the UKCSAPT website and social media. The submissions focused on perpetration, complicity and allegations of cover-up of child sex abuse.

This process was managed by the panel's two lawyers. Survivors and other witnesses were given the opportunity to call a UK telephone number to have an initial consultation, followed by an appointment either to meet in person or over Skype in order to tell their stories.

Once the submission was taken, the survivor or witness was able to read the statement to confirm its veracity and accuracy.

All persons that participated in the submission process were informed of the following:

- a The content of their submissions were strictly confidential and were for the tribunal only;
- b Their submissions would be anonymised;
- c The lawyers involved in taking the submissions would treat them as protected by lawyer-client privilege, and not discuss the contents with anyone on the Steering Committee or anyone else related to UKCSAPT;
- d Given the sensitive nature of the submissions process, the survivor or witness was free to narrate their story completely at their own discretion. If further details were required, they were informed that follow-up questions would be asked, but that if they felt uncomfortable at any time, they could withdraw their participation in the process.

Submissions were closed in August 2015, to allow for their collation and analysis.[9] Following receipt of this information, hearings were held on 2 and 3 October 2015 in London at which some survivors and witnesses gave live

8 Independent Panel United Kingdom Child Sex Abuse People's Tribunal, Preliminary Report, 'Healing and justice in defence of the survivors of child sexual abuse', 2016 <>www.hughjames.com/wp-content/uploads/2016/03/Healing-and-Justice-in-defence-of-the-survivors-of-child-sexual-abuse-preliminary-report-of-the-United-Kingdom-Child-Sexual-Abuse-Peoples-Tribunal.pdf>

9 The Tribunal received 24 written submissions: 18 from survivors, four from professionals, one from a journalist (described as a "whistleblower"), and one from the administrator of a charity that serves a survivor support group. Four witnesses testified in person in addition to giving their written testimony. The witnesses included nine female and 11 male victims. The age when the abuse started ranged from earliest childhood to 14 years. The oldest survivor was now in his sixties. The youngest was 23.

testimony to and answered questions posed by the Tribunal, after which its report was completed.

The Tribunal was conscious that it did not sit as a court of law and consequently did not apply strict evidential rules in arriving at its conclusions. The focus of its inquiry was to establish on a preliminary basis patterns of child sexual abuse and institutional failure, based on a sampling of testimony, research studies, and the expert judgement of the panel.[10] In this regard, although there is no way to determine the veracity of the testimony in some cases, it opined that there was no reason to believe that the patterns emerging therefrom are not representative of survivors in general. The patterns recognised in the testimony corresponded in the panel's opinion with those found in larger research studies, such as such as how children become vulnerable, circumstances whereby abusers gain access to children, and a range of impediments to the victims' ability to access the criminal justice system.

Findings

The UKCSAPT found that the UK Governmental institutions failed to provide survivors of sexual abuse with meaningful opportunities for either healing or justice, and that the mental health needs of survivors in the UK are not being met.

It made a series of recommendations including the establishment of a permanent and open forum for victims to share experiences and give evidence, better links between mental health services and police investigations, and training for police and judiciary professionals on the effects of undisclosed sexual abuse.

The final report made several findings. Some of the key findings were that there are clear links between children rendered vulnerable by institutional failures and predatory abuse on an organised scale, even if these links often remain obscure; that governmental institutions have failed to provide survivors with meaningful opportunities for either healing or justice, further police and other authorities often lack the training to understand the complex reasons for the inability of survivors to immediately disclose a history of abuse; and without far-reaching changes in institutional culture and practices, the sexual abuse of children will continue to be a significant scourge in the United Kingdom.

The report also outlined a series of recommendations for improving reporting and mental health provision, and access to justice for victims were made, including:

- A permanent, government-funded popular tribunal should be established to enable survivors to come forward and tell their stories.
- Survivors giving evidence should be assigned an advocate to assist their access to justice.

10 Some of the witnesses were only able to give a partial account of their experiences whereas others were very detailed. The panel reported that accounts as powerful, and many corroborative. It used its collective experience and expertise in assessing the submissions and allegations and is of the view that despite certain gaps and inconsistencies, the great majority are credible. This is a recognised approach to bearing witness to uncorroborated trauma, using the concept of reflective belief.

- Mental health services should be linked to police investigations to help victims disclose abuse.
- Victims who fear reprisals should be provided with a channel though which to give evidence anonymously.

Effectiveness?

UKCSAPT would never had been created had it not been for the survivors and their supporters who made it happen in spite of scepticism and lack of official funding. Such an initiative had never been attempted before in relation to child abuse issues and, therefore, for many there was a lack of a credible precedent and so all those involved had to instil confidence in to the process. All involved gave their time for free. This is of course in stark contrast to official inquiries which are invariably intensive and expensive exercises. The fact that it happened demonstrates an inert power and ability that can be galvanised to dictate how people want their inquiry to function as opposed to be told how.

Although the findings and recommendations were delivered in a report to the UK Parliament they were not of course legally binding, but that is, perhaps, to miss the point. The work of UKCSAPT was visible and recognised in the media and presented formally in its report to the UK Parliament, and so that it evokes a symbolic and political impact. Moreover there is the recognition of wrongs and suffering endured, and placed formally on record.

Critics can point of course to the work of the Royal Commission into Institutional Responses to Child Sexual Abuse[11] which undertook a comprehensive inquiry into child sexual abuse in Australia and has made a whole series of recommendations which have led to considerable legislative reform. The ability to investigate and effect change is of course on the face of it is on an entirely different scale to that enjoyed by UKCSAPT.

UKCSAPT was certainly successful as an engine that survivors could drive to achieve their objectives, but given its limited scale, its influence whilst real has been inevitably limited. For such a model to be used again in the context of child sexual abuse, key agencies in the world of safeguarding and representation need to be engaged in the process so as to provide political muscle which has the potential to influence change.

There is appetite for and recognition that survivors' "voices" be which is what UKCSAPT was arguably able to achieve. This necessity to engage survivors, perhaps, can be reflected in the work of the Citizen's Panel, in Jersey, which was established in the wake of the Independent Jersey Care Inquiry.[12] Survivors made up in part a panel which advised government and was and is a

11 Royal Commission into Institutional Response to Child Sexual Abuse <www.childabuseroyalcommission.gov.au/> accessed February 2019.

12 In 2018 the States of Jersey commissioned a Citizens Panel to make a set of recommendations 'which will ensure survivors can be respected and honoured in decades to come': The Jersey Citizens Panel 2018 and see <>www.jerseycareinquiry.org>

means of enabling survivors to be listened to and contribute to the public and political discourse.

Looking not just at the concept of the PT but more generally at how survivors of child sexual abuse are able to give evidence effectively, an inquisitorial approach certainly appears more effective than the traditional adversarial method with which those who practice in jurisdictions based on the common law are more familiar. UKCSAPT through its approach used an inquisitorial approach which enabled all those involved to understand in a more holistic way the experiences of the witnesses. Looking forward legislators and those concerned with advocacy should take note of the lessons learned during the UKCSAPT hearings.

The fate of many a report is to sit on a shelf and to be quietly forgotten about but the impact of UKCSAPT is more diffuse. Its report was published at a time of national attention on the issue of child sexual abuse in society and the need to face past failings. Societal attitudes have changed and continue to do so on the issue of child sexual abuse and its impact, and this is reflected is the legislative field. UKCSAPT reflects that change and in its own way has added its own contribution to the ongoing debate on child sexual abuse in a broad context. This can be seen at IICSA which has examined, for example, the issues of justice and accountability which was an issue raised by UKCSAPT in its report, and has again been examined by members of the UK parliament.[13]

Arguably of greater significance is the fact that UKCSAPT happened and now acts as a signpost to the direction of travel where society now sees survivors of child abuse as integral to civic discourse through, for example, citizens' panels.

References

Register of All Party Parliamentary Groups, Adult Survivors of Childhood Sexual Abuse (13 February 2019) <https://publications.parliament.uk/pa/cm/cmallparty/190213/adult-survivors-of-childhood-sexual-abuse.htm>

Royal Commission into Institutional Responses in Child Sexual Abuse www.childabuseroyalcommission.gov.au/

The United Kingdom Child Sex Abuse People's Tribunal <www.ukcsapt.wordpress.com>

UKCSAPT, 'Healing and Justice: In Defence of the Survivors of Child Sexual Abuse' Preliminary Report of the United Kingdom Child Sex Abuse People's Tribunal (1 March 2016) <www.hughjames.com/wp-content/uploads/2016/03/Healing-and-Justice-in-defence-of-the-survivors-of-child-sexual-abuse-preliminary-report-of-the-United-Kingdom-Child-Sexual-Abuse-Peoples-Tribunal.pdf>

13 Register of All – Party Parliamentary Groups <https://publications.parliament.uk/pa/cm/cmallparty/190213/adult-survivors-of-childhood-sexual-abuse.htm>

10 The China Tribunal

David Matas and Susie Hughes

The crackdown on innocents

Falun Gong is a traditional Chinese meditation and spiritual practice, a Chinese equivalent to yoga. It has three straightforward moral principles – truthfulness, compassion and tolerance. In the early years of Falun Gong (Buddha School Qi gong), the practice was encouraged by the Chinese Communist Party (CCP) because its exercises are good for health and cut down on the costs of the health system. The practice grew from a standing start in 1992 to an estimated 70 million practitioners in 1999 by government estimates and 100 million practitioners by private estimates.

Practitioners practised outdoors in groups. They were visible everywhere in China. There were 3,000 practice stations in Beijing alone. However, the rapid spread and wide popularity of the practice of Falun Gong led the CCP to fear for its supremacy. So a crackdown ensued. The CCP wanted to retain control and power. This was made difficult as the shift from socialism to capitalism meant that communist control was, allegedly, power without a purpose. There was no goal for the Communists to achieve other than their own continuation in office. The biggest threat Communists saw to this continuation in power was Falun Gong. The repression of Falun Gong was not, for the Communist party, one activity amongst many. It became, rather, their number one priority. There is a substantial gap between the Communist motivation for repression of Falun Gong and the public justification given for that repression. The CCP does not say that they are repressing Falun Gong because it is popular. They make up slanders against Falun Gong in order to discredit it. The CCP is known for calling Falun Gong an "evil cult."

There is, needless to say, no evidence for any of this. Falun Gong is not a cult. Falun Gong practitioners lead normal lives in their communities; they are a cross section of the global community, no different from their neighbours other than doing the exercises and striving to live by the moral principles of the Falun Gong teachings.

What the Communists say about Falun Gong does not tell us anything about Falun Gong. But it does tell us a lot about the CCP, that they are prepared to say more or less anything about Falun Gong, no matter what its connection to reality. It is not a big step from that to realise that the CCP are prepared to do anything against Falun Gong no matter what its connection to morality. The decision to repress Falun Gong was not unanimous in the CCP. It was led by former President Jiang Zemin when he was head of the Party, but many opposed it. The practice of Falun Gong was widespread within the Party before its repression and to many it seemed cruel, or at least pointless, to repress something which was beneficial, or at the very least harmless.

The persecution of Falun Gong developed in stages. The Standing Committee of the CCP met on 26 April 1999 to discuss the suppression of Falun Gong. In early May, Communist Party leader Jiang Zemin deputised the Party second in command Hu Jintao and the Party head of legal affairs Luo Gan to prepare a suppression plan.

Jiang Zemin, at a special Party meeting on 7 June, directed the creation of a special leading group within the Party's Central Committee to suppress Falun Gong. The leading group and its implementation arm, the 610 office, were then established on 10 June.

The 610 Office, deriving its internal name from the date of its founding, 10 June 1999 has a structure that extends from top to bottom throughout the Party, government, and military, and has the power to command all police and judicial organs. Its purpose dedicated to carrying out the systematic eradication of the practice of Falun Gong. An ad hoc agency endowed with extraordinary and extra-legal power, it later changed its name to the Central Leading Group on Dealing with Heretical Religions or Office of Maintaining Stability. The organisation is directly under the CCP Central Committee.

The Party made public the suppression campaign on 20 July. The Ministry of Civil Affairs issued a ban notice on 22 July. The Party together with the State Council issued a statement on 24 August that Falun Gong practitioners would be prosecuted for disturbing social order.[1]

The Supreme People's Court and the Supreme People's Procuratorate on 8 and 9 October 1999 together issued "Explanations . . . Concerning Laws Applicable to Handling Cases of Organizing and Employing Heretical Cult Organizations to Commit Crimes." The Standing Committee of the National People's Congress on 30 October 1999 passed a resolution on banning heretic cults.

All this had an impact. However, from the Party perspective, the impact was insufficient. The practice of Falun Gong was reduced but not eradicated.

1 The majority of evidence supporting the statements within the introduction and thereafter can be found on the China Tribunal website: www.chinatribunal.com. The submissions made to the Panel of the China Tribunal were made public, including all testimony from live witnesses. Other citations used by the authors of this chapter can also be found in the References section at the end of this chapter.

Moreover, the attempt at repression led to active pushback. Practitioners of Falun Gong began to work against the government's propaganda – distributing leaflets and displaying banners that clarified the truth about Falun Gong.

The Party had developed a view of Falun Gong out of touch with reality, that it was an organisation, when it was not; that it had a secret leadership, which it did not; that it was foreign directed or influenced, which it was not. The propaganda campaign against Falun Gong was even further divorced from reality, attributing to this mythical Falun Gong organisation a wide range of malpractices for which there was no factual foundation.

Falun Gong practitioners who came from all over the country to Tiananmen Square in Beijing to appeal or protest were systematically arrested. Those who disclosed their identities to their captors were shipped back to their home localities. Their families were implicated in their Falun Gong activities and pressured to join in the effort to get the practitioners to renounce Falun Gong. Their workplace leaders, their co-workers, their local government leaders would be held responsible and penalised for the fact that these individuals had gone to Beijing to appeal or protest. Despite this response from the CCP, peaceful demonstrations of protest continued.

The link between dehumanisation and brutality is a common place of persecution. Persecution almost always begins with words. As the chapter on the Iran Tribunal explained, the victims that died in the Iranian prisons were as a result of a fatwa issued by Ruhollah Khomeini. The case of Falun Gong is another example of this phenomenon because of the stark contrast between the propaganda against Falun Gong and the reality of Falun Gong.

On 30 November 1999, the 610 office called more than 3,000 officials to the Great Hall of the People in the capital to discuss the campaign against Falun Gong, which was then not going well. The then-head of the 610 office, Li Lanqing, announced the government's new policy on the movement: "defame their reputations, bankrupt them financially and destroy them physically."[2]

To protect their families and avoid the hostility of the people in their locality, many detained Falun Gong practitioners declined to identify themselves. The result was a large unidentified Falun Gong prison population. The authorities did not know who they were. The people who knew them did not know where they were. Falun Gong practitioners who renounced, denounced and cooperated with the authorities were released. If they did not, they were tortured. If after they were tortured, they still refused to recant, then, with few exceptions, they remained in detention indefinitely.

2 This information comes from an interview with Li Baigen who attended the meeting. He was then assistant director of the Beijing Municipal Planning office. He is now resident in the United States. The US Department of State Country Report for China for 1999 refers to the meeting, but not the quote.

As we will now discuss, soon after the crackdown on Falun Gong began, the number of organ transplants taking place in China took a dramatic rise.

Forced organ harvesting in China

According to The Declaration of Istanbul on Organ Trafficking and Transplant Tourism, organ trafficking consists of:

a removing organs without consent or in exchange for financial gain;
b any use of organs removed in this way;
c offering any undue advantage to a healthcare professional to perform this sort of removal or use;
d recruiting donors or recipients for financial gain;
e attempting to commit or aid any of these acts.

From the beginning of organ transplantation in China, the primary source of organs was prisoners. Typically, they were prisoners sentenced to death. Their organs were either extracted immediately after execution or they were executed through organ extraction. However, even in the early days, the Chinese health and prison system did not hesitate to source organs from prisoners of conscience. The earliest prisoners of conscience victims were Uyghurs. The Uyghurs are a Turkic people who are native to Asia and are estimated to be about 9 million people. They are an official recognised minority of China who mainly reside in the Xinjiang Uyghur Autonomous Region.

In the early days of transplantation in China, there was no national organ distribution system. All organs had to be sourced locally, that is to say from local prisons. As well, earlier transplantation technology allowed for only a short time for survival and utility of an organ once extracted from the source. This combination meant that, in the 1990s and 2000s organs harvested from Uyghurs were useable only in Xinjiang.

As the hospital and prison system had already institutionalised the killing of prisoners for their organs, albeit prisoners sentenced to death, it became a simple matter to shift from killing one set of prisoners to killing another. Indeed, as a source of organs, Falun Gong was preferable. They were in the prison system in large numbers. They were healthier than death penalty prisoners because of the health benefits of Falun Gong and because of the high rate of hepatitis B in the prison criminal population. They were available at any time in contrast to death penalty prisoners who, according to law, had to be executed within seven days of sentence. The killing of Falun Gong for their organs became an implementation and realisation of the CCP goal of destroying Falun Gong practitioners physically. Other prisoners of conscience also at risk included Uyghurs, Tibetans and House Church Christians.

The publicly available evidentiary record does not allow us to conclude when the first Falun Gong practitioner was killed for his or her organs. It may have been as early as December 1999. What we can see is that by 2001 transplant volumes across China shot way up, a rise that had no other explanation than the mass killing of Falun Gong for their organs.

There were many other evidentiary indications of these mass killings taking place. There are six notable reasons which are telephone calls with admissions, systematic blood tests, hate campaigns, waiting times, militarisation of hospitals, secrecy, lack of appropriate standards and safeguards.

The first pieces of telling evidence are the calls that have been made by different groups of investigators. Investigators made calls to hospitals throughout China, claiming to be relatives of patients needing transplants, asking if the hospitals had organs of Falun Gong practitioners for sale on the basis that, since Falun Gong through their exercises are healthy, the organs would be healthy. In the 2006 book, *Bloody Harvest*, Matas and Kilgour obtained on tape, transcribed and translated admissions throughout China. In 2018 the World Organisation to Investigate the Persecution of Falun Gong (WOIPFG) conducted phone call investigations which resulted in admissions of extremely short wait times and in a number of cases admissions that Falun Gong organs were available.

Another evidentiary indication of the mass killing of Falun Gong for their organs was that Falun Gong practitioners were systematically blood tested and organ scanned while in detention. Other detainees were not. The blood testing and organ examination could not have been for the health of the Falun Gong practitioners since they had been tortured; but it would have been necessary for organ transplants.

A third evidentiary indication was the prolonged, persistent, vitriolic national and international campaign of incitement to hatred against Falun Gong. The campaign prompted their marginalisation, de-personalisation and dehumanisation in the eyes of many Chinese nationals. To their jailors, Falun Gong practitioners are not human beings entitled to respect for their human rights and dignity.

A fourth evidentiary indication was waiting times for transplants of organs in China in days and weeks. Everywhere else in the world waiting times are months and years. Transplants, even for vital organs, could be booked in advance. A short waiting time for a deceased donor transplant, especially a transplant booked in advance for a vital organ, means that someone is being killed for that transplant.

Fifth, there is a heavy militarisation of transplantation in China. Hospitals with a ready supply of available organs are often military hospitals. Even in civilian hospitals, the doctors performing operations are often military personnel. The military have a common culture with prison guards and readier access to prisoners as organ sources than civilian hospitals and civilian personnel do. In China, the military is a conglomerate business and the sale of organs is a prime source of funds. Before the publication of *Bloody Harvest*, military hospital websites used to boast this fact. Though the hospitals have since taken down the information, the web pages have been archived so that independent researchers can still see them.

Sixth, there is an inordinate secrecy surrounding transplantation in China. The names of doctors are not identified. Patients are not allowed to bring their own doctors with them. Prior to 2006, Chinese doctors used to provide letters to patients indicating the treatment given and counselled. The letters ceased after the publication of the report.

Seventh, the standards and mechanisms which should be in place to prevent the abuse are not in place, neither in China nor abroad. International organ transplant abuse should be treated like international child sex tourism, an offence everywhere with extraterritorial effect. However, so far that is not the case.

On the one hand, we have organ transplant abuse which is possible without legal consequences. On the other hand, we have huge money to be made from this abuse, as well as desperate patients in need of transplants. This combination is a recipe for victimisation of the vulnerable.

Since the persecution of Falun Gong began, there has been a steady and large increase in transplantation superstructure – transplant hospitals, transplant wings of existing hospitals, dedicated beds, operating rooms and so on. This investment is predicated on the availability of an endless supply of organs into the indefinite future.

There is no other explanation for the transplant numbers other than primary sourcing from Falun Gong practitioners. China is the second-largest transplant country in the world by volume after the US Yet, until 2010 China did not have a deceased donation system and even today that system produces donations which are relatively small. The living donor sources are limited by law to relatives of donors and officially discouraged because live donors may suffer health complications.

China at first took the position that all organs came from donations, even though at the time they did not have a donation system. They then acknowledged that the overwhelming proportion of organs for transplants in China came from prisoners but asserted that the prisoners who are the sources of organs were all sentenced to death. Yet, the number of prisoners sentenced to death and then executed that would be necessary to supply the volume of transplants in China is far greater than even the most exaggerated death penalty statistics and estimates. Moreover, in recent years, death penalty volumes have gone down, but transplant volumes, except for a short downturn in 2007, have increased.

Recently, China has gone back to its original fable that all organs for transplants come from donations. The CCP has started buying organs from family members of patients near death. But this purchase and sale system does no more than account for the drop off in the death penalty sources. Today, organ transplant abuse with sourcing from prisoners of conscience continues at the high rate it reached after the persecution of Falun Gong began.

Still, and unsurprisingly, the CCP denies this practice.

Instead, China promotes itself as having one of the leading transplant practices in the world. Their boasts on brokerage websites for Chinese hospitals have been "thousands" of such operations being performed each year, of state-of-the-art hospitals and – most sinister of all – organ transplant operations available on demand. In the abhorrent, corrupt and inhumane system they have created, prisoners and prisoners of conscience exist – in essence – as live organ banks, whose genetic, tissue type, organ health and blood data, having been taken from them during detention, is added to a data bank. When a request was made, this data is matched to the recipient and the prisoner killed in order for their organs to be extracted at the time arranged with the recipient (be they Chinese nationals or international transplant tourists).

Whilst Falun Gong has remained the main target of forced organ harvesting between 1999 to the present, other vulnerable prisoners of conscience including Uyghurs, Tibetans and House Church Christians have also been targeted for their organs.

The Uyghur population is most at risk, with reports of people being detained or disappearing emerging in 2017. Those detained include men and women, the young and elderly, as well as people of various professions and social classes. The mass construction of detention centres in Xinjiang (East Turkistan) began in 2017 with the US government estimating as many as 2 million people currently detained – 20% of the Uyghur population. The CCP claims that the highly surveilled detention centres, where detainees are forbidden to speak or interact with each other and are required to write "self-criticisms" and admissions of "erroneous thinking," are in fact "vocational education centres" for the benefit of the people. Similar to the accounts from Falun Gong practitioners, victims report DNA testing, blood tests, ultrasound, x-ray, torture and deaths in custody.

When almost all of the victims of organ transplant abuse in China were Falun Gong practitioners, the global human rights community was mostly silent. There is a direct link between that silence and the killing of Uyghurs for their organs today.

The Tribunal's beginning

The International Coalition to End Transplant Abuse in China (ETAC), an international human rights charity, with headquarters in Australia and National Committees in the UK, US, Canada, New Zealand and Australia, was established in 2016 to provide the organisational structure needed to connect experts, primarily with backgrounds in law, academia, ethics, medicine and research, in order to facilitate further work and outreach on the issue of forced organ harvesting in China.

While past research had factually addressed forced organ harvesting of prisoners of conscience in China, it had not specifically addressed whether international crimes had been committed by the CCP's transplant practices.

In addition, a number of international leaders in organ transplantation had not engaged with investigations into forced organ harvesting in a meaningful way and were instead parroting the CCP line that anyone who spoke out about forced organ harvesting had motivations fueled with political intent. Many individuals and governments around the world were confused as to who to believe. One expert, without having spent time examining the reports in detail, stated that it was just too horrible to imagine and that it "just couldn't possibly be true."

ETAC believed that by approaching the question with reference to international law, and therefore by reference to the legal rights and obligations to which other states are subjected, a new perspective could be seen and a new, international dialogue could begin.

Initially ETAC approached Sir Geoffrey Nice QC, who worked at the ICTY and who had led the prosecution of Slobodan Milošević, in the hopes he would be interested to provide an independent legal opinion on the evidence available. After some consideration, Sir Geoffrey instead recommended that due to the gravity of the issue, and the seriousness of the allegations, ETAC could initiate a PT that would focus on reviewing all available evidence. After further discussion an ETAC Steering Committee was formed to look at the finer details for moving ahead. It was clear that ETAC did not want work to be redone since investigations had been conducted since 2006. Rather, it was important that the work of the Tribunal moved the issue forward.

As there had been no previous focus on what specific international crimes have been committed by forced organ harvesting, it was decided that the question of international criminal liability would be the focus of what the China Tribunal would address. Sir Geoffrey Nice was invited to fulfil the role, *pro bono publico*, of Tribunal Chair, which he accepted.

The ETAC Steering Committee then engaged Mr. Hamid Sabi as "Counsel to the Tribunal." Mr. Sabi, a lawyer from London, brought with him extensive experience and expertise from his role as Legal Counsel for the Iran Tribunal. The Tribunal Charter was developed with advice and guidance from Tribunal Chair and Counsel to the Tribunal. In these early stages a separation between the Tribunal and the initiating body, ETAC, was established and protocols established so that ETAC could manage the logistics throughout the Tribunal process but at no stage be privy to the internal work of the Tribunal and their deliberations of the evidence and determination of findings. In order to maintain this separation and preserve the independence of the Tribunal, evidence presented by ETAC to the Tribunal was via Counsel to the Tribunal.

An important part of the process was the determination of the structure and role of those involved. It was decided that as the Tribunal panel would have some of the characteristics of a jury it was essential that it was comprised of diverse individuals with the utmost integrity.

The process for choosing who to invite to participate was lengthy. The ETAC Steering Committee reached out to a number of professionals for nominations of who may be suitable and interested. Nominated individuals were not to be members of ETAC or have a close relationship to ETAC or have previously investigated the issue.

It was considered vitally important that the Tribunal panel be balanced in regards to gender, nationality, and cultural background, in accordance to the "*Commissions of inquiry and fact-finding missions on international human rights and humanitarian law – Guidance and Practice 2015*" and that a range of professional expertise be represented including expertise in transplant medicine, business (forced organ harvesting being a billion dollar business for the Chinese State), international relations and international law. It was decided that up to ten members could participate on the Tribunal panel. In order to maintain diversity, invitations were issued one at a time and consequently six additional members were secured over the course of three months.

Prof. Martin Elliott (UK), Andrew Khoo (Malaysia), Shadi Sadr (Iran), Nicholas Vetch (UK), Regina Menachery Paulose (US), and Prof. Arthur Waldron (US) joined Sir Geoffrey Nice, bringing with them professional expertise in international law, human rights, transplant medicine, international relations, Chinese history and business. The first China Tribunal meeting took place online in June 2018.

Over a period of 11 months, the China Tribunal members, working *pro bono publico*, conducted a robust legal analysis of all available reports and investigations into organ transplant practices within China, just as would any regular jury in a criminal trial. However, they were able to go further than jurors normally do by issuing a public call for evidence and counter evidence and questioning fact witnesses, investigators and experts during public hearings in order to reach conclusions in a transparent and evidence-based way. All of this evidence, as previously mentioned, has been placed on the website for the public to also review and make their own determinations based on what has been presented to the Tribunal.

The Tribunal also sought opinions from legal experts, as stated by Sir Geoffrey Nice,

> on certain possible factual conclusions that the Tribunal may reach but entirely without prejudice to the factual finding the Tribunal will actually make. These experts have been asked to express their opinions in short form, similar to directions of law that might guide a jury or panel of judges deciding a criminal case in a court.

Expert legal opinion was provided by Edward Fitzgerald QC (UK), and Datuk N. Savananthan (Malaysia). Tabitha Nice was later engaged as Co-counsel to the Tribunal and four assistants were appointed to assist the work of the Counsel.

The call for submissions began in September 2018. Among those who testified were independent investigators with expertise in international law who had researched the issue of forced organ harvesting from as early as 2006; fact witnesses who themselves had been blood tested and organ scanned in detention or who had family members as suspected victims of forced organ harvesting; a transplant surgeon whose patient had booked in advance for a heart transplant in China; Chinese medical professionals who themselves had been involved in harvesting organs from live prisoners; and experts in transplant medicine, ethics, international law, Chinese law, statistics and biomedicine.

In order to reach the communities of those who were known to be survivors of illegal detention in China, Falun Dafa (Falun Gong) Associations around the world were contacted. The Uyghur Human Rights Project and World Uyghur Congress were also contacted along with a researcher who had previously investigated forced organ harvesting of Tibetans, the Tibet Council and representatives from Free Tibet. ETAC also issued a call for submissions to independent experts, investigators and organisations who had previously spoken publicly on forced organ harvesting in China. This call included invitations to known experts as well as the request to pass the call for submissions on to other relevant individuals and/or organisations.

A call for submissions was also posted on the China Tribunal website in October 2018. ETAC decided not to reach out to witnesses from mainland China due to the personal safety risk posed to those individuals.

For the December 2018 hearings, in consultation with Counsel to the Tribunal, ETAC nominated 16 out of the 39 Falun Gong practitioners who had submitted testimony to appear before the Tribunal. Witnesses were nominated to maximise diversity in the oral testimonies, given that it was not possible for the Tribunal to take oral testimony from all Falun Gong practitioners who provided written testimony. In addition, practical considerations such as availability to appear in person were considered. To maximise diversity amongst these witnesses, the following criteria were taken into account: year/s of blood testing; nature and location of organ scanning (e.g. in detention centre, in bus, in medical facility); witnesses with family members who were deceased and/or missing; and current country of domicile (Canada, Australia, US, UK, New Zealand and Europe).

For the April 2019 hearings, Counsel to the Tribunal nominated six witnesses from the remaining 23 written submissions that had been received. ETAC received a further 12 submissions after the initial submission closing date of 10 November 2018; however these submissions were not translated into English and were not read by the Tribunal panel.

Four submissions from Uyghurs were received and submitted to the Tribunal with two Uyghur witnesses appearing at the December 2018 hearings and two in April 2019. Due to the limited number of submissions received, submissions remained open until the final report was finalised. No submissions were received from Tibetans.

Sir Geoffrey Nice QC, Tribunal Chair, publicly noted a number of times the need for exculpatory evidence.

> ETAC [the International Coalition to End Transplant Abuse in China] and the Tribunal remain aware of the need to have access to individuals who, or material that, suggests nothing criminal has been involved in China's organ transplant practices. The Tribunal would, accordingly, be grateful for notification of the names of any such individuals who could assist with exculpatory evidence, or of written material to a similar effect that it may not yet have had drawn to its attention.

To this end, the Counsel to the Tribunal contacted representatives of the World Health Organisation (WHO), an inter-governmental body which attempts to find consensus on global health policy; The Transplantation Society (TTS), the global association of transplant health professionals; the Declaration of Istanbul Custodian Group (DICG), the group which developed an internationally accepted definition of organ trafficking and a policy of opposition to it; and the Pontifical Academy of Sciences (PAS), which organised a transplantation summit in 2017; along with prominent Chinese transplant professionals and the Chinese government. The Tribunal invited them to provide evidence on past and present transplant practices in China.

During the opening statement for the December 2018 hearings, Sir Geoffrey Nice stated:

> Although this is not in any sense a criminal trial of an individual, the Tribunal will apply the presumption of innocence, will allow no presumptions or assumptions of any kind to play parts in its deliberations, will make its decisions on the basis of evidence considered by all of its members, nothing else. Any finding without qualification that commission of crimes has been proved will be based on the Tribunal members being satisfied of such a finding beyond reasonable doubt. Other findings, one way or another at lesser levels of certainty will be explained in the judgment.

It was also agreed that in the case that the China Tribunal concluded that crimes are being committed, the Tribunal would advise what actions, legal and otherwise, should be taken by the international community. The Tribunal will take into consideration the extent to which alleged perpetrators of forced organ harvesting can be named under relevant legislation and the effect of sovereign immunity on protecting wrongdoers from civil suits.

In the China Tribunal Charter, the Tribunal was also asked to consider the responsibilities of international hospitals, universities, doctors, professional societies, medical researchers, pharmaceutical and biotech companies, medical journals and publishers regarding collaboration with their Chinese counterparts and Chinese transplant professionals. The Tribunal was asked whether such collaboration might amount to complicity in forced organ harvesting, what constraints should apply to any future collaboration and to make recommendations regarding existing or proposed professional and legal sanctions.

Reasons for the Tribunal

Over the course of its existence, ETAC had recognised that the victims of this abuse knew it well, those researching it understood and believed the practice of forced organ harvesting to be widespread. However, outside those communities, there has not been awareness of that abuse.

The Tribunal gave voice to their accounts and provided a reference point for those who seek action. For those who find the ease in stating ignorance as a justification for inaction, the depth of work that the China Tribunal has produced makes such answers not simply uncomfortable to give, but inaccurate. The Tribunal's final report can therefore help to address the silence and inaction that exists within the international medical, legal, government and human rights sectors.

Although those who engage in research on the matter all come to the same conclusion – that widespread transplant abuse in China with prisoners of conscience as the victims is in fact occurring – it is nonetheless commonplace to find hesitation about that conclusion from institutions, governments, intergovernmental organisations and NGOs who do not have the willingness or the ability to replicate that research. The Tribunal's expertise and procedure, with public hearings, posted and available for viewing, provides ready access to an overwhelming accumulation of evidence which can dispel uncertainty about the conclusion of researchers.

Many institutions, governments, inter-governmental organisations and NGOs are more likely to defer to the Tribunal than to individual researchers; therefore the Tribunal conclusions are more likely to have more political if not evidentiary weight than are the work of individual researchers.

The European Parliament, United States Congress House of Representatives and the Subcommittee on International Human Rights of the Standing Committee on Foreign Affairs and International Development of the House of Commons Parliament of Canada have called reports of this sourcing from prisoners of conscience "persistent and credible." The United Nations Rapporteur on Torture, the United Nations Rapporteur on Religious Intolerance and the United Nations Committee on Torture have all called on China to explain the discrepancy between the volume of its transplants and the volume of its identifiable sources. The European Parliament and the UN Committee on Torture, in two separate years, and the United States Congress House of Representatives have all called on the Government of China to cooperate with a credible, transparent and independent investigation into organ transplant abuse in China. The Tribunal meets these criteria. It is credible; it is transparent; and it is independent. The Government of China has nonetheless not cooperated with the Tribunal. The failure to do so and the subsequent final report of the Tribunal will hopefully mobilise the institutions which have called for such an investigation to further action.

Prior research had established that prisoners of conscience have been and are being killed in large numbers for their organs. The work of the Tribunal can advance the dialogue: doubt can be settled and a constructive dialogue about what can be done can now begin.

The work of the Tribunal could also potentially become a basis for the work of any institution, including governments, universities and hospitals, in determining what can be done to avoid complicity in Chinese Government/CCP organ transplant abuse. The Tribunal, because of the credibility of its members and the process in which they are engaged, will produce a work which can be a basis both for institutional policies and for institutional implementation of those policies.

The official CCP response to the overwhelming evidence of organ transplant abuse which they perpetrate is denial, cover-up, bafflegab, insults directed at the researchers, and red-carpet invitations to anyone gullible enough to believe that dialogue with CCP officials can improve the situation in China. The work of the Tribunal and the final report can help immunise those who might be led astray by the Chinese government, facilitating an informed, evidence-based discussion to counter the enormous and – until now – elective propaganda machine that the CCP have so effectively created.

For the surviving victims, the work of the Tribunal has also provided a remedy. It validates their own experience and shows that they are not alone in their victimization, that they are taken seriously, and that outsiders do care.

This was particularly evident in messages received after the December hearings from Falun Gong and Uyghur witnesses who had appeared. Whilst their words were few, the thanks they expressed were heartfelt. Their experience was on record. It was meaningful particularly for the Falun Gong witnesses who had been subject to "testimonial injustice" for many years by the media, and even prominent members of the international transplant community who had publicly stated that their testimonies were of no value because they were fueled with "political intent." They had experienced the integrity of a court, a place where, whilst difficult questions were asked and their evidence scrutinised, their experiences were heard.

A number of those in attendance were deeply moved by the testimonies they heard. People taken from their homes by the Chinese authorities, often with children left behind, and locked up in detention centres without a fair trial, or any trial at all. Inhumane living conditions and horrendous torture inflicted upon innocent people simply for staying true to their spiritual beliefs. Descriptions of the forced blood testing and organ scanning that took place in the detention centres, with fellow prisoners of conscience regularly disappearing and prison guards threatening organ removal if Falun Gong believers did not recant. The pain for those who did recant and who were then forced to torture others to show their allegiance to the Party. The general feedback from the gallery was that hearing these stories first hand, seeing the demeanour of the witnesses and the pain they had suffered, gave them a much deeper insight into the tragedy of what was really going on.

The Tribunal's judgement

The China Tribunal delivered its final judgement to a full house on 17 June 2019 at the Grand Connaught Rooms in Central London. National and international press attended the event as did government representatives and professionals in the fields of human rights, law, research and medicine, members of the survivor communities and investigators. A summary of the full Tribunal report was delivered by Sir Geoffrey Nice QC, with all Tribunal members in attendance.

The Tribunal began by building upon their interim judgement that it was beyond a reasonable doubt that the mass killing of Falun Gong prisoners of conscience for their organs had occurred and was still occurring.

> Forced organ harvesting has been committed for years throughout China on a significant scale and that Falun Gong practitioners have been one – and probably the main – source of organ supply.

Evidence of Uyghurs being killed for organs was insufficient, however the Tribunal noted that they were a potential organ source and that evidence may well emerge.

> The concerted persecution and medical testing of the Uyghurs is more recent and it may be that evidence of forced organ harvesting of this group may emerge in due course.

> In regard to the Uyghurs the Tribunal had evidence of medical testing on a scale that could allow them, amongst other uses, to become an 'organ bank'.

They also without hesitancy found forced organ harvesting to be a crime against humanity. In order to prove a crime against humanity, there must be a widespread or system attack, directed at a civilian population with one or more certain acts. The Tribunal found the following acts to have been committed: murder, extermination, imprisonment or other severe deprivation of physical liberty in violation of fundamental rules of international law; torture, rape or any other form of sexual violence of comparable gravity; and persecution on racial, national, ethnic, cultural or religious grounds that are universally recognised as impermissible under international law and enforced disappearance.

The Tribunal also considered whether the act of forced organ harvesting constituted genocide. They concluded:

> The Tribunal considered whether this constituted a crime of Genocide; The Falun Gong and the Uyghurs in the PRC each qualify as a 'group' for purposes of the crime of Genocide. For the Falun Gong, the following elements of the crime of Genocide are clearly established: Killing members of the group; Causing serious bodily or mental harm to members of the group. Thus, bar one element of the crime, Genocide is, on the basis of legal advice received, clearly proved to the satisfaction of the Tribunal. The remaining element required to prove the crime is the very specific intent for Genocide.
>
> The Tribunal wishes to point out that specific intent does not necessarily make a crime of Genocide worse in real wickedness than an individual Crime against Humanity proved by the same set of facts. The Tribunal notes that forced organ harvesting is of unmatched wickedness even compared – on a death for death basis – with the killings by mass crimes committed in the last century. There is justifiable belief in the minds of some or many – rising to probability or high probability – that Genocide has been committed.

The Tribunal highlighted in the summary report the reason for uncertainty as to the intent for genocide was given the diversity and division in legal opinion on the requisite intent in the law on genocide. The Tribunal took notice of this division of opinion, finding that the act of genocide was, without doubt, made out (*actus reus*), but made no such finding for the requisite intent (*mens rea*).

One view on intent is that intent must be purpose based. The other view of intent is that intent may be knowledge based. A knowledge-based approach would include wilful blindness.

The arguments in favour of the knowledge-based approach, which would lead to a finding of genocide in the case of Falun Gong, are these: an article in the Rome Statute of the ICC provides that the intent for genocide has the same knowledge component as the intent for the other crimes over which the

Court has jurisdiction. The fact that tribunals have used to date a purpose-based approach for genocide is not in itself a rejection of a knowledge-based approach.

If a purpose-based approach is available, a knowledge-based approach is unnecessary. As well, the ICTY and the ICTR do not have an intent provision like one finds in the Rome Statute of the ICC, stating that the intent for genocide, like the intent for other crimes, includes knowledge.

The full text of the relevant Court provision is this:

> Unless otherwise provided, a person shall be criminally responsible and liable for punishment for a crime within the jurisdiction of the Court only if the material elements are committed with intent and knowledge.[3]

It would be harder to find the requisite intent for genocide if a purpose-based approach were used. An intention to harvest organs by force for profit is not the same as an intention to harvest organs by force to bring about the destruction of the group.

The arguments in favour of a purpose-based approach are these: a knowledge-based approach has yet to be supported by any court. Exclusion of the knowledge-based approach by the ICC could be based on the phrase in the Rome Statute "unless otherwise provided."[4]

There is nothing otherwise provided in the Court statute or the Court elements of crime. Moreover, the manner of phrasing suggests that what is being said is that strict requirements (intent and knowledge) must be met, unless otherwise required. The phrase "unless otherwise required" is meant, it would seem, to refer to a possible relaxation of requirements, not a possible enhancement of requirements. The argument about specific, purposive, intent instead interprets the phrase "unless otherwise provided" to allow for stricter requirements for intent than those set out in the statute.

The phrase "unless otherwise provided," so the argument goes, could refer to the origins and development of the prohibition against genocide. If one goes to the origins and development of the prohibition against genocide, there are indeed views which express the need to establish a specific, purposive, intent.

For instance, in its 1996 commentary to the Draft Code of Crimes Against the Peace and Security of Mankind, the International Law Commission stated that

> [t]he prohibited [genocidal] act must be committed against an individual because of his membership in a particular group and as an incremental step in the overall objective of destroying the group. . . . The intention must be to destroy the group 'as such,' meaning as a separate and distinct entity,

3 International Criminal Court, Rome Statute, Article 30(1).

4 The article refers to this position but argues against it. Alexander Greenawalt, "Rethinking Genocidal Intent: The Case for a Knowledge-Based Interpretation" Pace University School of Law, Digital Commons, 1999 <https://core.ac.uk/download/pdf/46713705.pdf>

> and not merely some individuals because of their membership in a particular group.[5]

The China Tribunal recommended that the UN General Assembly refer the interpretation of the intent component of the law of genocide to the International Court of Justice by way of resolution asking for an advisory opinion. We think it is important to clear up this uncertainty on the law of intent which has developed in the law of genocide. An advisory opinion from the International Court of Justice, which the Tribunal recommended, would do that.

The Tribunal concluded the judgement with a "call to action" to the international community:

> Governments and international bodies must do their duty not only in regard to the possible charge of Genocide but also in regard to Crimes against Humanity, which the Tribunal does not allow to be any less heinous. Assuming they do not do their duty, the usually powerless citizen is, in the internet age, more powerful than s/he may recognise. Criminality of this order may allow individuals from around the world to act jointly in pressurising governments so that those governments and other international bodies are unable *not* to act.
>
> Governments and any who interact in any substantial way with the PRC including:
>
> - Doctors and medical institutions;
> - Industry, and businesses, most specifically airlines, travel companies, financial services businesses, law firms and pharmaceutical and insurance companies together with individual tourists,
> - Educational establishments;
> - Arts establishments
>
> should now recognise that they are, to the extent revealed above, interacting with a criminal state.

Conclusion

Over 60 media outlets covered the China Tribunal judgement in the days following the final event, something never seen before, and whilst a handful of major outlets failed to report, the number of reputable sources that covered the judgement was significant. The CCP, through its Embassy in London stated prior to the release of the summary report, "we hope that the British people will not be misled by rumours." China reiterated that the "human organ donation must be

5 Report of the International Law Commission on the Work of Its Forty-Eighth Session, U.N. GAOR, 5lst Sess., Supp. No. 10, at 87, U.N. Doc. A/51/10 (1996) Chapter 11, the Draft Code of Crimes Against the Peace and Security of Mankind and commentary at 88.

voluntary and without payment." Unfortunately, the Embassy failed to respond to points raised in the summary report by the Tribunal.

The judgement also propelled numerous questions in the UK House of Lords. The United States Commission for International Religious Freedom (USCIRF) has publicly noted the Tribunal findings at length. University heads contacted in the US and Australia have stated that they are taking note of the judgement and looking into whether they have collaborations in place with China in relation to organ transplantation, and a number of NGOs are motivated to assist.

The Uyghur community abroad wants to further investigate forced organ harvesting of Uyghurs and is initiating efforts to spread the Tribunal judgement to propel government action. The judgement has also united the survivor groups to work together to mobilise stakeholders to act.

For human rights violations to be countered effectively, the violations have to be widely known. The work of the Tribunal is helping and will continue to help spread general public awareness. Communication of any sort can take a variety of forms. Different audiences are reached by different forms of communication. The work of the Tribunal, though addressing the same subject matter as a lot of other prior work, addresses it differently, both in form, as a Tribunal, and, in substance, in terms of its mandate. These differences mean that knowledge of the abuse itself and the concomitant determination to do something about it will spread more widely.

To begin with, outside of the victim community themselves, Dr. David Matas and David Kilgour were the only two people directed against the killing of prisoners of conscience in China for their organs. Now there are many. With the Tribunal, there will be many more. Ultimately, organ transplant crimes in China should stop and the perpetrators should be brought to justice. The work of the China Tribunal brings those aims within reach.

References

Bowcott, Owen, 'Tribunal to Investigate 1980s Massacre of Political Prisoners in Iran' *The Guardian* (18 October 2012) <www.theguardian.com/world/2012/oct/18/iran-tribunal-investigates-massacre>

China Tribunal <www.chinatribunal.com>

Cook, Sarah and Lemish, Leeshai, 'The 610 Office: Policing the Chinese Spirit' [16 September 2011] 11(17) China Brief <https://jamestown.org/program/the610officepolicingthechinesespirit/>

Embassy of the People's Republic of China in Canada, 'China Issued Anti-Cult Law' (2 November 1999) <http://ca.chineseembassy.org/eng/xw/xwgb/t38871.htm>

Forrest, Adam, 'China Harvesting Organs from Falun Gong Detainees, Tribunal Claims' (*Independent*, 17 June 2019) <www.independent.co.uk/news/world/asia/china-organ-harvesting-prisoners-falun-gong-deaths-tribunal-a8962661.html>

Greenawalt, Alexander, 'Rethinking Genocidal Intent: The Case for a Knowledge-Based Interpretation' (Pace University School of Law, Digital Commons, 1999) <https://core.ac.uk/download/pdf/46713705.pdf>

Human Rights Watch, 'Dangerous Meditation: China's Campaign Against Falun Gong' (7 February 2002) <www.refworld.org/docid/45cb148e2.html>

Human Rights Watch, 'China: Free Xinjiang "Political Education" Detainees, Muslim Minorities Held for Months in Unlawful Facilities' (10 September 2017) <www.hrw.org/news/2017/09/10/china-free-xinjiang-political-education-detainees>

Hutzler, Charles, 'Chinese Leaders Prepare Careful Crackdown Against Secretive Group' (Associated Press, 8 May 1999) <https://culteducation.com/group/1254-falungong/6710chineseleaderspreparecarefulcrackdownagainstsecretivegroup.html>

International Coalition to End Transplant Abuse in China (ETAC) <https://endtransplantabuse.org/>

Kilgour, David, Gutmann, Ethan and Matas, David, 'Bloody Harvest/The Slaughter: An Update' (22 June 2016) <https://endtransplantabuse.org/an-update/>

Matas, David and Kilgour, David, 'Bloody Harvest: The Killing of Falun Gong for Their Organs' (Seraphim Editions, 2006) <https://endtransplantabuse.org/2006-report/>

Matas, David and Trey, Dr. Torsten, 'State Organs: Transplant Abuse in China' (Seraphim Editions, 24 February 2015).

Radio Free Asia, 'Who Are the Uyghurs' (9 July 2009) <www.rfa.org/english/news/uyghur/uyghurs_facts-07092009163637.html/>

Report of the International Law Commission on the Work of Its Forty-Eighth Session, U.N. GAOR, 5lst Sess., Supp. No. 10, at 87, U.N. Doc. A/51/10 (1996) Chapter 11, the Draft Code of Crimes Against the Peace and Security of Mankind and commentary at 88.

Senate Foreign Relations Committee Subcommittee on East Asia, the Pacific, and International Cybersecurity Policy, 'Testimony of Deputy Assistant Secretary Scott Busby' (4 December 2018) <www.foreign.senate.gov/imo/media/doc/120418_Busby_Testimony.pdf>

United Nations Human Rights Office of the High Commissioner, Commissions of Inquiry and Fact-Finding Missions on International Human Rights and Humanitarian Law Guidance and Practice (New York and Geneva, 2015) <www.ohchr.org/Documents/Publications/CoI_Guidance_and_Practice.pdf>

'Xinjiang's Uyghurs Were Enslaved and Forced to Convert to Islam, Chinese White Paper Claims' (*ABC*, 22 July 2019) <www.abc.net.au/news/2019-07-22/china-report-says-xinjiangs-uyghurs-forced-to-convert-to-islam/11330490>

11 Transitional justice delayed is not transitional justice denied

Contemporary confrontation of Japanese human experimentation during World War II through a People's Tribunal

Zachary D. Kaufman

The modern need to address Japanese wartime human experimentation

Both the historical and political background of Japanese human experimentation and recent geopolitical developments in East Asia make this issue particularly crucial to address today.

Historical and political background

During World War II, Japanese officials experimented on thousands of civilians and Allied soldiers, including US prisoners of war.[1] The Imperial Japanese Army's Unit 731, led by Lieutenant General Shiro Ishii, conducted the most notorious research, in Manchuria.[2] These experiments, sometimes referred to as the "Asian

An earlier version of this chapter was published by the *Yale Law & Policy Review* in its volume 26 (2008) and is reprinted here with that journal's permission.

1 Although no consensus exists about whether American POWs were among the human guinea pigs of Unit 731 specifically, they certainly were victims of Japanese human experiments elsewhere. See Zachary D. Kaufman, *United States Law and Policy on Transitional Justice: Principles, Politics, and Pragmatics* 117, 249 n. 209 (2016).

2 Unit 731 is discussed in various sources. See, e.g., Yves Beigbeder, *Judging War Criminals: The Politics of International Justice* 53, 72–74 (1999); John L. Ginn, *Sugamo Prison Tokyo: An Account of the Trial and Sentencing of Japanese War Criminals in 1948, by a U.S. Participant* 242–245 (1992); Hal Gold, *Unit 731 Testimony: Japan's Wartime Human Experimentation Program* (1966); Sheldon H. Harris, *Factories of Death: Japanese Biological Warfare, 1932–45, and the American Cover-Up* (rev. ed. 2002); Kaufman, *United States Law and Policy on Transitional Justice*, (note 1), 108, 117–118, 249 n. 209; Yuki Tanaka, *Hidden Horrors: Japanese War Crimes in World War II* 135–165 (1996); Peter Williams and David Wallace, *Unit 731: Japan's Secret Biological Warfare in World War II* (1989); John Saar, Japan Accused of WWII Germ Deaths, *Washington Post* (19 November 1976), A1. Declassified US government documents relating to Japanese medical experimentation during World

Auschwitz," included vivisections, dissections, weapons testing, starvation, dehydration, poisoning, extreme temperature and pressure testing and deliberate infection with numerous deadly diseases (such as bubonic plague, cholera, anthrax, smallpox, gangrene, streptococcus bacteria and syphilis).[3] Had the war continued, the Japanese planned to use the biological weapons developed from these experiments to attack the US military in the Pacific and possibly even the west coast of the United States itself.[4]

When the war ended, the US government offered immunity and other incentives – including money, food and entertainment – to over 3,600 Japanese government agents, physicians and scientists involved in these experiments. Declassified US government documents and testimony from Japanese involved in or knowledgeable about the experiments reveal that the US government was interested in the potential utility of the work of Ishii and other Japanese, however unethical, to the US military.[5] Senior US officials felt that obtaining data from the experiments was more valuable than bringing those involved to justice, because the information could be used to advance the US government's own weapons development programme. US officials were also concerned about preventing other countries, particularly the Soviet Union, from obtaining the data.[6] Unlike Josef Mengele and some of his Nazi colleagues who performed similar experiments on humans but who were, according to a former US Department of Justice official and an investigative reporter, "too well known for their war crimes" to become collaborators with the United States,[7] the Japanese human experimenters were relatively anonymous. As a result, the US government could pursue its strategy undetected, and US policymakers could partner with implicated Japanese officials without much fear of a public relations backlash. After being granted

War II can be found online. See The Nazi War Crimes and Japanese Imperial Government Records Interagency Working Group, National Archives <www.archives.gov/iwg> accessed 31 July 2019.

3 See generally sources cited supra (notes 1–2).

4 See Gold, (note 2), 86–92.

5 See, e.g., C. A. Willoughby, Report on Bacteriological Warfare (1947) (on file with author); Letter from C. A. Willoughby, US Army Forces, Pac., Military Intelligence Section, Gen. Staff, to Major Gen. S. J. Chamberlin, Dir. of Intelligence, War Dep't Gen. Staff (22 July 1947) (on file with author).

6 See Beigbeder, (note 2), 72–74; Gold, (note 2), 86–143; Harris, (note 2), 147–233; *The Tokyo War Crimes Trial: An International Symposium* 85–86, 131, 134 (Chihiro Hosoya et al. eds., 1986); Awaya Kentarō, In the Shadows of the Tokyo Tribunal, in *The Tokyo War Crimes Tribunal: An International Symposium* 79, 85–86 (C. Hosoya et al. eds., 1986); B. V. A. Röling, The Tokyo Trial and the Quest for Peace, in *The Tokyo War Crimes Tribunal: An International Symposium*, supra, at 125, 131, 134; Shane Green, The Asian Hell of Unit 731, *Age* (Melbourne, Australia) (29 August 2002), 11; Kyodo, US Paid for Japanese Human Germ Warfare Data, *Australian Broadcasting Corporation* (14 August 2005) <www.abc.net.au/news/2005-08-15/us-paid-for-japanese-human-germ-warfare-data/2080618>; Justin McCurry, 'Japan's Sins of the Past' *The Guardian* (London, 28 October 2004) <www.guardian.co.uk/elsewhere/journalist/story/0,7792,1338296,00.html>.

7 John Loftus and Mark Aarons, *The Secret War Against the Jews: How Western Espionage Betrayed the Jewish People*, 290 (1994).

immunity, some Japanese participants in these experiments assumed prominent roles – including senior positions in the health ministry, academia and the private sector – in post-war Japanese society, allegedly with the assistance or at least knowledge of the US government.[8]

Through its conscious decision not to hold these alleged atrocity perpetrators accountable, the US government implicitly provided amnesty to thousands of Japanese suspected of direct involvement in some of the most horrific crimes of World War II, including those who planned offences against Americans. The incipient Cold War – and the superpowers' attendant desire to secure competitive advantages and scientific advancements – thus chilled the US government's enthusiasm for investigating and prosecuting Japanese human experimenters. US officials believed that their research would be useful in the arms race developing between the United States and the Soviet Union. US war memorials and history books gloss over these facts.

Recent developments

In recent years, Japanese nationalism and revisionism have grown, particularly about the country's wartime atrocity crimes.[9] For example, early in his term, Shinzo Abe, who initially served as the Japanese prime minister from September 2006 to September 2007, erroneously claimed that there was no evidence that Japan instituted sexual slavery during World War II.[10] Abe's whitewashing of Japanese history has continued since he became prime minister again in 2012.[11]

Meanwhile, Japan has steadily increased its military spending, despite having been constitutionally barred since the end of World War II from maintaining

8 Gold, (note 2), 139–143; Williams and Wallace, (note 2), 235–242.

9 See, e.g., Howard W. French, 'Specter of a Rearmed Japan Stirs Its Wartime Generation' *New York Times* (20 June 2001), A1; Francis Fukuyama, 'The Trouble with Japanese Nationalism' *Project Syndicate* (2007) <www.project-syndicate.org/commentary/fukuyama2>; Shane Green, 'Japan's Lack of Remorse Troubling as It Manoeuvres to Rearm' *Sydney Morning Herald* (19 June 2003), 15; Norimitsu Onishi, 'Long After War Trials, Japan Still Honors a Judge' *New York Times* (31 August 2007), A4; George F. Will, Editorial, 'The Uneasy Sleep of Japan's Dead' *Washington Post* (20 August 2006), B07; Paul Wiseman, 'Nationalism Gains Strength in Japan' *USA Today* (27 July 2007), 6A.

10 See, e.g., Editorial, 'No Comfort' *New York Times* (6 March 2007), A20; Norimitsu Onishi, 'Denial Reopens Wounds of Japan's Ex-Sex Slaves' *New York Times* (8 March 2007), A1; Norimitsu Onishi, 'Premier's Sudden Resignation Leaves Japan in Disarray' *New York Times* (13 September 2007), A3; Editorial, 'Shinzo Abe's Double Talk' *Washington Post* (24 March 2007), A16.

11 See, e.g., Hugh Cortazzi, 'Opinion, Abe's Unconvincing Attempt to Whitewash Japan's History' *Japan Times* (17 August 2015) <www.japantimes.co.jp/opinion/2015/08/17/commentary/japan-commentary/abes-unconvincing-attempt-to-whitewash-japans-history/>; Editorial, 'Whitewashing History in Japan' *New York Times* (4 December 2014), A30; Martin Flacker, 'Rewriting War, Japanese Right Goes on Attack' *New York Times* (3 December 2014), A1.

its own "land, sea, and air forces."[12] In 2018, Japan spent the equivalent of $47.3 billion on its military, the eighth largest annual military budget of any country in the world.[13]

Japan's changing attitudes and capabilities have alarmed its neighbours, particularly China and Korea, which suffered numerous atrocity crimes at the hands of Japanese in World War II.[14] As I have argued elsewhere, Japan's failure to acknowledge these and other offences it has committed casts uncertainty over its recent military resurgence. To assuage the fears of China, Korea and other countries in the Pacific Rim – where memories of a brutal, imperialistic Japanese government remain vivid – modern-day Japan should both acknowledge and apologise for the atrocity crimes its military perpetrated in World War II. Japan's neighbours will, in part, look to how the current Japanese government treats the wrongdoing of previous Japanese regimes to interpret how Japan will manage its newfound military might in the years to come.[15]

In addition to the practical benefits for Japan's diplomatic relations, the Japanese government should come to grips with its past for ethical reasons: out of respect for survivors, victims and their families. Other governments have recently issued apologies for their past wrongs, recognising that doing so is a necessary first step on the path towards reconciliation and achieving long-term peace and stability.[16]

12 Nihonkoku Kenpo [Kenpo] [Constitution] art 9, para. 2 (Japan).

13 International Institute for Security Studies, Top Defense Budgets, 2018 (US$bn), Including Total European NATO Spending <www.iiss.org/-/media/files/publications/military-balance-2019/mb2019-defence-budgets-branded.ashx> accessed 31 July 2019.

14 See, e.g., French, (note 9); see also Green, (note 9).

15 See Zachary D. Kaufman, Recent Development, 'No Right to Fight: The Modern Implications of Japan's Pacifist Postwar Constitution' [2008] 33 Yale Journal of International Law 266.

16 For example, on 13 February 2008, Australian Prime Minister Kevin Rudd officially apologised for past wrongs committed by his country's government against Aborigines and Torres Strait Islanders. As part of his apology statement, Rudd declared, "The Parliament is today here assembled to deal with this unfinished business of the nation, to remove a great stain from the nation's soul, and in a true spirit of reconciliation to open a new chapter in the history of this great land, Australia." Tim Johnston, 'Australia Says "Sorry" to Aborigines for Mistreatment' *New York Times* (13 February 2008), A14 (quoting Rudd). The offences some Aborigine rights advocates claim the Australian government committed against Aborigines include human experimentation, particularly on children. See, e.g., 'Aborigines "Used in Experiments"' *BBC News* (15 April 2008) <http://news.bbc.co.uk/2/hi/asia-pacific/7348144.stm>. The Canadian government has similarly apologised for its past offences against the country's indigenous people. See, e.g., Ian Austen, 'Trudeau Apologizes for Abuse and "Profound Cultural Loss" at Indigenous Schools' *New York Times* (24 November 2017) <www.nytimes.com/2017/11/24/world/canada/trudeau-indigenous-schools-newfoundland-labrador.html>; Steve Scherer, 'Canadian Inquiry Calls Deaths of Indigenous Women "Genocide"' *Reuters* (3 June 2019) <www.reuters.com/article/us-canada-aboriginal/canadian-inquiry-calls-deaths-of-indigenous-women-genocide-idUSKCN1T41XF> (Prime Minister Justin "Trudeau made Canada's reconciliation for its colonial past a major plank of his 2015 campaign, and he has apologized for some of the country's historical wrongs since taking office.").

At the same time, other countries, including the United States, could do more to help establish an accurate record not only of Japanese atrocity crimes but also of the conduct of post-war American authorities who were able but unwilling to punish them.[17] The door is therefore open to a new US policy, grounded in morality, which acknowledges the United States' politically expedient cover-up of Japanese wartime transgressions. Just as Japan's leaders should be more forthcoming about their dark past, so too should the United States recognise that it was complicit in hiding that shameful affair. A change in US policy may even help motivate a change in Japan's.

A People's Tribunal as a means to examine past atrocity crimes

Even if acknowledging Japanese wartime atrocity crimes is sound policy, the reality is that the United States and Japan may continue to be silent about their respective involvement in human experimentation during World War II. Absent government action, civil society should pursue alternative means of obtaining official acknowledgement. Because the particular circumstances and challenges of confronting Japanese wartime human experimentation limit the appropriateness and practicality of the most common transitional justice mechanisms,[18] a more innovative – or at least more unusual – approach is required.

A so-called PT – an ad hoc organisation of private citizens – may offer the most promising method of addressing the atrocity crimes. Beyond expressing general outrage, non-governmental actors can assemble to create a forum to register public protest about state actions. Such civil society members can draw upon their particular backgrounds and expertise in order to provide analysis and recommend remedies for violations of international law.[19] Undoubtedly, PTs have significant drawbacks: their history and operation demonstrate the potential pitfalls of civil society's attempt to provide reconciliation, retribution or restitution for past crimes. However, these institutions present a compelling means for addressing Japanese human experimentation in World War II.

17 To be sure, the US government has taken some steps to address Japan's wartime human experimentation. In December 1996, the US Department of Justice's Office of Special Investigations announced that it had added to its watch list of atrocity perpetrators banned from entering the United States 16 Japanese veterans of World War II, which included some participants in Unit 731. See Beigbeder, (note 2), 73.

18 See infra, pp. 173–176.

19 See, e.g., José E. Alvarez, *International Organizations as Law-Makers* (2005); Anna-Karin Lindblom, *Non-Governmental Organisations in International Law* (2006); Farouk Mawlawi, 'New Conflicts, New Challenges: The Evolving Role for Non-Governmental Actors' [1993] 46 Journal of International Affairs 391.

Background and critique of People's Tribunals

It is difficult to catalogue all of the PTs that have been instituted across the world and throughout history, as they have taken a wide variety of forms and have been created for multifarious purposes. By some accounts, the first PT originated during the interwar period in response to perceived inefficiencies in the rule of law at the time. Private citizens established panels to examine the 1933 fire that damaged the Reichstag, the Parliament building in Berlin in what was then Nazi Germany, as well as to confront the mid-1930s Moscow show trials, part of the "Great Purge" in the Soviet Union. In both cases, prominent Americans, including attorney Arthur Garfield Hays and public intellectual John Dewey, promoted and participated in the PTs.[20] Throughout the 20th and early 21st centuries, PTs have been organised to address a range of alleged violations of international law, from US involvement in Vietnam to the rights of asylum seekers, psychiatric patients and indigenous peoples. As this volume illustrates, survivors have often played a crucial role in PTs.

But no matter the purpose or personnel, the greatest strength of PTs is that, precisely because they are driven by civil society and are thus, unlike state-sanctioned courts and truth commissions, independent from political authorities, they may be more willing and better able to reveal damning information and to present critical findings and recommendations.[21] A report of a PT's hearings and conclusions can be disseminated either by the tribunal itself or by news agencies, thus raising public awareness about the tribunal's operations and the subject matter of its inquiries.

20 Arthur Jay Klinghoffer and Judith Apter Klinghoffer, *International Citizens Tribunals: Mobilizing Public Opinion to Advance Human Rights* (Palgrave Macmillan US, 2002), 11–101. The first PT the Klinghoffers identify was named the Commission of Inquiry into the Origins of the Reichstag Fire, also known as the International Juridical Investigatory Commission on the Reichstag Fire. This PT held hearings in London from 14 September through 18 September 1933, and announced its "final conclusions" two days later. Klinghoffer and Klinghoffer, supra, 21–25. The second PT the Klinghoffers identify was named the Preliminary Commission of Inquiry into the Charges Made against Leon Trotsky in the Moscow Trials, also known as the Dewey Commission, after its chairman, John Dewey. This PT held hearings in Coyoacán, outside Mexico City, from April 10 through April 17, 1937; released a transcript of those hearings and summary of findings on 21 September 1937; and announced its verdict in New York on 12 December 1937. Klinghoffer and Klinghoffer, supra, 72–73, 80–82, 96–97.

21 For general discussion of such tribunals created and staffed by civil society, see Klinghoffer and Klinghoffer, (note 20); Arthur Jay Klinghoffer, 'International Citizens' Tribunals on Human Rights' in *Genocide, War Crimes and the West* 346 (Adam Jones ed., 2004). The Klinghoffers provide the most thorough treatment of this developing area of scholarship.

A PT may therefore provide compelling shaming pressures,[22] much like other features of international law and politics.[23] As Andrew Moravscik argues in a case study of the European human rights regime, shaming

> seeks to enforce individual human rights and promote democracy by creating an international and domestic climate of opinion critical of national practices. Shaming exploits the symbolic legitimacy of foreign pressure and international institutions. . . [and] is instigated through the dissemination of information . . . and exploitation of international practical institutions.[24]

That shaming function, which Moravscik found in European Union institutions, is also indicative of a PT. As Arthur Jay Klinghoffer and Judith Apter Klinghoffer state in their extensive study of PTs, such institutions

> can . . . serve as a corrective mechanism through which public intellectuals mobilize world public opinion against powerful countries shielded from sanctions under international law. If the absence of effective and permanent legal structures is the problem, then [people's] tribunals may offer an appropriate solution.[25]

To be sure, commentators have levelled substantial criticism against PTs. One major critique concerns their nomenclature, as the term "People's Tribunal" is controversial. For some, the first word is reminiscent of "totalitarian and terrorist concepts of justice," leading the Klinghoffers, for instance, to refer to these institutions instead as "international citizens' tribunals."[26] The second word, "tribunal," suggests a juridical function, but, as the Klinghoffers observe, "[a]pplying legalistic terminology is often confounding,"[27] as these civil society initiatives employ staff and methods that depart from traditional notions of courtroom procedure.

22 Professors Dan Kahan and Eric Posner define shaming as the "process by which citizens publicly and self consciously draw attention to the bad dispositions or actions of an offender, as a way of punishing him for having those dispositions or engaging in those actions." Dan M. Kahan and Eric A. Posner, 'Shaming White-Collar Criminals: A Proposal for Reform of the Federal Sentencing Guidelines' [1999] 42 Journal of Law and Economics 365, 368.

23 See, e.g., Robert F. Drinan, *The Mobilization of Shame* (2001); Lesley Wexler, 'The International Deployment of Shame, Second-Best Responses, and Norm Entrepreneurship: The Campaign to Ban Landmines and the Landmine Ban Treaty' [2003] 20 Arizona Journal of International and Comparative Law 561, 563–567.

24 Andrew Moravcsik, 'Explaining International Human Rights Regimes: Liberal Theory and Western Europe' [1995] 1 European Journal of International Relations 157, 161.

25 Klinghoffer and Klinghoffer, (note 20), 5.

26 Ibid., 3.

27 Ibid., 9.

Indeed, PTs have often been criticised for their mechanics. First, they have lacked generally accepted guarantees of due process. Some tribunals, for example, have conducted hearings *in absentia* and have relied on hasty and possibly predetermined deliberations.[28] Second, because PTs are often created, staffed, and defended by famous liberal Western professors and philosophers – Simone de Beauvoir, Richard Falk, Bertrand Russell and Jean-Paul Sartre, for example – these institutions have been dismissed as Eurocentric, elitist, left-leaning and radical.[29] Third, many PTs have focused on atrocity crimes allegedly committed by the United States,[30] leading some to criticise these institutions as politically motivated and anti-American.[31] Because of past PTs' procedural defects and thinly-veiled political agendas, some may therefore consider PTs to be kangaroo courts rather than legitimate, fair quasi-judicial institutions.

The greatest criticism of PTs may be their inherent lack of an enforcement mechanism. PTs share the same impotence as truth commissions, which "hold fewer powers than do courts. They have no powers to put anyone in jail, they can't enforce their recommendations."[32] In fact, PTs may be even less powerful than truth commissions, as many truth commissions have been sanctioned by the state and thus have "had the power to compel anyone to come forward to answer questions."[33] As Russell acknowledged of his first eponymous tribunal, "Our tribunal . . . commands no State power. It rests on no victorious army. It claims no other than a moral authority."[34] Because they have no teeth, PTs have been largely ineffective, and they have been accused of being nothing more than political activism cloaked in legal imagery. Indeed, as even neutral commentators such as Sally Engle Merry have recognised, PTs often "appropriate[ ] legal forms and symbols in an effort to harness the power and legitimacy of law in a movement of resistance."[35]

28 See, e.g., Ibid., 5, 8.

29 See, e.g., Ibid., 1, 5–7, 10, 103–162, 163, 165, 171. For the inaugural statement to the first Russell Tribunal by Jean-Paul Sartre, who served as its executive president, see Jean-Paul Sartre, Inaugural Statement to the Russell Vietnam War Crimes Tribunal (1966), in *Genocide, War Crimes and the West*, (note 21), 181.

30 For example, the first Russell Tribunal, established in 1966, charged the United States with committing war crimes, crimes against humanity and genocide in Vietnam, and found the United States guilty of violating international law through aggression, targeting civilians, and using prohibited weapons. Later PTs focused on US involvement in, among other places, Guatemala, Hawaii, Iraq, Nicaragua and Panama. See Klinghoffer and Klinghoffer, (note 20), 1, 4, 7–8, 103–177; Caroline Moorehead, *Bertrand Russell: A Biography* 520–530 (1993); Sally Engle Merry, 'Resistance and the Cultural Power of the Law' [1995] 29(11) Law & Society Review 20–23. For Russell's views on American responsibility for the Vietnam War, which informed his decision to establish the first Russell Tribunal, see Bertrand Russell, *War Crimes in Vietnam* (1967).

31 See, e.g., Klinghoffer and Klinghoffer, (note 20), 7, 134, 178.

32 Priscilla B. Hayner, *Unspeakable Truths: Facing the Challenge of Truth Commissions* (2002), 16.

33 Ibid.

34 Russell, (note 30), 125.

35 Merry, (note 30), 21.

Yet proponents of PTs respond that they can succeed despite – or perhaps *because of* – some of their flaws. As Arthur Jay Klinghoffer argues,

> International citizens' tribunals cannot impose their decisions upon transgressing states, but this apparent weakness may be turned into an advantage, at least in theory. Such tribunals are not indebted to states, and are not influenced by them. Powerlessness may thus prove to be a virtue, and contribute to [international citizens'] tribunals' legitimacy.[36]

Furthermore, given that so many critiques of PTs derive from their design and operation, many of those criticisms could be addressed through more careful planning, as I suggest below.

Application to Japanese wartime human experimentation

A PT was used once before to respond to Japanese wartime atrocity crimes. In 2000, a Women's International War Crimes Tribunal (WIWCT) on Japan's Military Sexual Slavery was held in Tokyo to establish the history of, and recommend action on, Japan's use of "comfort women" during World War II.[37] This PT was organised and staffed exclusively by individuals acting in their private capacities, including Gabrielle Kirk McDonald, a distinguished US jurist.[38] The WIWCT was designed to supplement the International Military Tribunal for the Far East (IMTFE), which the Allied victors of World War II held in Tokyo from 1946 to 1948 to try the perpetrators of Japan's most egregious wartime atrocity crimes.[39] The IMTFE was insufficient because, among other flaws, it failed to include rape, sexual enslavement and other sexual crimes in the litany of Japanese offences it confronted.[40]

36 Klinghoffer, (note 21), 347.

37 "Comfort women" is the euphemistic term for the tens of thousands of women, the majority of whom were from China and Korea, whom the Japanese forced into prostitution and sexual slavery during World War II. See, e.g., George Hicks, *The Comfort Women: Japan's Brutal Regime of Enforced Prostitution in the Second World War* (1994); Dai Sil Kim-Gibson, *Silence Broken: Korean Comfort Women* (1999); *Legacies of the Comfort Women of World War II* (Margaret Stetz and Bonnie B. C. Oh eds., 2001); Yuki Tanaka, *Japan's Comfort Women: Sexual Slavery and Prostitution During World War II and the US Occupation* (2002); *True Stories of the Korean Comfort Women* (Keith Howard, ed., Young Joo Lee, trans., 1995); Yoshimi Yoshiaki, *Comfort Women: Sexual Slavery in the Japanese Military During World War II* (Suzanne O'Brien, trans., Columbia University Press 2000) (1995).

38 McDonald is a former judge on the US District Court for the Southern District of Texas, a former arbitrator on the Iran-U.S. Claims Tribunal, and the former president (chief judge) of the ICTY.

39 For background discussion of the IMTFE, see, e.g., Kaufman, *United States Law and Policy on Transitional Justice*, (note 1), 93–120.

40 See Klinghoffer and Klinghoffer, (note 20), 166–167; see also, e.g., Christine M. Chinkin, Editorial Comments, 'Women's International Tribunal on Japanese Military Sexual Slavery' [2001] 95 American Journal of International Law 335; Christine Chinkin, 'Rape and Sexual Abuse of Women in International Law' [1994] 5 European Journal of International Law

Because the IMTFE also failed to address Japan's human experimentation,[41] a PT should be convened for those crimes as well. Civil society should demand the declassification of documents about human experimentation, including information about which Japanese officials were involved in these activities and the Allied forces' decision not to seek the trial of Ishii or his cohorts before the IMTFE or other post-war courts. Civil society should also demand a full and public apology by Japan for carrying out – and by the United States for covering up – these horrendous events.

If private citizens do pursue such an initiative, the aforementioned criticisms of PTs could be addressed in the process. The initiative should be referred to as a "commission of inquiry" or something similarly descriptive of its extrajudicial nature. Efforts should be made to have a fair and balanced group of panellists that, if possible, includes individuals from across the political spectrum and from several different countries, including China, both North and South Korea, and Japan itself. The Japanese government should be afforded the opportunity to present a defence. The panellists should take that defence and all other evidence into consideration *before* arriving at their conclusion. That conclusion should not be a "verdict," but rather a statement of findings and should include any dissenting views among the panellists. By virtue of its primary focus on Japan, even though the matter considered involves the United States, the institution would not necessarily be deemed anti-American.

Of course, neither Japan nor the United States would be obligated to acknowledge the findings or follow the recommendations of such a grassroots initiative. Still, a PT could help raise public awareness about Japanese wartime human experimentation, and it could pressure Japan and the United States finally to take responsibility for their actions. Indeed, Japan would be especially susceptible to the shaming function of a PT, as Japanese society is more sensitive to shame than many other cultures.[42] Moreover, as Japan seeks greater involvement in international affairs – for example, through its ongoing campaign to obtain a permanent seat on the United Nations Security Council (UNSC)[43] – Japan is likely to be increasingly concerned about its public image.

326; 'Hirohito "Guilty" Over Sex Slaves' *BBC News* (12 December 2000) <http://news.bbc.co.uk/1/hi/world/asia-pacific/1066658.stm>; Stacy Sullivan, 'Symbolic War Crimes Tribunal for Japanese "Comfort Women"' (10 December 2002) <www.crimesofwar.org/onnews/comfort.html>.

41 Beigbeder, (note 2), 73.

42 For one of the seminal works describing Japan as "a shame culture," see Ruth Benedict, *The Chrysanthemum and the Sword: Patterns of Japanese Culture* (1946).

43 Since at least the early-1960s, Japan has campaigned for a permanent seat on the UNSC. See Jose E. Guzzardi and Mark J. Mullenbach, 'The Politics of Seeking a Permanent Seat on the United Nations Security Council: An Analysis of Japan' [2007–2008] 9 Midsouth Political Science Review 35, 46. In recent years, Japan has continued to seek such a permanent seat. See, e.g., 'Japan to Run for 2023–2024 Seat on UNSC, Continue Reform Push' *Japan Times* (16 December 2017) <www.japantimes.co.jp/

A court of last resort? Why other transitional justice options would not work

Beyond the possible effectiveness of shaming Japan and the United States into finally publicly addressing Japanese human experimentation during World War II, a PT might also be the most appropriate transitional justice mechanism in this case simply because other options would be unsuccessful or impractical. While a process of elimination is perhaps not always the most desirable means of arriving at a conclusion or recommendation, in this case it is an honest and realistic one. Implementing a PT, even with its significant controversy and weaknesses, is better than the current situation of inaction. In this Part, I discuss why transitional justice options besides a PT would be unlikely to effectively address Japanese wartime human experimentation. I find, as Benjamin Duerr does in Chapter 2 and Ronald Rogo does in Chapter 3, that PTs may fill a gap that international courts and truth commissions, respectively, can't or won't.

International criminal tribunals, if formally and officially established by recognised authorities such as international organisations, can have large budgets and staffs, widespread legitimacy, binding judgements and strong enforcement mechanisms.[44] For example, the UN ICTR and ICTY each cost roughly $100 million per year to operate.[45] These now-defunct tribunals were established by the UNSC using its Chapter VII powers as outlined in the UN Charter[46] – the first international war crimes tribunals so created. Consequently, these courts had the official imprimatur and support of the UNSC, the division of the UN charged with "primary responsibility for the maintenance of international peace and security,"[47] in their existence, operation, and working relationship with all state members of the UN (effectively the entire world).[48]

However, such international tribunals have always had limited temporal, subject matter, personal and territorial jurisdictions. For instance, the competence of

news/2017/12/16/national/politics-diplomacy/japan-seek-nonpermanent-u-n-security-council-seat-2023-2024> (Japanese Foreign Minister Taro Kono "pushed Japan's case for reforming the council, which includes the goal of getting Japan and other nations added as permanent members."); 'Japan Steps Up Campaign for Full UN Security Council Seat' *Deutsche Welle* (Germany, 27 January 2016) <www.dw.com/en/japan-steps-up-campaign-for-full-un-security-council-seat/a-19007001>.

44 See generally Howard Ball, *Prosecuting War Crimes and Genocide: The Twentieth-Century Experience* (1999); Gary Jonathan Bass, *Stay the Hand of Vengeance: The Politics of War Crimes Tribunals* (2000); Beigbeder, (note 2); Richard J. Goldstone, *For Humanity: Reflections of a War Crimes Investigator* (2000).

45 Kaufman, *United States Law and Policy on Transitional Justice*, (note 1), 49.

46 S.C. Res. 827, U.N. Doc. S/RES/827 (25 May 1993); S.C. Res. 955, U.N. Doc. S/RES/955 (8 November 1944).

47 U.N. Charter art. 24, para. 1.

48 S.C. Res. 827, (note 46), ¶ 4; S.C. Res. 955 (note 46), ¶ 2.

the ICTR, established by the UNSC to address the 1994 genocide against the Tutsi in Rwanda,[49] was confined to prosecuting

> persons responsible for genocide and other serious violations of international humanitarian law committed in the territory of Rwanda and Rwandan citizens responsible for genocide and other such violations committed in the territory of neighbouring States, between 1 January 1994 and 31 December 1994.[50]

Given their constrained mandate, ad hoc tribunals that have been created, like the ICTR, could not exercise jurisdiction over Japanese wartime transgressions.

The jurisdictional constraints on even existing *permanent* international tribunals preclude them from trying cases concerning Japanese human experimentation during World War II. The International Court of Justice (ICJ), "the principal judicial organ of the United Nations,"[51] can only try cases between states,[52] and thus individual Japanese could not come under its jurisdiction. It is also unclear whether the ICJ would have jurisdiction over crimes such as these, which were committed before the court was established as part of the UN in 1945.[53] The ICC, the world's first permanent international war crimes tribunal, would be a similarly inapplicable forum. Although Japan is a state party to the Rome Statute, the treaty that established the ICC,[54] and therefore the ICC could have jurisdiction over atrocity crimes committed in Japan or by Japanese,[55] the ICC's temporal jurisdiction extends back only to July 1, 2002, the date on which the Rome Statute entered into force.[56]

But even an ad hoc war crimes tribunal created specifically to address these offences would likely not be effective. Such tribunals, which establish an historical account of atrocity crimes and impose sentences on convicted defendants, usually require alleged perpetrators of crimes to be in custody,[57] and often the accused

49 S.C. Res. 955, (note 46).

50 Ibid. ¶ 1.

51 U.N. Charter art. 92.

52 Statute of the International Court of Justice Art. 34(1), June 26, 1945, 59 Stat. 1031, 1059.

53 See generally Shabtai Rosenne, *The Time Factor in the Jurisdiction of the International Court of Justice* (1960).

54 Japan acceded to the Rome Statute on 17 July 2007. International Criminal Court: Japan <https://asp.icc-cpi.int/en_menus/asp/states%20parties/asian%20states/Pages/japan.aspx> accessed 31 July 2019.

55 See Rome Statute of the International Criminal Court art. 12, adopted and opened for signature 17 July 1998, 2187 U.N.T.S. 90 [hereinafter Rome Statute].

56 See Marlise Simons, 'Without Fanfare or Cases International Court Sets Up' *New York Times* (1 July 2002), A3. The Rome Statute provides: "The Court has jurisdiction only with respect to crimes committed after the entry into force of this Statute." Rome Statute, (note 55), art. 11, para. 1.

57 For example, the ICTY and the ICTR both provided that the accused shall be entitled to be tried in their presence and to defend themself in person or through their own chosen legal assistance. Statute of the International Tribunal for Rwanda art. 20, para. 4(d), 8

choose to testify.[58] In the case of Japan's wartime human experimentation, most, if not all, suspected offenders are likely to have died, while old age, poor health or the passing of almost eight decades may cloud the memories of those who are still alive. The Extraordinary Chambers in the Courts of Cambodia, the ad hoc hybrid war crimes tribunal created in 2003 to address the Cambodian genocide of 1975 to 1979,[59] suffers from these very problems, even though the crimes it covers occurred decades *after* World War II.[60]

For the same reason, a truth and reconciliation commission, as most famously implemented in South Africa[61] (but also used elsewhere in Africa, Latin America, Europe, Asia and even recently in the United States),[62] would be problematic. Priscilla Hayner, an expert on truth commissions, suggests that

> a truth commission may have any or all of the following five basic aims: to discover, clarify, and formally acknowledge past abuses; to respond to specific needs of victims; to contribute to justice and accountability; to outline

November 1994, 33 I.L M. 1602; Statute of the International Tribunal art. 21, para. 4(d), 25 May 1993, 32 I.L.M. 1192.

58 For example, Saddam Hussein and Slobodan Milošević both testified at their own trials. See Gary J. Bass, 'Milosevic in The Hague' *Foreign Affairs* (May–June 2003), 82; Edward Wong, 'Hussein Urges Iraqis to Unify in War on U.S.' *New York Times* (16 March 2006), A1.

59 Laura Dickinson describes "hybrid" tribunals as those for which 'both the institutional apparatus and the applicable law consist of a blend of the international and the domestic. Foreign judges sit alongside their domestic counterparts to try cases prosecuted and defended by teams of local lawyers working with those from other countries. The judges apply domestic law that has been reformed to accord with international standards'. Laura A. Dickinson, 'The Promise of Hybrid Courts' [2003] 97 American Journal International Law 295.

60 See, e.g., Editorial, 'The Killing Fields' *New York Times* (6 July 2006), A20 ("[Because] the leaders of the Khmer Rouge are either old or dead. . . [w]e can only hope that there will be enough of a trial in the end to give Cambodia's survivors some sense of justice done."); Seth Mydans, 'Khmer Rouge Tribunal's Record: 11 Years, $300 Million and 3 Convictions' *New York Times* (11 April 2017), A5.

61 See generally Alex Boraine, *A Country Unmasked: Inside South Africa's Truth and Reconciliation Commission* (2000); Hayner, (note 32), 40–45; *Truth v. Justice: The Morality of Truth Commissions* (Robert I. Rotberg and Dennis Thompson eds., 2000); Desmond Mpilo Tutu, *No Future Without Forgiveness* (1999); Timothy Garton Ash, 'True Confessions' 44 *New York Review Books* (17 July 1997) 33.

62 See generally Jon Elster, *Closing the Books: Transitional Justice in Historical Perspective* 62–66, 70–72, 196, 215 (2004); Mark Freeman, *Truth Commissions and Procedural Fairness* 3–87 (2006); Hayner, (note 32), 32–40, 45–71; Kaufman, *United States Law and Policy on Transitional Justice*, (note 1), 28–29 (noting truth commissions in the United States that have been established or proposed); Martha Minow, *Between Vengeance and Forgiveness: Facing History after Genocide and Mass Violence* 52–90 (1998); Ruti G. Teitel, *Transitional Justice* 69–117 (2000); 1 *Transitional Justice: How Emerging Democracies Reckon with Former Regimes* 223–333 (Neil J. Kritz ed., 1995); Jack Snyder and Leslie Vinjamuri, 'Trials and Errors: Principle and Pragmatism in Strategies of International Justice' [Winter 2003–2004] 28 International Security 5, 31–33; Jonathan D. Tepperman, 'Truth and Consequences' *Foreign Affairs* (March–April 2002), 128.

> institutional responsibility and recommend reforms; and to promote reconciliation and reduce conflict over the past.[63]

Such commissions, which sometimes offer amnesty in exchange for truthful testimony, are most successful when they are sanctioned by the state in which they operate, engage alleged perpetrators and victims of crimes over which they have jurisdiction, and function in the shadow of prosecution.[64] However, given the recent resurgence of Japanese nationalism and the dubious availability of competent witnesses to or perpetrators of these heinous crimes, none of these conditions would be likely to apply in the case of Japanese human experimentation during World War II.

Conclusion

This chapter illustrates the reality that legal responses to atrocity crimes may not always be appropriate, practical or effective. Political solutions, including those pursued by civil society, may be the only alternative. Even though such entities may be controversial and lack the ability or authority to investigate, prosecute or punish, they can command the attention of the public – particularly as information-disseminating and shaming mechanisms – and possibly achieve those ends.

Justice for those who suffered Japanese human experimentation during World War II is long overdue. Though even a PT could not provide full accountability for the perpetrators or reconciliation for the victims of this atrocity, it could at least help promote greater historical awareness and acknowledgement about the respective roles of Japan and the United States in this horrific crime. A PT on Japanese human experimentation offers a means of addressing the past while promoting reconciliation among peoples and states for the future.

63 Hayner, (note 32), 24.
64 Ibid., 1–9, 14, 239–240.

12 From painkillers to cures

Challenges and future of People's Tribunals

Shadi Sadr

Introduction

Hafner and Tsutsui demonstrate in their statistical findings on states' compliance with human rights treaties that international human rights law often works only in democratising or already democratic states, or in states with strong civil society activism.[1] They conclude that "the human rights regime can help only a small number of states and a small percentage of the world's population, leaving behind those who are worst abused."[2] This highlights an existential problem with international law; given state sovereignty, enforcement of international human rights principles and norms to combat impunity is next to impossible without the compliance of the state.

International human rights law in the field of truth, justice and reparation has historically been shaped mainly by transitional justice processes in societies emerging from conflict, with heavy involvement from victims' groups, human rights NGOs and other societal actors.[3] The norms and response mechanisms constructed within such contexts have largely sidelined the experiences of undemocratic non-transitional countries, where civil societies are also often fragile. Nevertheless, societal actors working in the contexts of impunity employ international human rights law language and frameworks to articulate and legitimise their demands, and to contribute to the advancement of people's rights. A popular example is the use of People's Tribunals. As pointed out by Byrnes & Simm, "they reflect a broader claim that asserts the rights of peoples (and people)

1 Emilie M. Hafner-Burton and Kiyoteru Tsutsui, 'Justice Lost! The Failure of International Human Rights Law to Matter Where Needed Most' [2007] 44(4) Journal of Peace Research 407, 422.

2 Ibid.

3 In defining societal actors, I cast a wide net and draw upon Kaiser and Meyer's definition: 'groups of individual or collective bodies representing certain collective preferences that can arise from their normative commitments and/or material or other interests' [Jan-Henrik Meyer and Wolfram Kaiser, 'Polity-Building and Policy-Making: Societal Actors in European Integration' in Jan-Henrik Meyer and Wolfram Kaiser (eds), *Societal Actors in European Integration: Palgrave Studies in European Union Politics* (Palgrave Macmillan, 2013), 22.]

to claim for themselves the benefit of international and other forms of law, and to interpret and develop international law."[4]

This chapter examines international PT driven by societal actors, whether as on-off initiatives established by groups of people who are directly affected by atrocities, or organised by the PPT based on requests they receive from such beneficiary groups.

I have served as a member of the jury in three international People's Tribunals[5] and I use this chapter to share some reflections in my capacity as both an insider and a legal scholar. This chapter avoids repeating the usual critiques of PT being political, partisan, illegitimate, procedurally flawed and proceeded with default judgements due to the refusal of perpetrators or defendant states to participate, as these criticisms have been adequately described and addressed by other scholars in recent years.

Although each tribunal is unique in its form, mandate and outcome, and thus deserves to be examined on its own goal and principles, this chapter attempts to find common challenges that most tribunals have encountered and identifies strategies that may have helped them overcome past challenges. The chapter concludes with recommendations for future tribunals in light of the examined challenges.

The paradoxical nature of People's Tribunals

In a blatant critique of the global justice order, PT claim to fill gaps in the international legal system that effectively prevent some victims from accessing justice. In many instances the international legal system has neglected to investigate atrocities or failed to adequately address them in the minds of victims' communities. Tribunals thus address a chronic pain point in the current regime – that despite claims to the contrary, the law is not, in fact, for all.

Tribunals promise a more inclusive system of law or a reclamation of the law. In doing so, People's Tribunals usually adopt a "court-style" format and a semi-judicial procedure. They argue, as Manfredi articulated, that they "persistently contest dominant visions of international law's purpose – and through their enduring practice new futures for international justice may yet emerge."[6]

The challenge is that the tribunals, which are shaped as radical responses to the dominant system of international law on the one hand, increasingly apply the very same laws on the other. That is, they address an existential flaw in international

4 Andrew Byrnes and Gabrielle Simm (eds), *Peoples' Tribunals and International Law* (Cambridge University Press, 2018), 13.

5 They include: The International People's Tribunal on 1965 Crimes against Humanity in Indonesia, the Permanent People's Tribunal on Myanmar State Crimes, and the Independent Tribunal into Forced Organ Harvesting from Prisoners of Conscience in China.

6 Zachary Manfredi, 'Sharpening the Vigilance of the World: Reconsidering the Russell Tribunal as Ritual' [2018] 9(1) Humanity Journal <http://humanityjournal.org/issue9-1/sharpening-the-vigilance-of-the-world-reconsidering-the-russell-tribunal-as-ritual/> accessed 1 May 2019.

law, but invite their own existential issue by utilizing the same laws. The paradoxical nature of the People's Tribunal derives from the fact that its participants revolt against a system while subsequently using its languages. These conflicting notions are present within the majority of tribunals' structures and proceedings, as Jayan Nayar suggested about the PPT:

> The constitution of the 'judges', the hierarchical positioning of 'experts', the conceptual and literal languages of communication, the mechanics of the presentation of 'evidence' and the formulaic construction of 'indictments' and 'verdicts' within the PPT process all retain within them some assumptions and prescriptions of dominant legality.[7]

In her analysis on Iran's Tribunal, Sakhi illustrates her critiques on the use of international language by the tribunals from the perspective that the centrality of victimhood in international law language, recognised in the Covenants, falls short of representing all aspects of witnesses' life experiences that thus "codified and narrowed them to the truth of the state's practice of power over their psyches and bodies" in a tribunal.[8]

In response, one may argue that People's Tribunals do more to underscore the incapabilities and non-inclusivity of the global justice system than to undermine the international human rights law. In other words, People's Tribunals are invented only to address the issue of implementing international laws in the absence of state compliance and to grant the power of implementation of international law to the people.

However, some tribunals have pushed the boundaries of international law and contributed to its broader development. One example is the Conclusion of the Second Session of International War Crimes Tribunal (the Russell Tribunal), which recognised the US as guilty of genocide on a broader basis than the definition established by the Genocide Convention.[9]

Another area in which tribunals, and in particular the PPT, have gone beyond the boundaries of international law are in their works, mainly in the early 1990s, that

> appear to be a noticeable shift in focus – from considerations of what can be regarded as state violations within a conventional 'international law' context, to considerations of structural, transnational violence, increasingly by 'private' actors in the context of 'globalisation' that include the IMF and the

7 Jayan Nayar, 'A People's Tribunal Against the Crime of Silence? – The Politics of Judgement and an Agenda for People's Law' [2001] 2 Law, Social Justice & Global Development Journal <https://www2.warwick.ac.uk/fac/soc/law/elj/lgd/2001_2/> accessed 28 March 2019.

8 Shekufe Sakhi, 'Ethical – Political Praxis: Social Justice and the Resistant Subject in Iran' in Peyman Vahabzadeh (ed), *Iran's Struggles for Social Justice* (Palgrave Macmillan, 2017), 157.

9 Geoffrey Nice, *Justice for All and How to Achieve It: Citizens, Lawyers and the Law in the Age of Human Rights* (Scala Arts & Heritage Publishers Limited, 2017), 110.

World Bank,[10] the international garment industries,[11] and the French oil/energy corporation Elf-Aquitaine.[12]

Only very few tribunals have overruled the dominant legal order and moved completely beyond it. An example of such a radical approach is the lesser-known International Tribunal on Crimes against Women, which was inspired by the Russel Tribunal's idea that "oppressed people have the right to dissociate themselves from those definitions of crimes which have been developed by their oppressors to serve their own interest" and opened with a message from Simone De Beauvoir who was unable to attend in person.[13] With more than 2,000 women from 40 countries participating, there was no panel of judges, but all participants had equal votes as judges. This 1976 tribunal was revolutionary in its both procedure and content. It refused to apply existing laws as male-products and, in a rejection of normative orders, introduced the new notion of crimes against women – a set of criminal actions such as forced motherhood, compulsory non-motherhood, persecution of non-virgins and unmarried mothers, sexual objectification of women, etc.[14]

Nevertheless, most tribunals, and frequently even the PPT, have chosen to more or less remain within the boundaries of the law, even if they vary in the degree to which they utilise international law.[15] This may owe partly to the fact that People's Tribunals are usually overly cautious of appearing biased or having their judgements discredited by the respective government and other observers. Such concerns lead most tribunals to take a more conservative approach towards international law. This, however, has not made them immune of criticisms that they adopt a "pick and choose" method in applying international law; e.g. finding a government that is not a signatory to the Genocide Convention guilty of such a crime, which in a court of law would not be applicable to the accused.

Another important reason is that, no matter how problematic, the only available, credible and common language for recognising the most heinous acts that have occurred in the contemporary world is international law. The judgements of People's Tribunals need to be framed in an understandable common knowledge that conveys the gravity of acts described as international crimes. In order

10 Tribunal on the Policies of the International Monetary Fund and the World Bank (1988) <http://permanentpeoplestribunal.org/13-the-policies-of-the-international-monetary-fund-and-the-world-bank-ii-west-berlin-26-29-september-1988/?lang=en> accessed 28 March 2019.

11 Gianni Tognoni, 'The History of the Permanent Peoples' Tribunal' in Andrew Byrnes and Gabrielle Simm (eds), Peoples' Tribunals and International Law (Cambridge University Press, 2018), 147.

12 Ibid.

13 Diana E. H. Russell and Nicole Van De Ven, *Crimes Against Women: International Tribunal* (Less Femme, 1976), Introduction.

14 Ibid.

15 Arthur W. Blaser, 'How to Advance Human Rights Without Really Trying: An Analysis of Nongovernmental Tribunal [1992] Human Rights Quarterly 339, 357.

to accuse the most powerful actors such as states and multinational entities, one needs to apply the powerful language of the law that rules above all.

As Manfredi pointed out,

> in calling our attention to mass atrocities the tribunals impart skills and virtues in how "we watch" the commission of mass atrocities; they provide a critical forum and space for the cultivation of the sensibilities necessary to recognise atrocities as such and to take responsibility for them. In so doing, they ritualise, and thereby concretise, a practice of speaking in the language of international law.[16]

The final judgement of the PPT on Myanmar is a good example of such functions. The judges applied a very conventional interpretation of the law in recognising the atrocities against Rohingya as genocide.[17] However, given the context in which the tribunal took place – when, despite the existence of every consisting element of genocide, the UN and even international NGOs such as Human Rights Watch and Amnesty International avoided using the term and instead, calling the situation "ethnic cleansing" which has no meaning in international law[18] – the Tribunal judgement was radical and groundbreaking.

In addition, as initiatives by societal actors aimed at achieving policy changes, People's Tribunals often find the language of international law and court-style set up to be the most effective model for their advocacy.

The tendency to ensure that the tribunal is a "credible judicial inquiry"[19] within the boundaries of existing international laws and norms has only grown stronger in recent years. Even PPT has mostly shifted toward that direction and rarely uses its self-invented law – Universal Declaration of the Rights of Peoples (Algiers Charter)[20] – which takes a socialist approach to universal rights.

As bodies that are already struggling with issues of credibility and legitimacy, People's Tribunals are too weak and generally lack the resources, above all, to

16 Manfredi, (note 6).

17 Judgment of the People's Tribunal on Myanmar (31 October 2017) <https://tribunalon-myanmar.org/2017/10/31/judgment-of-the-peoples-tribunal-on-myanmar> accessed 28 March 2019.

18 For example see: UN Human Rights Chief Points to 'Textbook Example of Ethnic Cleansing' in Myanmar, *UN News* (11 September 2017) <https://news.un.org/en/story/2017/09/564522-un-human-rights-chief-points-textbook-example-ethnic-cleansing-myanmar> accessed 28 March 2019; Myanmar: Accountability for Ethnic Cleansing Urgently Required, Human Rights Watch (12 March 2018) <www.hrw.org/news/2018/03/12/myanmar-accountability-ethnic-cleansing-urgently-required> accessed 28 March 2019.

19 Payam Akhavan, 'Is Grassroots Justice a Viable Alternative to Impunity? The Case of the Iran People's Tribunal' [2017] 39(1) Human Rights Quarterly 73, 82.

20 Algiers Charter Universal Declaration of the Rights of Peoples (4 July 1976) <http://permanentpeoplestribunal.org/wp-content/uploads/2015/01/Carta-di-algeri-EN-1.pdf> accessed 28 March 2019.

challenge the entire international law domain and replace it with "an alternative 'legal' forum for the voices of those suffering to denounce the power of dominant law which refuses to name their violation a crime."[21]

That being said, as humanity's conscience erodes along with the once-revolutionary idea that people's invented laws can be applied in People's Tribunals, those tribunals are in danger of becoming yet another routine enterprise, a part of the *status quo* that they were designed to revolt against.

"Standing in between" truth and justice

Although truth and justice are often "locked together as the corollary components for considerations on law,"[22] the UN Sets of Principles to Combat Impunity draws a sharp line between the notions of truth and justice, both in terms of the consisting elements of the rights to truth and to justice and in the duty bearers in upholding those rights. The Principles hold that "every people has the inalienable right to know the truth about past events concerning the perpetration of heinous crimes and about the circumstances and reasons that led, through massive or systematic violations, to the perpetration of those crimes."[23] It also recognises the right of "victims and their families to know the truth about the circumstances in which violations took place and, in the event of death or disappearance, the victims' fate."[24]

While the right to truth starts with the "rights" of beneficiaries, i.e. every human being, the Principles introduces the right to justice as a "duty" to be fulfilled only by the State, which"

> shall undertake prompt, thorough, independent and impartial investigations of violations of human rights and international humanitarian law and take appropriate measures in respect of the perpetrators, particularly in the area of criminal justice, by ensuring that those responsible for serious crimes under international law are prosecuted, tried and duly punished.[25]

The question is, can court-style initiatives led by societal actors, i.e. PT, also be considered to be upholding human rights, and thus render justice, or, at least, an alternative form of justice as some authors suggest?[26]

Such arguments appear to challenge the Principles' definitions of the rights to truth and justice. The lack of enforceability and the absence of the State – the

21 Nayar, (note 7).

22 Ibid.

23 Diane Orentlicher, 'Updated Set of Principles for the Protection and Promotion of Human Rights Through Action to Combat Impunity' (8 February 2005) E/CN.4/2005/102/Add.1 <https://undocs.org/E/CN.4/2005/102/Add.1> accessed 28 March 2019.

24 Ibid.

25 Ibid.

26 See for example: Regina Paulose, Imagining People's Tribunals as the Promoter of Human Rights, in Ekaterina Yahyaoui Krivenko (ed), *Human Rights and Power in Times of Globalisation* (Brill, 2017), 271; Blaser, (note 15), 354; Akhavan, (note 19), 73.

only duty-bearer in international law – prevent tribunals from realising victims' rights to justice.

Thus, societal actors' utilisation of international law is more effective in preserving the truth about gross human rights violations and raising public awareness than in achieving justice and rendering reparation to victims, which require some state-level compliance with the obligation to investigate crimes. Taking this a step further, tribunals work better in establishing historical truth than individuals' right to know.

The individual rights of survivors' and victims' next of kin to obtain "incident-specific truths"[27] refers to information such as the human rights violations suffered or the identity and responsibility of the perpetrator. Incident-specific truths" usually establish "legal truth" which, as Naqvi said, "is merely a by-product of a dispute settlement mechanism,"[28] such as an investigation and prosecution. A more holistic "historical truth" that can be achieved through measures such as truth commissions, public access to government archives, and the founding of museums and memorials, which together satisfy the right of the entire society to the truth, would fall more squarely within the functions that People's Tribunals could have.

Geoffrey Nice even raises questions about the inevitability of PT fulfilling the function of establishing historical truths. In his analysis on the impact of the Russell Tribunal, he writes: "only with . . . public trial will public memory of what has been done be certain to remain strong."[29] "Ask an American how they would characterise the US involvement in Vietnam, Cambodia, and Laos and they are unlikely to say 'war crimes.'" "Had there been a formal international court making the same findings the position would inevitably be different," he added.[30]

However, the majority of scholars have little doubt that PT collect and document truths that can repudiate the versions of events offered by states and serve the function of "memorialization" and establishing historical memories. Some even called several tribunals an "unofficial but credible truth commission."[31] This argument is disputed by others in that, although People's Tribunals "shed light on historical or ongoing issues to help foster discussion, create a legitimate record of evidence, and suggest constructive solutions to the issues raised," they are different than truth commissions in many aspects including the lack of formality and state's engagement.[32]

But what separates People's Tribunals from other truth-telling and truth-seeking projects initiated by societal actors lies "in the extent to which the forms

27 Sam Szoke-Burke, 'Searching for the Right to Truth – The Impact of International Human Rights Law on National Transitional Justice Policies' [2015] 33(2) Berkeley Journal of International Law 533.

28 Yasmin Naqvi, 'The Right to the Truth in International Law: Fact or Fiction?' [2006] 88(862) International Review of the Red Cross 246.

29 Nice, (note 9), 112.

30 Ibid., 116.

31 Akhavan, (note 19), 74.

32 Paulose, (note 26), 273

and procedures of a legal proceeding are observed, as well as in the cogency of the analysis of evidence and legal reasoning adopted"[33] which makes it massively unfair to them to be reduced merely to truth initiatives.

People's Tribunals not only contribute to rewriting the history previously dominated by the ruling elites – the "history of the winners" – and replacing the public "archive of the oppressors", or at least complementing it with an "archive of the oppressed."[34] They also, much more importantly, validate such history with an "authoritative body"[35] established by the tribunals in the forms of "the panel of judges," "the panel of experts" or "the jury." Moreover, though appointed by the organisers, not by a state or the UN, these authoritative bodies usually, if not always, go beyond the confirmation of the historical truths and determine whether specific international crimes have occurred. This goes far beyond fact finding or establishing truth, but falls short of a proper and enforceable judgement, which involves a defendant in the dock and provides justice, and mandates reparation. Such validations and recognitions by an "authoritative body" assist victim suffering to be acknowledged on a much higher level than the acknowledgements they would gain through a civil society fact-finding project.

In other words, drawing on elements of truth and justice throughout the process up to their final products, tribunals stand somewhere between the realms of right to truth and right to justice, or somewhere between truth commissions and criminal trials. They achieve measures of both but deliver neither completely, as they issue a verdict without sentencing the accused.

Perhaps only such a unique setting can achieve the impacts described in the case of the International People's Tribunal on 1965 Crimes against Humanity in Indonesia "the pronouncement of the Panel of Judges on the applicability of the term 'genocide' for the mass killings in Indonesia after 1 October 1965 . . . [was] . . . the first occasion on which a legal institution has come to this conclusion for Indonesia."[36]

However, though a unique mechanism for accountability, the "stand-in-between truth and justice" nature of tribunals may also lead to unease and even tension among different stakeholders by creating the wrong expectations among witnesses and victims' communities. The mere adoption of forms and procedures of legal proceedings, as well as the practice of issuing "decisions" or "judgments," may mislead the audience or stakeholders about the authority of such tribunals, as pointed out by Paulose who indicates that "society may doubt the legitimacy of

33 Gabrielle Simm and Andrew Byrnes, 'International Peoples' Tribunals in Asia: Political Theatre, Juridical Farce, or Meaningful Intervention?' [2014] 4 Asian Journal of International Law 103, 105.

34 Saskia Wieringa, 'The International People's Tribunal on 1965 Crimes Against Humanity in Indonesia' in Andrew Byrnes and Gabrielle Simm (eds), *Peoples' Tribunals and International Law* (Cambridge University Press 2018), 130.

35 Ibid., 156.

36 Ibid., 129.

People's Tribunals because it is not sanctioned by the state and it may be viewed as a farce or ruse to manipulate people into believing it has power."[37]

In order to avoid such confusion, some People's Tribunals call their final outcome "reports" and resist the preference of the organisers to use possibly misleading words like "decision" or "judgement." Some also refrain from using the title "judge" and replace it with "expert" in order to avoid creating an expectation of judicial authority Some tribunals use both methods.

PT can be considered a mechanism of accountability that supports the realisation of the rights of victims and societies to know the truth, as well as the right of victim communities to justice. However, actual achievement of the rights to truth and justice will only be achieved through formal legal proceeding, which should use tribunals' outputs as important collections of primary and secondary material.

Internal tensions

Other tensions that may arise in tribunals are the those between members of the panels, in particular between lawyers and non-lawyers, and between the organisers and panels.

PT are the "courts of people's opinion," thus usually consisting of lawyers and non-lawyers, including intellectuals, scholars, writers, politicians, and even celebrities. These hybrid panels are expected to apply law in order to deliver a legal document called "judgement," "decision" or "report," which differentiates them from other civil society initiatives such as conferences and rallies. These circumstances can create conflict between members of the panels, or an uneven power dynamic within panels in which the opinions of lawyers are, in practice, given more weight on the final decision. Such situation occurs when the law, presumably being guarded by lawyers, contradicts the opinion of other members, including witnesses and organisers, who are often non-lawyers.

Some tribunals have tried to overcome this challenge by obtaining independent legal opinions from lawyers outside the panel. However, this again reaffirms the hierarchy between lawyers and non-lawyers.

In almost all temporary PT, the jury is appointed by organisers. In the case of the PPT, when it receives a general mandate from a victim's community and the PPT decides to accept it, the organisation appoints a panel. In either case, while the expectations of the organisers are often apparent in the mandate they give to the tribunal when it is first appointed, panels will subsequently and independently decide on details such as the procedure, the questions they must address, and so on. Usually, such independent decision-making is sacredly maintained throughout the tribunal.

PT are labour-intensive, time-consuming and relatively expensive endeavours. Although panel members, prosecutors, counsels and registrars work on a voluntarily basis, the organisers have to raise a considerable amount of funding to cover

37 Paulose, (note 26), 275.

the cost of a venue, travel, simultaneous interpreters, etc. In exchange for facilitating such backbreaking work, the organisers expect an outcome that proves what had remained unproven to the world. They want to use the tribunal as a tool for further advocacy that ultimately achieves meaningful policy changes. The panels, on the other hand, obtain their credibility from being completely independent from the organisers, and thus inevitably indifferent to their expectations. The panel's conclusion sometimes disappoints the organisers and victims' community, particularly when applying to law to the evidence and recognising acts as particular international crimes.

For instance, with regards to the question of genocide in the Indonesia Tribunal, the prosecution did not include it in the indictment, mainly for security reasons.[38] However, the organisers, as demonstrated in one of their writings,[39] expected the tribunal to address it. There was also the issue of applicability of the definition of the convention on "protected groups" to the victims of the 1985–86 mass atrocities in Indonesia, who were mainly leftist activists. After hours of deliberations, heated discussions, and even the danger of collapse, the tribunal finally "sought to extend the concept of genocide to the human rights violations it considered."[40] However, the dissenting opinion was neither written nor spoken of.

As the record of minority or dissenting opinions and internal discussions are seldom documented or, if documented, are rarely, if ever, released, such internal tensions between members of the panels and between panels and organisers, no matter how paralysing or collapsing, have barely come to the surface in the history of tribunals. Consequently, the current studies on People's Tribunals fail to address the impact of such challenges. One exception was the 2001 Russell Tribunal on Human Rights in Psychiatry which concluded with a majority and a minority verdict. Unlike the majority of the jury, the Brazilian novelist Paulo Coelho and Israeli Law Professor Alon Harel took a more cautious position in accusing psychiatry of being guilty of widespread and serious abuses of human rights.[41]

Healing or chilling effect?

Other than breaking the silence and raising awareness about mass atrocities at a wider scale, and establishing the historical truth as previously mentioned, it is commonly assumed that People's Tribunals provide healing and closure to victims,

38 Wieringa, (note 34), 118.
39 Ibid., 130.
40 Andrew Byrnes and Gabrielle Simm, 'Reflections on the Past and Future of International Peoples' Tribunals' in Andrew Byrnes and Gabrielle Simm (eds), *Peoples' Tribunals and International Law* (Cambridge University Press 2018), 263.
41 Russell Tribunal on Human Rights in Psychiatry & "Geist Gegen Genes", 30 June–2 July 2001, Berlin [2001] 27 PINS (Psychology in Society) <www.pins.org.za/pins/pins27/pins27_article12_Parker.pdf> accessed 1 May 2019.

especially for those who participate and testify. Some suggest that such effects are the result of public acknowledgement, which restores the dignity of the victims[42] and rehumanises them.

Similarly, Akhavan describes the feeling of Mother Esmat, who lost her entire family in the 1980s mass atrocities, after testifying before the Iran Tribunal:

> Mother Esmat's catharsis, her heart-breaking but graceful exposition of the truth, captured the surprising, healing power of merely sharing a story, of putting an end to suffering in silence. It was remarkable to see her relief after she had finished her testimony; her elation that the Commission, the audience, the Iranian people, and the world, had listened to her woes with such patience and empathy.[43]

Nevertheless, Shekufe Sakhi, a witness in the same tribunal, contested the absolutism of such arguments, describing her feelings after giving her testimony:

> In fact, I was not relieved from any past suffering. Instead, I was ecstatic, witnessing the persistence of a people's resistance to and in the face of all the powerful forces of the *nezam's*[44] deliberate annihilation.[45]

She then continues:

> That process of the Iran Tribunal, including its preceding Truth Commission, the gathering of documents, the gaining of the indispensable and heartfelt (forever appreciated), and the participation of the international judges and lawyers, volunteers, and private donors, signified for me the long-enduring resistant subjectivity and manifestations of the agency of a people in spite of the systematic attempt to remove it from the Iranian public sphere and its historical memory. Creating our own institution, practicing our subjectivity, and fulfilling our responsibility to the executed and disappeared and for the generations after us: that was our subjectivity in action, a process of hope and inspiration – and it was filled with agony not relief.

The chilling effect of testifying before the People's Tribunals can be analysed from another perspective. Recent research on trauma and testifying strongly challenges the common claim that truth-telling is healing. Studying the results of a random survey of 1,200 Rwandans about the Rwandan village tribunals for truth and reconciliation after the 1994 genocide (gacaca), Brounéus demonstrates that

42 Wieringa, (note 34), 121.

43 Akhavan, (note 19), 86.

44 The entire power structure of the Islamic Republic of Iran is called by the regime officials and its followers as *Nezam* which can be literary translated into "system".

45 Sakhi, (note 8), 156.

gacaca witnesses suffer from higher levels of depression and PTSD than non-witnesses.[46] Exposure to truth-telling did not lower their levels of psychological ill-health nor the prevalence of depression and PTSD over time.

This is important especially because People's Tribunals rarely have resources to provide professional assistance to witnesses, either before or after giving testimony, which can lead to revictimization of the testifying and participating witnesses.

Communications and outreach

Non-governmental tribunals are tribunals of conscience, and their legitimacy and effectiveness depend upon public reactions[47] and propelling further conversation about their subject matter. Wider outreach is an indicator of success of these tribunals. Some scholars even suggest that merely "to raise awareness on a particular issue that was silenced for decades can already be viewed as a tremendous success."[48]

As with litigation in official courts, activists who instigate People's Tribunals may aim to bring evidence into the public domain, to shift public opinion and to assert political pressure. Judgments are usually communicated to governments, international organisations and corporations accused in the proceedings and to the media and NGOs in order to publicise a particular cause.

It seems that for measuring the effectiveness of each tribunal, there should be an "audience that matters" where, as Nayar categorises, there are three "constituencies of audience" for PT: "The policy formulators and lawyers, the general public within societies of "engineered consent," and communities (and supporters) of the victimised."[49]

Nevertheless, many tribunals lack proper communications and outreach strategies, which require organisers to determine the target audience based on their goals and develop specific strategies to engage with and influence each group within that audience.

Except for a very few cases, People's Tribunals have faced challenges in attracting members of the public to attend, and the mainstream media to report, the hearing or its outcome.

In the absence of a proper communications and outreach strategy, the tribunals tend to adopt the most traditional communications strategy for civil society initiatives, which entails engaging with the mainstream media in order to attract their coverage.

46 Karen Brounéus, 'The Trauma of Truth Telling: Effects of Witnessing in the Rwandan Gacaca Courts on Psychological Health' [2010] 54(3) Journal of Conflict Resolution 408.
47 Blaser, (note 15), 361.
48 Paulose, (note 26), 275.
49 Nayar, (note 7).

The mainstream international media usually work through established working relationships with press officers and media advisors of international human rights NGOs. The ad hoc tribunals that are formed just a few months before launching a hearing are less credible to the media than long-standing human rights organisations like Amnesty International and Human Rights Watch, diminishing the likelihood of tribunals attracting the coverage they deserve, and their "conclusions are seldom quoted,"[50] even if, as in the case of the UKCSAPT, the issue might sound attractive.[51]

Resonating in new and social media also depends on factors such as having online platforms or active social media accounts with a large following, or a massive budget for advertising and hiring people who are savvy at using social media.

Some tribunals engage with celebrities and high-profile figures to increase their resonance in both old and new media and draw more public attention. For instance, the Russell Tribunal on Palestine had a plethora of actors and actresses in its well-populated Support Committee.[52] However, without an impact report documenting reach and engagement figures, it is difficult to assess the effectiveness of such strategies.

Furthermore, the influence of corporate and "branding" culture and competitions in covering human rights issues[53] have required People's Tribunals to engage the quality of professional public relations companies in order to gain public attention, a luxury that the People's Tribunal can barely afford.

For these reasons, even the PPT – a permanent, well-established, reputable NGO – faces the same challenges with almost every other tribunal. For instance, the PPT Tribunal on Myanmar took place in September 2017, when the Burmese government's crackdown against the Rohingya population peaked and the human rights violations that it committed was widely covered by the international mainstream media. However, beyond regional news outlets, the tribunal failed to attract international mainstem media coverage.[54]

In addition to the lack of adequate resources to hire PR companies, small NGOs and networks around the world are generally poor communicators for various reasons, such as considering professional communications and outreach to be unnecessary and beyond their reach.[55] As a result, the excellent work of many PT, the touching testimonies of witnesses to the most heinous crimes, the

50 Blaser, (note 15), 361.

51 Paulose, (note 26), 280–281.

52 For more information see: Russel Tribunal on Palestine. Patrons, <www.russelltribunalonpalestine.com/en/about-rtop/patrons> accessed 28 March 2019.

53 Lilie Chouliaraki, *The Ironic Spectator: Solidarity in the Age of Post-Humanitarianism* (Cambridge, Polity Press, 2013), 71.

54 See the section 'In the News' of the Tribunal web site, <https://tribunalonmyanmar.org/category/news/> accessed 28 March 2018.

55 Trevor Thrall1, Dominik Stecula and Diana Sweet, 'May We Have Your Attention Please? Human-Rights NGOs and the Problem of Global Communication' [2014] 19(2) The International Journal of Press/Politics 135, 148–150.

impressive, well-articulated statements and judgements of the tribunals, and the impact that they have on policy and society often do not receive the media coverage and, in turn, the public attention that they deserve.

Another factor that should be considered is the fact that many tribunals take place outside the concerned country, often engaging exiled activists. National media outlets usually censor them or publish distorted accounts about them,[56] local media in the host country do not find them newsworthy for their own national audience, and the international media discount them, especially when tribunals investigate past crimes, often having occurred in small countries in the global south.

Dealing with such a complex situation requires sophisticated, professional, thorough and well-thought-out communications and outreach plans. The plans must be developed early in the tribunal's conception and executed well in advance of the actual hearing sessions. Communications and outreach should be considered as important as appointing the judges for a People's Tribunal, with an urgency and necessity that is typically overlooked by organisers in their initial planning and only comes up at a much later stage, often when the announcement of the hearing sessions is due, which is ultimately too late.

Despite all adversarial factors, a few tribunals were quite successful in using both traditional and new media and attracted thousands of people to watch their sessions or engage with them in other ways. For instance, as Payam Akahvan, the prosecutor of Iran Tribunal, argues, it attracted "a diverse and significant audience, including both those physically present at the hearing and those watching through Internet live-streaming or satellite television broadcasts." It was covered by major outlets such as the BBC, Al Jazeera, *The Economist*, and *New York Times*, "as well as every significant Persian language media that broadcasted into Iran from abroad, given that local media in Iran was subject to strict censorship,"[57] which, to his analysis, led to effectively capturing "the popular imagination in order to confront the long-standing policy of denial by the Iranian government."

Nevertheless, some scholars raise difficult questions regarding the relationship between media coverage and tribunals' effectiveness. For instance, Dolgopol points out that as "an important issue to consider in the context of People's Tribunals: Whom precisely are we (organisers) seeking to influence and how do we measure our impact? Is media attention alone sufficient, or are we able to find mechanisms for gauging changes in attitude over time?"[58]

Without an external examination of the impact of each PT, including the impact of media coverage, it is difficult to conclude that any tribunal achieved its aim. Such evaluations are seldom part of a People's Tribunal's organising plan. The author has not been able to locate any "impact report" in the public records

56 Akhavan, (note 19), 98–100.

57 Ibid., 83.

58 Ustinia Dolgopol, 'The Tokyo Women's Tribunal' in Andrew Byrnes and Gabrielle Simm (eds), *Peoples' Tribunals and International Law* (Cambridge University Press 2018), 97.

from any People's Tribunals, despite the remarkable results some of them have achieved. For instance, as discussed in Chapter 1, the report "Buried Alive," published by the International Peoples Tribunal on Kashmir led the Indian government to establish an ad hoc commission to investigate the 3,000 plus unmarked graves in Kashmir.

This is part of a wider problem in documenting PT themselves, which itself is a part of a bigger issue of planning, from lack of a media engagement strategy to follow-up plans that ensure the tribunals' objectives are realised.

Lack of concrete follow-up plans

People's Tribunals are exhausting endeavours that mainly rely on hundreds, if not thousands, of hours of voluntarily work for the organisers, members, lawyers, translators and so on. Holding public hearing sessions and announcing final judgements or reports are both significant milestones. However, exhausted organisers, with their depleted resources and lack of prior planning of concrete follow-up actions, have difficulty carrying out activities beyond publishing their tribunal's judgements. The ambiguity of follow-up actions is reflected in vague statements such as this: "The findings of the UKCSAPT are now accessible to the public and the next leg of the journey for the People's Tribunal is to continue to share its finding worldwide with various communities in and out of the United Kingdom."[59]

As mentioned earlier, most tribunals are merely an episode in a longer series of activities that one or several societal actors carry out to combat impunity in their cases of concern. Organisers may understandably not see the need for a follow-up plan after the "judgement" or "report" of the tribunal is delivered and published because the broader movement that the tribunal is a part of will continue its path toward defined goals. However, the reality of a People's Tribunal proves that assumption wrong more often than not. The tribunals create a huge amount of energy and enthusiasm, especially among participating victims, for further action around the "judgement" or "report" such as conducting UN advocacy, running more traditional and social media campaigns to raise awareness, holding seminars and public events and more. However, such propositions usually only come after the tribunal has finished its task and organisers are often too exhausted and lacking the financial resources. In fact, there are very few tribunals that had a comprehensive written follow-up plan ahead of the hearing and deliberation sessions. One reason for this may be that the final outcomes of the tribunals are largely unpredictable for the organisers.

A tribunal's follow-up plan should not only include strategies and actions concerning the future, but also actions concerning the past. The challenge is that the history of the tribunal and its process, internal and external challenges, and impact are rarely documented or reported. A review of websites of many past

59 Paulose, (note 26), 281.

tribunals and pages designated to each PPT tribunal proves this, as they have usually remained static after publishing their panels' findings. While People's Tribunals may excel at establishing a historical memory of oppression, they are not equally capable of transmitting their own historical records and memory.

The Tribunal on Crime against Women, however, provides a strong counterexample. Written by two of the organisers, the book portrays a detailed account of the past and future of the tribunal. It offers an honest, open, and interesting reading about the "herstory" of the tribunal, including the internal debates and "fights," as well as some tangible impacts on laws and policies in the countries where the participants of the tribunal used its findings.[60]

An ideal tribunal?

In most cases, PT address a fundamental, chronic pain within the international legal order. However, in using the same language of international law, they are in danger of acting more as painkillers than cures. Trapping itself within the constraints of international law is a departure from a tribunal's existential rationale. The ideal tribunal should "not only engage in holding states and others accountable informally" but also articulate claims about the right of civil society to own, interpret, and develop international law.[61] Otherwise, tribunals may briefly alleviate suffering in the global justice order, but not solve injustices themselves.

Tribunals should be transparent about their internal challenges and tensions, creating space for scientific examination and recommendations to overcome their challenges. Publishing dissenting opinions of panel members would be a major step in the right direction. Clearly communicating to participating and non-participating witnesses, members of the public, media representatives and other targeted audience members about the expectations that the tribunal can meet, especially those outside the capacity of a PT, is equally important. Past experiences demonstrate that, in order to avoid misunderstanding, disappointment and unrealistic expectations, it is not enough to provide a list of what the tribunals can do without mentioning what they cannot do, side-by-side. Sending a clear message about its incapabilities should be an empowering and legitimising exercise for the ideal tribunal.

Compiling good quality research, reliable evidence and witnesses, and handing them over to a panel of credible individuals who form an authoritative body to judge grave human rights violations, is not a recipe for a successful tribunal. Without a proper and professional communications and outreach strategy tailored for different audiences and a tentative and working follow-up plan from the very beginning, a tribunal's impact will remain limited.

60 Russell and Van De Ven, (note 13), 284–294.

61 Andrew Byrnes and Gabrielle Simm, 'International Peoples' Tribunals' in Andrew Byrnes and Gabrielle Simm (eds), *Peoples' Tribunals and International Law* (Cambridge University Press, 2018), 41.

It is commonly argued that measuring the impact of PT is too difficult or perhaps impossible, as the real impact will only become apparent in the future.[62] Tribunals are also usually part of a broader sequence of activities to achieve desired change, not stand-alone actions. Therefore, their success or failure depends on many other factors and initiatives outside the framework of the tribunal, including unpredictable political developments.

Having said that, an external, independent impact assessment should be part of any tribunal's follow-up plans, designed to vigorously monitor and evaluate the progress of an ideal tribunal against its aims. Tribunals should also plan to release reports to insiders and the public, such as scholars, journalists and human rights activists, for further research, advocacy or planning. This is important because much of the current analysis on the impact of tribunals are written by those who were involved in the tribunal or close to them, "the insiders," which would fall short of scientific.

While the current scholarship has focused mainly on describing the contexts in which different People's Tribunals have been initiated, their procedures and their findings, the contributions of tribunals to international law remains largely unexplored. For instance, reviewing and analysing the contribution of People's Tribunal judgements on the current debates around genocide and, in particular, on broadening the applicability of the definition of the convention from protected groups to those who might be considered as unprotected is one such unexplored subject. The broader questions of whether the international legal order would be transformed by increasing the contribution of societal actors' tribunals to the development of international law, and what critical legal questions of the world could be resolved in doing so, is yet to be explored.

62 Nice, (note 9), 126.

Index

FSC
www.fsc.org
MIX
Papier | Fördert
gute Waldnutzung
FSC® C083411

Kolibri 360 GmbH
Ferdinand-Jühlke-Straße 7
99095 Erfurt, Deutschland
produktsicherheit@kolibri360.de